THE CHRISTIAN PRIESTHOOD

THE CHRISTIAN PRIESTHOOD

Edited by Nicholas Lash
and
Joseph Rhymer

Darton, Longman & Todd
London

Dimension Books, Inc.
Denville, New Jersey

First published in 1970 by
Darton, Longman & Todd Limited
85 Gloucester Road, London SW7
England
and
Dimension Books Inc.
Denville, New Jersey
USA

Printed in Great Britain by
Western Printing Services Limited, Bristol
ISBN 0 232 51136 5 *paper*

We acknowledge The Hutchinson Publishing Group
for a quotation from *Friday the Rabbi Slept Late*
by Harry Kemelman.

Contents

BIOGRAPHICAL NOTE ON THE EDITORS

NICHOLAS LASH *is a Research Fellow of St Edmund's House, Cambridge. Born in 1934, educated at Downside and Oscott, he is a priest of the Northampton diocese, for which he was ordained in 1963. Author of* His Presence in the World (*London 1968*); *contributing editor of* Doctrinal Development and Christian Unity (*London 1967*), Authority in a Changing Church (*London 1968*); *contributed to* The Church is Mission (*London 1969*), Understanding the Eucharist (*Dublin 1969*).

JOSEPH RHYMER *is a Senior Lecturer in the Theology Department of Notre Dame College of Education, Liverpool. Born in 1927, he is author of* The Prophets and the Law (*London 1964*), The Beginnings of a People (*London 1966*), The Good News: St Mark's Insight (*London 1966*), The Covenant and the Kingdom (*London 1968*), The Old Testament (*London 1970*), *contributor to* The People of God (*London 1965*), Theology in Modern Education (*London 1965*), The Committed Church (*London 1966*), *editor of the series* The Bible in History (*London 1968–70*) *and of the journal* Catholic Education Today. *He is a layman.*

Preface

THE DOWNSIDE SYMPOSIUM GROUP CONSISTS OF A NUCLEUS
of priests and laymen who meet together several times a year for
theological discussion. From time to time these discussions
crystallise into a theme which the group decides is worth exploring
in more depth by means of a symposium. The contributors to
this book accepted the group's invitation to read papers at a
symposium held at the Benedictine Abbey of Notre-Dame-du-Bec
in Normandy from 14th to 19th of April, 1969.

The members of the Downside Symposium Group, who spon-
sored this ninth symposium, were as follows: Dom Raphael
Appleby, Laurence Bright O.P., Simon Clements (Chairman and
Secretary), John Coulson, Dom Philip Jebb, Nicholas Lash, Dom
Sebastian Moore, Joseph Rhymer, Dom Ralph Russell, Lance
Shepherd, Hamish Swanston, John M. Todd and Christopher
Williams.

The group is deeply indebted to many people for help in
mounting the symposium. In particular we are most grateful to
Dom Paul Grammont, Abbot of Bec, for inviting us again to Bec
for a symposium, and to the Prior, Dom Philibert, and the members of the community at Bec, for the great kindness and warm
hospitality which was so generously given to all who attended the
symposium.

We are also very grateful to the Downside Centre for Religious
Studies, whose Director, John Coulson, is a member of the group,
for the grant made towards the costs of the symposium.

Finally the group again takes this opportunity of recording its
deep gratitude to the Abbot and monks of Downside Abbey who
for sixteen years have given hospitality and a very agreeable
meeting place for the group's regular discussions.

Nicholas Lash
Joseph Rhymer
Editors

PART ONE

INTRODUCTION

At first sight, the Christian community depicted in the New Testament appears to be an entirely lay one, particularly when it is considered against the background of the main-stream of Judaism from which it sprang, or when it is compared with its contemporary, the Qumran sect. In the religion both of the Jerusalem temple and of Qumran, a clearly defined and recognised priesthood was essential.

Bishop Robinson argues that it would be a mistake to conclude from this that the first Christian communities were unpriestly. In them, the priestly element in Judaism had been transmuted, not discarded, through the emphasis placed on Christ as the fulfilment of the Jewish law. The Jewish priesthood and its functions were fulfilled and superseded in Christ, rather than abolished; consequently (and in sharp contrast with the treatment of the scribes and Pharisees) there is no suggestion in the New Testament that Jesus attacked priesthood and sacrifice as such.

With the destruction of the temple in A.D. 70 Judaism was left as a purely lay organisation, or at best with a priesthood which could no longer perform its cultic functions. Christianity, on the other hand, found a completely satisfactory replacement for the temple in the true high priesthood of Christ, and in the true high priesthood of the whole body of the Church. This was made possible by the Christian insistence that all the members of the Christian community share in the sphere of the holy, and so in the priesthood. The partition between the sacred and the secular has been eliminated in Christ, thus creating a holy people of God in which each member shares in the priesthood of Christ.

Consequently, the ordained Christian ministry, in contrast to the Jewish priesthood, is representative, not vicarious, for it is commissioned to do in the name of the whole what in principle all can do.

BIOGRAPHICAL NOTE

J. A. T. ROBINSON *was Anglican Bishop of Woolwich from 1959 to 1969, when he resigned to return to Cambridge as Dean of Trinity College. Amongst the many books which he has written are* In the End God; The Body; Jesus and His Coming; Twelve New Testament Studies; Honest to God; The New Reformation?; Liturgy Coming to Life; Exploration into God; On Being the Church in the World; *and* Christian Freedom in a Permissive Society. *He is married and has four children.*

I Christianity's 'No' to Priesthood

THE RT. REVD. JOHN A. T. ROBINSON D.D.

I HAVE BEEN DELIBERATELY INVITED TO BE ONE-SIDED.
Father Robert Murray s.j. will supply the corrective. This is
somewhat ironical because, on a previous occasion (now some
twelve years ago), I was asked to fulfil his role in an address to the
Rochester Diocesan Clergy School on 'The Priesthood of the
Church', subsequently published in my book *On Being the Church
in the World*.[1] I started that address by some opening paragraphs
on the *other* side – which is now my side. So I will begin by
quoting them:

> In speaking of the priesthood of the Church it may sound para-
> doxical to begin by emphasising how *little* ground there is for
> speaking of it. Yet surely one of the most remarkable facts in
> the history of religion is the astonishing and well-nigh total
> eclipse in the New Testament of the priestly side of the Old
> Testament religion. The great exception is, of course, the
> Epistle to the Hebrews. But while this Epistle affords a magni-
> ficent interpretation of the priesthood of Christ, it is virtually
> silent on the priestly aspect of the Church. As is well known,

[1] New edition (Pelican Books 1969) pp. 89–101.

nowhere in the New Testament nor in the early period of the Church is the word *hiereus*, priest, used of the Christian ministry, though all the other offices – bishop, presbyter and deacon – were evidently adapted from Jewish models.[2] The whole elaborate liturgy of the temple and the sacrificial system which lay at the very centre of Jewish religion was given up with extraordinarily little heart-searching; the ritual requirement of circumcision was officially waived within twenty years; and the still more pervasive provision for ceremonial cleansing was abandoned almost at the drop of a hat. The *un*priestly character of early Christianity must surely have been one of the first things to strike an outsider, whether he were Jew or pagan. And we find Justin Martyr having in fact to defend the faith precisely on this score.

It is instructive to contrast the early Christian Church at this point with the Qumran community on the shores of the Dead Sea, with which so many other parallels have been drawn. There is indeed even here a superficial resemblance between them, for both found themselves at odds with official Sadducean priest-hood and cut off from the temple worship and its sacrifices. Moreover, the Qumran Covenanters had a conception of spiritual sacrifice very like that which we find in the New Testament. But we should not be led into thinking that this was in any sense a 'lay' movement, rather like early Quakerism. On the contrary, they prided themselves on being the *true* Zado-kites, and from their Manual of Discipline and the so-called Damascus Document we are left in no doubt that they were as priest-ridden as any section of Judaism. The leadership was overwhelmingly in priestly hands. In any group of ten or more there must be one priest. Their inner circle of twelve priests and three laymen contrasts strongly with the lay character of Jesus' chosen group. Again, in the Covenanters' hopes for the future the priestly 'Messiah of Aaron' always takes precedence

[2] I cannot resist quoting the striking anticipation of the episcopal ideal which occurs in 'The order for the superintendent of the camp' in the Damascus Docu-ment, xvi, of the Qumran Community: 'And he shall have mercy on them as a father on his sons, and shall bring back all their erring ones as a shepherd does with his flock. He shall loose all the ties that bind them, so that there shall be none op-pressed and crushed in his congregation.'

over the secular 'Messiah of Israel', whereas in the main body of Judaism the royal, Davidic hope is strongly to the forefront. If, as I believe to be a plausible hypothesis,[3] John the Baptist was brought up at Qumran, or at any rate had such a way of life as the background of his mission, we should not forget that he too was of priestly descent on both sides. And finally, the decisive difference between Qumran and Christianity lay in the centrality given by the former to constant acts of ablution and purification: the judgement of Jesus that nothing from without can defile a man would not have met with much response on the shores of the Dead Sea.

But if this *un*priestly quality was the characteristic of early Christianity that would have struck the casual observer most forcibly, the casual observer would, not for the last time, have been superficial in his judgement. For the priestly element in Judaism had not disappeared without trace: it had been transmuted. It is indeed the speed and the thoroughness of this transmutation that is the truly remarkable fact.

I think the word 'transmutation' is the clue. As St Paul said, Christ is the *telos* or end of the law, which of course included the levitical as well as the moral law, which were not distinguished in Judaism. He is the *telos* in the double sense of being both its supersession and its fulfilment. My emphasis is to be its supersession.

A key passage is Matt. 12:1–8:

1. At that time Jesus went through the grainfields on the sabbath; his disciples were hungry, and they began to pluck ears of grain and to eat.
2. But when Pharisees saw it, they said to him, 'Look, your disciples are doing what is not lawful to do on the sabbath.'
3. He said to them, 'Have you not read what David did, when he was hungry, and those who were with him:
4. how he entered the house of God and ate the bread of the Presence, which it was not lawful for him to eat nor for those who were with him, but only for the priests?

[3] See my article 'The Baptism of John and the Qumran Community', *Harvard Theological Review*, L (1957), pp. 175–91, subsequently reprinted in my *Twelve New Testament Studies* (1962), pp. 11–27.

5. Or have you not read in the law how on the sabbath the priests in the temple profane the sabbath, and are guiltless?
6. I tell you, something greater than the temple is here.
7. And if you had known what this means, "I desire mercy, and not sacrifice", you would not have condemned the guiltless.
8. For the Son of man is lord of the sabbath.'

This is a Markan passage expanded by Matthew, writing in a Jewish Christian milieu, to give the Church's 'answer' to the priesthood and the temple system. Verses 5-7 are Matthew's addition. 'Something greater than the temple is here' is for him the heart of the Christian claim. And he alone quotes Hos. 6:6, 'I desire mercy and *not* sacrifice', both here and in Matt. 9:13. It is interesting also that he omits, in his parallel to Mark 12:32-3, the scribe's citation of 1 Sam. 15:22: 'To love one's neighbour as oneself is *much more* than all whole burnt offerings and sacrifices'. Evidently Matthew wanted to go beyond the 'much more' of traditional Judaism and justify the actual supersession of sacrifice in the Christian community.

There is no doubt that there is a polemical interest at work here. Matthew's additions and omissions provide evidence of early Christian apologetic rather than of the teaching of Jesus. There is no suggestion that Jesus himself attacked priesthood or sacrifice as such. Indeed, there is remarkably little to show that he even regarded the priests of his day as enemies of his teaching. True, the priest and the levite in the parable of the Good Samaritan do not exactly show up well – though neither does the Pharisee who went up to the temple to pray. But, in contrast to the withering series of attacks on the scribes and Pharisees (Matt. 23:1-36), there is no attack on the priests as a group – Matthew, again, alone adds to the warning 'Beware of the leaven of the Pharisees' the words 'and Sadducees' (Matt. 16:6 and 11). The chief priests, as members of the Sanhedrin, were for political reasons concerned both in the Gospels and Acts for the threat posed by the Christian movement. But early Christianity appears to have been marked by no anti-priestly strain, and both Jesus and Paul carefully refuse at their trials to be trapped into disrespect for the high priesthood

(John 18:22–3; Acts 23:4–5). The legalism of the scribes and Pharisees was evidently seen as a much greater menace. It should not therefore surprise us as much perhaps as it does that Acts 6:7 casually records that 'a great many of the priests were obedient to the faith'.

As I said, there is no suggestion that Jesus himself attacked priesthood and sacrifice as such. He had come to fulfil rather than abolish the law. Yet there is no doubt either that the early Christian community was right in seeing that this 'fulfilment' had quite radical implications.

The same conclusion must be drawn from consideration of the charge at Jesus's trial that he wished to destroy the temple:

> And some stood up and bore false witness against him, saying: 'We heard him say, "I will destroy this temple that is made with hands, and in three days I will build another, not made with hands." ' Yet not even so did their testimony agree. (Mark 14:57–9)

It is stressed that this is false witness and that even on this version agreement was impossible. The report may in fact have been a garbled version of what Jesus is recorded as saying in John 2:19: 'Destroy this temple, and in three days I will raise it up.' There is no ground for thinking that *Jesus* wished to destroy the temple. He cleansed the temple – but only in order to restore it to its proper function of being 'a house of prayer for all nations' (Mark 11:15–18), or, as we might put it, to make it a genuinely ecumenical centre. He foresaw the inevitable desolation of the temple (Mark 13:1–4; Luke 19:43–4), but there is no evidence that he deliberately attacked it. Indeed he wept and lamented over it (Luke 13:34–5; 19:41–2). His whole attitude was that of the radical, who wants to go to the roots of his tradition, not of the revolutionary, who wants to overthrow the tradition.

The same seems to be true of the attitude of Stephen in Acts. In Acts 6:12–14 we read:

> And they stirred up the people and the elders and the scribes, and they came upon him and seized him and brought him before the council and set up false witnesses who said, 'This man never ceases to speak words against this holy place and the

law; for we have heard him say that this Jesus of Nazareth will destroy this place, and will change the customs which Moses delivered to us.'

Again it is 'false witnesses', and this time Stephen (unlike Jesus) makes a careful and spirited defence. He outlines the history of God's dealing with his people and makes it clear that there is nothing wrong with sacrifice, except when it becomes idolatry (Acts 7:41). Yet sacrifice is plainly not essential. He quotes Amos 5:25: 'Did you offer to me slain beasts and sacrifices, forty years in the wilderness, O house of Israel?' (Acts 7:42). And he goes on to take the same attitude of the temple. Israel managed perfectly well simply with a 'tent of witness' 'until the days of David'. Yet even though God granted David's desire and Solomon built a house for him, nevertheless: 'The Most High does not dwell in houses made with hands; as the prophet says, "Heaven is my throne, and earth my footstool. What house will you build for me, says the Lord, or what is the place of my rest? Did not my hand make all these things?" ' (Acts 7:44–50). The temple, like sacrifice, is ultimately dispensable. Yet the final sentence of Stephen's defence makes it clear that he is not against Moses and the law, but against those 'who received the law delivered by angels and did not keep it' (Acts 7:53).

A similar attitude is to be seen in the conversation between Jesus and the woman of Samaria in John 4:20–6. Again, there is no attack on the temple. On the contrary says Jesus: 'We worship what we know, for salvation is from the Jews.' Yet the *necessity* of the temple is questioned: 'The hour is coming, and now is, when the true worshippers will worship the Father in spirit and truth'. And it will be superseded because a greater than the temple is already here: 'The woman said to him: "I know that Messiah is coming (he who is called Christ); when he comes, he will show us all things". Jesus said to her, "I who speak to you am he." ' This is precisely the theology of John's comment in 2:21 on the raising up of the new temple: 'But he spoke of the temple of his body.' And this theology receives its final expression in the New Testament in Rev. 21:22: 'I saw no temple in the city, for its temple *is* the Lord God the Almighty and the Lamb.'

The temple is abolished only because it is replaced. When the substance is come the shadows retreat. This is the message of the Epistle to the Hebrews, which must be quoted just as much for Christianity's 'no' to priesthood as for its 'yes'. Indeed there is no more sustained argument *against* the levitical priesthood in the whole Bible than Heb. 7–10. The argument comes to its climax in 10:1–14:

> For since the law has but a shadow of the good things to come instead of the true form of these realities, it can never, by the same sacrifices which are continually offered year after year, make perfect those who draw near. Otherwise, would they not have ceased to be offered? If the worshippers had once been cleansed, they would no longer have any consciousness of sin. But in these sacrifices there is a reminder of sin year after year. For it is impossible that the blood of bulls and goats should take away sins. Consequently, when Christ came into the world, he said, 'Sacrifices and offerings thou hast not desired, but a body hast thou prepared for me; in burnt offerings and sin offerings thou hast taken no pleasure. Then I said, "Lo, I have come to do thy will, O God," as it is written of me in the roll of the book.' When he said above, 'Thou hast neither desired nor taken pleasure in sacrifices and offerings and burnt offerings and sin offerings' (these are offered according to the law), then he added, 'Lo, I have come to do thy will.' He abolishes the first in order to establish the second. And by that will we have been sanctified through the offering of the body of Jesus Christ once for all. And every priest stands daily at his service, offering repeatedly the same sacrifices, which can never take away sins. But when Christ had offered for all time a single sacrifice for sins, he sat down at the right hand of God, then to wait until his enemies should be made a stool for his feet. For by a single offering he has perfected for all time those who are sanctified.

For Christianity priesthood and the temple are abolished only because they are *fulfilled*. And this is the great point of contrast with Judaism. The contrast comes out very clearly in the anxiety of the chief priests in John 11:48:

If we let him go on thus, every one will believe in him, and the Romans will come and destroy both our holy place and our nation.

The verb is 'take away', the same word as is used in John 1:29 of the Lamb of God taking away the sin of the world. It means to rub out all together, leaving nothing. This, as Jesus saw, was the only prospect left for Judaism: 'Behold your house is forsaken and desolate' (Matt. 23:37). This is the end not as *telos* but as bare *finis*: nothing is left but a hole.

And this is in fact what happened to Judaism. With nothing to put in the place of the temple and its sacrifices, the synagogue and the rabbinate had to cope. The priestly element simply went into abeyance – pending its restoration – and today in orthodox Judaism the shadow of it is still there. There are, I am told, certain blessings in the liturgy that can only be given by descendants of the house of Aaron. These are pronounced not by the rabbi but by anyone in the congregation who happens, as the case may be, to have the surname Cohen (priest) or Levy (levite). The rabbi is essentially a layman, inheriting the mantle of the teacher, and to some extent the prophet and the judge, but not the priest.

Perhaps I can illustrate this from an unlikely theological source, the American detective story by Harry Kemelman, *Friday the Rabbi Slept Late*. The rabbi is speaking:

'When I got my S'michah – you call it ordination – I was not questioned on my beliefs and I took no oath of any sort.'
'You mean you are not dedicated in any way?'
'Only as I feel myself dedicated.'
'Then what makes you different from the members of your flock?'
The rabbi laughed. 'They are not my flock in the first place, at least not in the sense that they are in my care and that I am responsible to God for their safety and their behaviour. Actually, I have no responsibility, or for that matter no privilege, that every male member of my congregation over the age of thirteen does not have. I presumably differ from the average member of my congregation only in that I am supposed to have a greater knowledge of the law and of our tradition. That is all.'

'But you lead them in prayer –' He stopped when he saw his guest shaking his head.

'Any adult male can do that. At our daily service it is customary to offer the honour of leading the prayers to any stranger who happens to come in, or anyone who is not usually there.'

'But you bless them and you visit the sick and you marry them and you bury them –'

'I marry them because the civil authorities have empowered me to; I visit the sick because it is a blessing that is enjoined on everyone; I do it as a matter of routine, largely because of the example set by your priests and ministers. Even the blessing of the congregation is officially the function of those members of the congregation who happen to be descendants of Aaron, which is the custom in Orthodox congregations. In Conservative temples like ours, it is really a usurpation on the part of the rabbi.'

'I see now what you mean when you say you are not a man of the cloth', said Lanigan slowly. Then a thought occurred to him. 'But how do you keep your congregation in line?'

The rabbi smiled ruefully. 'I don't seem to be doing a very good job of it, do I?'

'That's not what I meant. I wasn't thinking of your present difficulties. I mean, how do you keep them from sinning?'

'You mean how does the system work? I suppose by making everyone feel responsible for his own acts.'

'Free will? We have that.'

'Of course, but ours is a little different. You give your people free will, but you also give them a helping hand if their foot slips. You have a priest who can hear confession and forgive. You have a hierarchy of saints who can intercede for the sinner, and finally you have a Purgatory, which is in the nature of a second chance. I might add that you have a Heaven and a Hell that help to right any wrongs in life on this earth. Our people have only the one chance. Our good deeds must be done on this earth in this life. And since there is no one to share the burden with them or to intercede for them they must do it on their own.'[4]

[4] Penguin ed. (1967), pp. 118-20.

The comparison and contrast with the early Christians is, I think, interesting. They shared with Judaism the end of the temple, even before its destruction. They too got on without it. They had no priests, and the Epistle to the Hebrews rubs in the fact that Jesus was a layman:

> For the one of whom these things are spoken belonged to another tribe, from which no one has ever served at the altar. For it is evident that our Lord was descended from Judah, and in connection with that tribe Moses said nothing about priests (Heb. 7:13–14).

Moreover, the early Church was not anti-priestly – though, as we have seen, it soon found itself involved in polemic against the *necessity* of the sacrificial system, as it was also against the necessity of circumcision and ritual ablutions. But, unlike Judaism, it found a completely satisfying *replacement* for it (*a*) in the true high priesthood of Christ (this is the great theme of the Epistle to the Hebrews) and (*b*) in the true priesthood of the whole body of the Church (which interestingly enough receives no treatment in the Epistle to the Hebrews).

In support of the latter, early Christian apologetic (as we find it reflected both in 1 Pet. and in the Apocalypse) brought together two Old Testament texts:

> You shall be to me a kingdom of priests and a holy nation (Exod. 19:6)

and

> You shall be called the priests of the Lord, many shall speak of you as the ministers of our God (Isa. 61:6).

For comment perhaps I may be allowed to refer back once again to my earlier address on 'The Priesthood of the Church':

> It is very significant that, of the hundreds of Old Testament references to the priesthood, it should be these two alone which are applied to the Church. For here, almost uniquely in the Old Testament, it is the whole people of Israel who are designated priests, and not, as usually, one tribe or family succession

within Israel. In a situation such as ours where the vocation to the ordained ministry is essentially a personal and spiritual calling, we can hardly appreciate the position which prevailed in Judaism, where to be a priest one had to belong to a certain line, and then all one had to do was to prove it. This idea of a closed hereditary priesthood is again one of the things that the Christian revolution abolished so summarily that we are scarcely aware from the New Testament that anything has happened at all. The theme, to be found in these isolated passages of the Old Testament, that the whole of Israel was a priesthood was in practice obscured by the much more obvious fact that there was one tribe in Israel which was priestly and eleven that were not.[5]

The crucial thing that Christianity did was to end the distinction on which late Judaism rested between the holy and the common. This end was symbolised by the rending of the temple-veil from top to bottom at Jesus's death (Mark 15:38). Henceforth nothing could be common or unclean (Acts 10:14-15) – or therefore unpriestly. Christianity celebrated as one of its distinctive marks the *koinonia hagiōn*[6] – the making holy of the common and the communalisation of the holy. And with the communalisation of the holy went the communalisation of the priesthood. For this was its sphere of operation. There is for the New Testament no longer any separated space or holy time, no sacred realm or hieratic caste, no particular order of ministry that is priestly – for the whole is. The New Testament, as opposed to the Old Testament, would agree with the modern rabbi (against many sacerdotalist Christians) that the ordained ministry is representative, not vicarious. It does not stand over against the laity, mediating

---

[5] Pelican ed., p. 92.

[6] This phrase carries a multitude of nuances – from the communion of saints to the sharing of the sacraments. But basically it means common participation in the sphere of the holy – which was hitherto the preserve of a privileged elite. Thus in Acts 2:17-18 Peter announces on the day of Pentecost as the great fact of the new age the fulfilment of the eschatological promise that the holy Spirit would be the possession not only of a select few – prophets, kings and outstanding individuals – but of everyone, down to menservants and maidservants. The *koinonia tou hagiou pneumatos*, the common ownership of holy Spirit, was as much a summary of the Gospel as 'the grace of our Lord Jesus Christ' or 'the love of God' (2 Cor. 13:13).

between them and God, and doing what they cannot. It is commissioned – by Head and Body alike – to do in the name of the whole what in principle all can do. But, unlike the ministry of the rabbi, this is essentially a priestly ministry – the ministry of a priestly people, the *plebs sancta dei*, the holy common people of God.

The theme of this paper can perhaps be summarised by saying that Christianity stands not for the abolition of priesthood but for its secularisation. (This is why Gogarten and Harvey Cox are able to see the process of secularisation in our contemporary world not as the enemy of the Gospel, but as its fruit.) There is no longer any separate sacral realm, because the partition between the sacred and the secular, religion and life, is in Christ done away. John Macmurray once said that the great contribution of Judaism to religion was to abolish it. This in fact it never succeeded in doing. Indeed, it strengthened the middle wall of partition. But, in this as in other respects, Christ came as the fulfilment of Judaism – making possible what the law could not do.

Starting from the definition of a priest as "a cult official recognised by a given religious group as having a mediatorial function and status with regard to the deity and to men, such that he is understood in some sense to act and speak for each to the other," Fr Murray traces the early historical stages of applying the language of priesthood and the sacrificial cult to the ministry of the Christian Church.

In examining this process it is essential to recognise that it is not sufficient to discover the sources from which the language about the ministry, or the ceremonies, were borrowed. The apostolic Church borrowed freely, but it transformed what it borrowed and changed it radically to make it say to the needs of the Christian community and to give it a specifically Christian significance.

In all the language of priesthood and sacrifice, the priority remains clearly with Christ. We see in Christ all that priesthood can mean when the concept is at the service of the God revealed by Jesus. Priesthood language is also applied to the Church, but in a transferred or figurative sense; transferred, in so far as it reflects a widespread pattern of dependent sharing in Christ's status and function, since he has made men able to pray and act "in" and "through" him; figurative, in so far as the Church claims, as the new people of God, to fulfil the meaning of the institutions of the former people without actually having a cult priesthood.

Essentially, this paper develops the position opened by Bishop Robinson, but with the clear understanding that even in the New Testament there is no one theology — which should encourage 'mutual tolerance between the alternatives of differing theological views'. There is no single, systematic New Testament theology of priesthood because the apostolic ministry did not need or want such a foundation: its true basis was (and is) participation in Christ's ministry of priesthood and service, not conformity to the old law. In the sub-apostolic period the emergence of problems of ecclesiastical and sacramental procedure show that an explicitly priestly ministry had become normal, but only as the actualisation of Christ's work in the Church, and as something latent in the apostolic ministry. In this context the attempts to establish the validity of Jesus's priesthood by tracing it from Moses through John the Baptist by means of levitical 'ordination' rites were misguided.

Whatever language or ceremonial was used, in conjunction with the Church's official ministry during the first three centuries of the Church's existence, it was never forgotten that priesthood is predicated more properly of the Church as a whole.

BIOGRAPHICAL NOTE

ROBERT MURRAY was born in Peking in 1925, where his father was missionary. He became a Catholic in 1936 while reading Greats at Corpus, and joined the Jesuits in 1945. He was ordained priest in the theology of the Church and its various scriptural studies at Heythrop College since 1963. Chief Papal correspondent for reviews and periodicals.

INTRODUCTION

Starting from the definition of a priest as 'a cult official recognised by a given religious group as having a mediatorial function and status with regard to the deity and to men, such that he is understood in some sense to act and speak for each to the other', Fr Murray traces the early historical stages of applying the language of priesthood and the sacrificial cult to the ministry of the Christian Church.

In examining this process it is essential to recognise that it is not sufficient to discover the sources from which the language about the ministry, or the ceremonies, were borrowed. The apostolic Church borrowed freely, but it transformed what it borrowed and changed it radically to make it serve the needs of the Christian community and to give it a specifically Christian significance.

In all the language of priesthood and sacrifice, the priority remains clearly with Christ; 'We see in Christ all that priesthood can mean when the concept is at the service of the God revealed by Jesus. Priesthood language is also applied to the Church, but in a transferred or figurative sense; transferred, in so far as it reflects a widespread pattern of dependent sharing in Christ's status and function, since he has made men able to pray and act "in" and "through" him; figurative, in so far as the Church claims, as the new people of God, to fulfil the meaning of the institutions of the former people without actually having a cult priesthood.'

Essentially, this paper develops the position opened by Bishop Robinson, but with the clear understanding that even in the New Testament there is no *one* theology – which should encourage 'mutual tolerance between representatives of differing theological tastes'. There is no single, systematic New Testament theology of priesthood because the apostolic ministry did not need or want such a foundation: its true basis was (and is) participation in Christ's ministry of priesthood and service, not conformity to the old law. In the sub-apostolic period the emergence of problems of ecclesiastical and sacramental procedure show that an explicitly priestly ministry had become normal, but only as the actualisation of Christ's work in the Church, and as something latent in the apostolic ministry. In this context the attempts to establish the validity of Jesus's priesthood by tracing it from Moses through John the Baptist by means of levitical 'ordination' rites were misguided.

Whatever language or ceremonial was used in conjunction with the Church's official ministry during the first three centuries of the Church's existence, it was never forgotten that priesthood is predicated more properly of the Church as a whole.

BIOGRAPHICAL NOTE

ROBERT MURRAY *was born in Peking in 1925, where his father was a missionary. He became a Catholic in 1946, while reading Greats at Oxford, and joined the Jesuits in 1949. He has been a lecturer in the theology of the Church and in various scriptural subjects at Heythrop College since 1963. Apart from contributions to various symposia*

2 Christianity's 'Yes' to Priesthood

ROBERT MURRAY s.j.

AS WE HAVE SEEN, THERE ARE STRANDS IN THE NEW Testament, both in the Gospels and elsewhere, which suggest, even more sharply than some passages in the prophets, that since the definitive act of God in Jesus all previous ideas of cult, temple and priesthood have, at best, a relative value; their meaning has been fulfilled and they are either already superseded or clearly dispensable. Yet it is equally clear that the language of priesthood and formal cult is adopted, in one context or another, by several New Testament writers, and that the immediate heirs of the apostolic Church came comparatively quickly to accept this sort of language in speaking of the Church's ministry. It is the purpose of this paper to trace the history of this acceptance; first to elucidate the contexts and senses in which cult and priesthood language are used in the New Testament, and then, by examining the evidence left us by the early Church, to trace the stages up to the point when, in the third century, it is generally assumed that this language is applicable in the direct and proper sense to the Church's ministry.

and journals, he has written Behold the Lamb of God, and Newman on the Inspiration of Scripture (in collaboration with J. D. Holmes).

This is not, therefore, an essay on the origins and original nature of Christian ministry. I presuppose that from the beginning the Church and the local churches had leaders who preached and taught the 'good news' of Jesus himself, and who exercised functions in the community which were determined either by Jesus or by the original apostles, and organised by the latter so that they should continue in the Church. It is not my task to add to the studies of ministry in the early Church.[1] It is enough to observe the often-noted fact that none of the words used for the New Testament ministry are 'priestly', and conversely, 'priestly' words are not applied to Christian ministers as such.

Of the terms used for the latter, *apostolos* means an authorised emissary; *episkopos* means an overseer or manager; *presbyteros* means a senior person or dignitary, especially the member of some board or guild; *diakonos* means some kind of servant, and the related noun *diakonia* is used to designate what all these do, which is service in the Church in the spirit of Jesus the servant. The stress is entirely on function or activity, not on sacred status. *Diakonia* covers the activities of others besides those just mentioned – teachers (*didaskaloi*), prophets, 'healers', 'helpers' and all those mentioned in passages such as 1 Cor. 12:27–8. Only some of these functions have ever become institutionalised and connected with the ordained ministry, but all of them (and whatever other service the Church needs or is called to render) are *diakonia*, functions undertaken in response to the *charismata* given by the holy Spirit; the word *charisma* likewise covers both the authoritative functions such as apostle and *episkopos* and the free activities of witness and charity. The ceremony for appointing church members to any function seems to have been, from the beginning, the laying-on of hands with prayer for the holy Spirit to come upon the candidate. The origins of this practice are not in any ceremony of priestly ordination but rather in that for authorising rabbis;[2] but, as so often, the apostolic Church radically changed what it adopted, and made the laying-on of hands the outward sign of

---

[1] For a useful recent summary with bibliography, cf. J. H. SCHELKLE, 'Ministry and Minister in the New Testament' in *Concilium* 3, 5 (March 1969), pp. 5–11.

[2] Cf. D. DAUBE, *The New Testament and Rabbinic Judaism* (London 1956), pp. 224–46.

the gift of the holy Spirit in all the various appropriate contexts – at baptism, ordination or designation for special ministries, the difference being no doubt expressed in the accompanying prayer.

In contrast with all this is the language and activity of cult priesthood, Jewish or pagan. On this also the reader is referred to standard studies.[3] The primary words to consider are 'priest' or 'high priest' (Greek *hiereus* or *archiereus*, Latin for both *sacerdos*) with the related nouns for the priestly state or order, *hierateia* or *hierateuma* (Latin *sacerdotium*) and the verb meaning 'to function as a priest', (arch-)*hierateuein* (*sacrum facere* etc.). Of the many other relevant words it is, perhaps, enough to mention *thüein*, to slay or offer in sacrifice (*mactare*, *immolare* etc.) and *thüsiasterion*, place or altar of sacrifice (*altare*, etc.). In the New Testament words of this kind are found in their common or everyday sense applied only to Jewish or pagan priests.

To conclude this introduction we need some agreeable description (if not a definition) of priesthood as a religious phenomenon.[4] Here again we must tread warily past the workshops of the comparative religion scholars, but I hope that some such account as this may be acceptable: a priest is a cult official recognised by a given religious group as having a mediatorial function and status with regard to the deity and to men, such that he is understood in some sense to act and speak for each to the other. The characteristic priestly activity is leading worship and especially performing sacrifice, often in a sanctuary to which priests have privileged access; such sacrifice, correctly performed, is understood to be acceptable to the deity and to win his favour for men. Often the successful outcome of the rites is seen as *conditional* upon correct performance, with a consequent elaboration of rubrics and casuistry to solve all uncertainties; the body of priestly learning which thus comes about fosters the development of priestly castes. In many religions priesthood also involves oracular functions, whereby the priest acts as a mediator also by presenting men's

[3] E.g. the articles by G. SCHRENK on the word-family *hieros* in KITTEL's *Theol. Dict. of the N.T.*, tr. G. W. Bromiley, vol. III (Grand Rapids, Mich. 1965), pp. 221–83. The non-specialist reader may consult Y. CONGAR, O.P., 'The different priesthoods: Christian, Jewish and Pagan', in his *Priest and Layman* (London 1967), pp. 74–89.

[4] For a similar but more succinct account, cf. K. H. SCHELKLE, art. cit. (*Concilium*, 3, 5, 1969), p. 5.

questions and replying in the name of the deity; in other religions the place of such mediatorship may be taken by prophecy, which may even be in conflict with cult priesthood. The above sentences have been phrased with the intention that they should apply to various religions which use or accept the idea of priesthood, including Judaism and Christianity.[5] My intention is not to attempt a definition (which would almost inevitably beg questions) but to give a focus to what follows by locating the idea of priesthood approximately and descriptively.

THE ADOPTION OF PRIESTHOOD LANGUAGE
IN THE NEW TESTAMENT

The apostolic Church clearly understood its ministry to be different in kind from Jewish or pagan priesthood, though it saw itself as the heir to the authentic tradition of prophecy. When priesthood language is adopted in the New Testament it is in order to express theological ideas about the work and role of Christ, and secondly of the Church. The priestliness of Christ and the Church is certainly asserted as true, yet this cannot be in the ordinary or obvious sense, both because Jesus was not a levitical priest and because all the New Testament writers hold that he has fulfilled and superseded all that the former cult signified or effected. Rather we should say that priesthood language is adopted symbolically, provided that this is not misunderstood (through that kind of panic with which some Catholics immediately react to the word 'symbolic', for example when the real presence in the eucharist is discussed) as though the expression undermined or weakened the assertion of truth. Symbolic discourse, in fact, is simply one of the ways men can express what they mean, including what they mean to assert as true.

When we come to consider the application of priesthood language to the Church or any of its members, a further distinction is needed. The application to Christ is proper and direct,

---

[5] The accident that 'priest' comes etymologically from *presbúteros* in the New Testament will not, it is hoped, mislead any unwary reader into misunderstanding the above remarks, which are neither primarily about Christian ministry, nor intended to criticise anything.

because though the language is used symbolically, it is asserted as absolutely and transcendentally true; we see in Christ all that priesthood can mean when the concept is at the service of the God revealed by Jesus. Priesthood language is also applied to the Church, but in a transferred or figurative sense; transferred, in so far as it reflects a widespread pattern of dependent sharing in Christ's status and function, since he has made men able to pray and act 'in' and 'through' him; figurative, in so far as the Church claims, as the new people of God, to fulfil the meaning of the institutions of the former people without actually having a cult priesthood. My thesis, then, is that in the New Testament priesthood language is applied symbolically, in the proper sense to Christ and in a transferred or figurative sense to the Church. This thesis must now be substantiated, but this can be attempted summarily, since there are excellent surveys of the New Testament teaching on this theme.[6]

Priesthood Language used of Christ

1. Christ is the Mediator of the New Covenant. This statement is rightly taken first, though 'mediator' (mesitēs, 'middleman' or 'go-between') is not necessarily a word connoting cult priesthood, because here we are closest to actual words of Jesus. At the Last Supper Jesus gave the bread and the cup a special meaning with reference to his imminent death, and spoke of the new covenant in his blood. (The slight verbal divergence between the Matthew-Mark tradition and the Luke-Paul tradition need not detain us here.) There is an evident reference both to the sacrificial ceremony of sealing the covenant in Exod. 24:1–11 and to Jeremiah's promise of the new covenant (31:31–4). Other aspects of the Last Supper reveal the same double reference; Luke stresses the gathering of the twelve heads of the new Israel (22:29–30) and John the 'new commandment', all in the context of a sacred meal like that in Exod. 24, whether the Last Supper was the Passover meal or not.[7]

As offerer of the new covenant sacrifice Jesus is regarded as

[6] Especially recommended is J. LÉCUYER, C.S.SP., Le Sacerdoce dans le mystère du Christ (Paris 1957).

[7] On this problem cf. J. JEREMIAS, The Eucharistic Words of Jesus (2nd edn., London 1966); probably we simply do not possess enough evidence to settle the question.

antitype of Moses (though also, as we shall see, of other aspects of sacrifice – victim, altar and temple); this typology is explicit in Heb. 9:15–22 and 12:24, where Jesus is called mediator of the new covenant in his own blood, and also in 2 Cor. 3, though there the aspect of mediation which is stressed is the revelation of God's commandments and the gift of the Spirit – the interior reality of the new covenant rather than the offering of the covenant sacrifice. In 1 Tim. 2:5 Jesus is called the 'one mediator between God and men', words which would not necessarily connote priestly activity were it not for the next phrase, 'who gave himself as a ransom for all'; this alludes, presumably, to the synoptic saying 'The Son of Man came not to be served but to serve, and to give his life as a ransom for many' (Matt. 20:28 and par.), behind which surely lies Isa. 53:10 with its use, unique in non-rubrical contexts, of a word belonging to the ritual of expiatory sacrifice. The theme of Jesus as victim as well as offerer, however, will be treated below.

2. Jesus by his sacrifice is seen as fulfilling the meaning of the Old Testament priesthood and cult. This is, of course, the theme of the whole central section of Hebrews. The writer calls Jesus our great high priest (Heb. 3:1; 4:14 etc.) and draws freely on the Old Testament and Jewish tradition in order to interpret Jesus's redemptive work in priestly terms. For this purpose he dwells especially on the high priest's annual entry, on the day of atonement, into the Holy of Holies to sprinkle expiatory blood (Heb. 9:1–10); but he is at pains to explain that the sole and entire significance of the former dispensation was symbolic, to be made clear when Christ had come (8:5; 9:23–10:4). The activities of the former priesthood can serve as a type to illustrate Christ's work, but that is all; he has superseded the former dispensation and abolished it (10:9), just as Jeremiah had declared that the former covenant, broken by Israel, was to be renewed on new and different terms (Heb. 8:6–13; 10:15–18). Consequently the priesthood which served under the former covenant has been superseded by Jesus, who was not even of the priestly tribe (7:11–14); the writer finds a more suitable type for Jesus in Melchizedek, the priest-king of Salem to whom, though a 'gentile', Abraham gave tithes (Gen. 14:18–20). Though the mysterious figure of Melchizedek

had not played much part in the Old Testament, the writer finds his key text in Ps. 110:4, 'Thou art a priest for ever after the order of Melchizedek'.[8] In Hebrews, Melchizedek's presentation of bread and wine is not yet interpreted sacrificially or related to the eucharist; what interests the author is that he was not a levitical priest but (since Abraham gave him tithes) greater in dignity than the whole people of Abraham including its priests (7:9), while Melchizedek's lack of genealogy and his 'priesthood for ever' can well symbolise Christ's divine origin and eternal destiny.

As Christ is the antitype who supersedes the former priesthood, so is he of the temple (as we saw in Bishop Robinson's paper) and of the altar, as is probably implied by Heb. 13:10, 'We have an altar . . .' This passage, though it is better discussed below in the context of the Church, views Christ's death as the antitype of the destruction of the sacrificial victims 'outside the camp'; 'our altar', that is, his death as understood by Christians, supersedes the altar in the tabernacle and is not for the worshippers at the latter.[9]

3. Jesus is a self-offering victim whose blood effects expiation and redemption. While priestly language is acceptable inasmuch as Jesus 'offered the sacrifice of our redemption', the fact that he suffered and poured out his blood (a fact to which he referred in his words over the cup) makes it appropriate to call him a priest only of a special kind, namely a self-offering one. This is expressed succinctly by the Johannine phrase 'Lamb of God', used in connection with Jesus's baptism (John 1:29, 36). The accounts of this event (especially that of John) symbolically suggest both Jesus's status as mediator, identifying himself with sinners yet acknowledged by the Father, and his self-consecration to death. (Compare his allusion to his death as a 'baptism' in two quite different sayings, Mark 10:38 and Luke 12:50.) John implicitly takes up the figure again at the death of Jesus by quoting a

---

[8] Heb. 5:6; 7:1–25. Ps. 110:4 may have played a part in the Christian development of the word 'order' (Gr. *taxis*, Lat. *ordo*) as designating the sacred status given by ordination, but the word has a Jewish background, as we shall see below.

[9] Cf. IGNATIUS, *Magn.* 7, 2: 'Hasten all together as to one temple of God, as to one altar (*thüsiastērion*), to the one Jesus Christ, who came forth from the one Father.' For Ignatius, Clement and the *Didache* cf. *Early Christian Writings*, tr. M. Staniforth (Penguin Classics 1968). On the imagery of the temple cf. R. J. MCKELVEY, *The New Temple : The Church in the New Testament* (Oxford 1969).

'rubrical' passage about the paschal lamb (Exod. 12:46) as if it were a prophecy (John 19:36). The Johannine theology of the efficacy of the 'blood of the Lamb' comes out equally in Rev. 5:6–12 and implicitly in 1 John where, though without the lamb image, the passage 5:6–8 is surely linked with the piercing of Jesus's side in the gospel (19:34), while in 1 John 2:2 Jesus is called the propitiation or expiation for our sins and those of the whole world, language which is both definitely sacrificial and close to the phrase in John's baptism narrative. Of the many other New Testament passages which stress the redemptive power of Christ's blood, it may suffice to refer here to one very similar to the last though quite independent of it, 1 Pet. 1:19, 'You were ransomed . . . with the precious blood of Christ, like that of a lamb without blemish or spot.'

The lamb image does not in itself express Jesus's voluntary self-offering. This is clear, however, in the synoptic saying 'to give his life as a ransom for many' (Matt. 20:28 and par.), and in the Johannine equivalent where Jesus speaks of freely laying down his life and taking it up again (10:17–18; cf. 'I consecrate myself', 17:19). On two counts, both the use of the lamb image and the self-offering, we are justified in relating all such passages to the early Church's meditation on what was perhaps its favourite piece of the whole Old Testament, the fourth 'Servant-song' in Isaiah (52:13 – 53:12). But it is very possible, even likely, that behind this whole range of religious imagery, both in the New Testament and perhaps already in the exilic prophets, lies a Jewish tradition of great importance for the understanding of redemption at the time when the New Testament was born. This tradition, to which scholars have given attention only in comparatively recent years, concerns Abraham's readiness to offer Isaac in sacrifice (Gen. 22). In Jewish tradition Isaac was by no means passive but voluntarily offered himself as a victim to win blessings for his posterity.[10] In the Targums Isaac is described as

---

[10] Cf. G. VERMES, *Scripture and Tradition in Judaism* (Leiden 1961), pp. 193–227, 'Redemption and Genesis xxii – The Binding of Isaac and the Sacrifice of Jesus', and R. LE DÉAUT, C.S.SP., *La Nuit pascale; Essai sur la signification de la Pâque juive à partir du Targum d'Exode XII.42*, pp. 133–212, where Pére Le Déaut traces the increasing importance of the Isaac theme in the developing Passover tradition even before Jesus.

a lamb, and it is very possible that even 6th-century passages such as Jer. 11:19 and Isa. 53:7 are related to the development of this imagery. If the suffering servant can never be 'identified', at least the picture squares exactly with the late Jewish view of Isaac; in any case, by the time of Jesus it was understood that the primary meaning of the morning and evening sacrifice of a lamb was to remind God of the merits of Isaac. If this theology under-lies the picture of Jesus as the 'Lamb of God who takes away the sin of the world', a lot of things click into place, including, for example, the echo of Gen. 22:16 in Rom. 8:32, 'He who did not spare his own Son but gave him up for us all'.

There are other ways in which the earliest Christian writers regard the priesthood of Christ in the light of Jewish symbolic theology; for example, the theme of Christ as the second Adam, head of the human race restored, which is explicit in St Paul (Rom. 5; 1 Cor. 15) and may be implicit in John, has its background in Jewish meditations on Adam which saw him as cosmic priest, a role to be fulfilled by the Messiah.[11] But within the limits of this paper the above summary must suffice.

Priesthood Language used of the Church

Though there are clear instances of such use, they are far less frequent than references to Christ in priestly terms. The thesis proposed above is that priesthood language is adopted more figuratively than when Christ himself is the subject. It is used to express a truth about the Church, but this truth is not a matter of the Church's social and ministerial structure; it concerns the Church's role and status in relation to God and the world. This is in contrast with the writings of the Qumran community, which claimed to be the authentic Israel and the community of the new covenant, and laid stress on its possession of true and pure priests, even if, at the time their documents were written, these were not exercising their ritual functions. Likewise in main-stream Judaism, after the destruction of the temple and the end of the sacrificial

---

[11] Cf. R. SCROGGS, *The Last Adam: A Study in Pauline Anthropology* (Oxford 1966). These speculations were eagerly pursued by the early Judaeo-Christians, as is shown by (e.g.) the Pseudo-Clementine literature, e.g. *Recog.* I, 47 (ed. B. Rehm, G.C.S., Pseudo-Klementinen II, p. 35).

cult, the Jewish people's religious life was organised with great stress on the rabbinate; but in the primitive Church there does not seem to have been any such concern with status, only with function. Of course the apostles, as Jesus's own witnesses and emissaries, had a special status, but the rest of their work as witnesses, teachers, leaders of worship and directors of the Church's works of service and charity was to be shared with and continued by the ministers whom they appointed. In all this the dominant and directing reality was the Spirit, the inner reality promised in the new covenant, from now on to work in the hearts of all who came to believe in Jesus as Messiah and God incarnate.

1. The Church as the 'Royal Priesthood'. The application of priesthood language to the Church is clearest wherever the New Testament refers to the covenantal passage in Exod. 19:6, 'You shall be to me a kingdom of priests and a holy nation', combined with Isa. 61:6, 'You shall be called the priests of the Lord'. The primary original sense of the Exodus passage is not easily fixed; it may mean a people which will be ruled by kings and priests, or a people whose status as a whole is priestly, bound to the covenant-God as a priest is bound to his sanctuary. This sense seems to be that of the Septuagint rendering *basileion hierateuma*, 'royal priestly body'.[12] The phrase is adopted in 1 Pet. 2:9, 'You are a chosen race, a royal priesthood, a holy nation, God's own people'. Exod. 19:6, rather in its Hebrew form, is echoed also in Rev. 1:6, where it says that Christ 'has made us a kingdom, priests to his God and Father', and likewise in 5:10, 'Thou . . . hast made them a kingdom and priests to our God'. Both passages refer to Christ's ransoming men by his blood.

Though I have taken Peter's use of the Exodus phrase first, this is only the climax of a passage in which, by means of a catena of well-loved 'testimonia', the imagery of the temple and its building is applied to the Church. Earlier, in 2:5, Peter says 'like living stones be yourselves built into a spiritual house, to be a holy priesthood (*hierateuma*), to offer spiritual sacrifices (*pneumatikas thüsias*) acceptable to God through Jesus Christ'. On this passage E. G. Selwyn remarks that it implies a much more favourable

---

[12] For a recent discussion of this theme and its use in the N.T. cf. J. H. ELLIOTT, *The Elect and the Holy* (*Supplements to Novum Testamentum* XII, Leiden 1966).

view of the temple and the levitical priesthood than the Epistle to the Hebrews;[13] the Judaeo-Christian spirituality which this reflects may be the starting-point for the tradition which will concern us again as it appears in 1 Clem. and Hippolytus.

In Hebrews and the Pauline letters, when priestly and sacrificial language is used of the Church, though verbally it may be close to 1 Pet.,[14] it is 'spiritualised'. The whole Christian people now has, like a priest, 'access' to the Father, through Christ, in the Spirit (Eph. 2:18), but the sacrifice of Christians is explained in spiritual and ethical terms, as happened also in Judaism after the destruction of the temple. Thus in Heb. 13:10–16, after the mention of Christ's death in terms of 'our altar', referred to above, sacrificial language is used of the Church, but in a different, eschatological, context (v. 14). Through Christ Christians now 'offer up a sacrifice of praise to God, that is, the fruit of lips that acknowledge his name. Do not neglect to do good and to share what you have, for such sacrifices are pleasing to God' (vv. 15–16). Likewise St Paul tells the Romans (12:1): 'Present your bodies as a living sacrifice, holy and acceptable to God, which is your spiritual (or rational) worship (*logikē latreia*).' The constant stress laid by the apostolic writers on 'holiness' echoes a theme of the priestly code, 'You shall be holy, for I the Lord your God am holy' (Lev. 19:2), which is quoted in 1 Pet. (1:16) to introduce one of the Epistle's main themes; but since Jesus's adaptation of this, 'You must be perfect, as your heavenly Father is perfect' (Matt. 5:48), the primary aspect of the Hebrew word (consecration and setting-apart from everyday life) is enriched in the New Testament with a more ethical, less 'sacral' sense, corresponding much more to the biblical sense of 'righteous'.

2. Priesthood language used of individual members of the Church. Where this occurs it is evidently figurative, and though the subject is usually Paul himself, it does not express a cult-priestly view of the apostolic ministry. This is true even in a passage so loaded with priesthood language as Rom. 15:16, where Paul describes himself as 'a minister (*leitourgos*) of Christ Jesus to the gentiles in the priestly service (*hierourgein*) of the gospel of God,

---

[13] *The First Epistle of St Peter* (London 1946), Add. Note H, pp. 285–98.
[14] Compare Rom. 15:16, discussed below, with 1 Pet. 2:5.

so that the offering (*prosphora*) of the gentiles may be acceptable, sanctified by the holy Spirit'; the language is borrowed from pagan rather than biblical usage. Elsewhere Paul uses sacrificial language to express his own readiness to lay down his life; in Phil. 2:17 he speaks of being poured as a libation on the sacrificial offering (*thüsia kai leitourgia*) of the Philippians' faith, and in 2 Cor. 2:15–16 he speaks of the apostles and himself in terms of the 'sweet savour' of sacrifice. The very rarity of such language combines with the evidently figurative usage to underline the fact that, for the New Testament writers, the Church is indeed the heir to the privileges of Israel and its priests, but the status of the Church's members and the functions of its ministers alike are a new gift of God under the new covenant, whereby the Spirit has been poured out and now directs the life of the Church in a radically new way.

THE ADOPTION OF PRIESTHOOD LANGUAGE
IN THE SUB-APOSTOLIC CHURCH

We have seen how the New Testament writers use and do not use this language. To jump ahead two centuries, we may take as a typical sentiment from the mid-third century this sentence of St Cyprian's: 'That priest truly acts in Christ's stead who imitates what Christ did, and he offers a true and complete sacrifice in the Church to God the Father if he sets about offering in the way that he sees Christ to have offered.'[15] Cyprian is in the middle of a heated argument about correct ecclesiastical and sacramental procedure. The terms he uses are those he can assume will be generally understood. Priesthood language in the direct and natural sense, involving the characteristic stress on correct performance, is now at home in the Church. In this section it is our task to trace how this came about.

The Problem of Ministry and Priesthood
The early Church continued in its conviction that the former dispensation of priesthood and sacrificial cult had already been

[15] Ep. 63: 14 (C.S.E.L. III. 2, p. 713).

superseded by Christ before the destruction of the temple in
A.D. 70 put an end to the temple ceremonial. The early Fathers all
insist that God has no need of sacrifices, and that he accepts such
cult only if it expresses true 'spiritual worship' of the heart. This
theme is general in the second and third century Fathers; the
sacrifice of the new 'priestly people' is a pure and holy life and the
offering of prayer.[16] In such contexts the early Fathers seem
never to think of the ministry as exercising priesthood.

On the other hand, the early Church followed the apostolic
writers in seeing Christ's redemptive work in priestly terms. They
understood that he had taught the Church to continue certain
symbolic actions – baptism and the 'breaking of bread', together
with the laying-on of hands with prayer for the holy Spirit in
various contexts, and the ministries of healing and forgiveness –
and they understood, likewise, that he had given his apostles his
authority and his spiritual power to make these actions effective
when they were accepted with faith. The eucharist was understood as Christ's eucharist, forgiveness as Christ's forgiveness.
The Church's witness and preaching was the work of the word of
God. In all this the early Church understood that it had been
empowered, through the apostles, to make Christ's saving work
available to be experienced, through faith, by new generations
who had known neither him nor the apostles. His saving work
was essentially mediatorial, the reconciliation of sinful man with
God and the 'adoption' of undeserving mankind as God's sons in
and through Christ; by this adoption, men could speak the word
of God and symbolically 're-present' or actualise Christ's grace-
giving actions, and likewise they could approach God with confidence that their worship was no mere human effort but was
acceptable in and through Christ. Since priesthood language had
been found appropriate in speaking of Christ's own work, it was
inevitable that it would likewise be found appropriate in speaking
of the continued 'actualisation' of his work in the Church. It is idle
to discuss whether the early Church regarded the eucharist as a
sacrifice; if one considers all the data and its overtones, one cannot

---

[16] E.g. Ps.-Barnabas 2ff.; Justin, *Dial.* 117; Irenaeus A. H. IV, 29ff. (Harvey II,
pp. 193ff.; *Didascalia*, R. H. Connolly (ed.) pp. 98, 226, 238 etc.); in the Latin Fathers,
e.g. Minucius Felix, *Octavius* 32, 1–3, and often in Tertullian, e.g. *De Orat.* 28.

doubt that they saw it through and through as *sacrificial*, and this is true already in 1 Cor. 10:14–21. As soon as we learn who were the ministers of the eucharist we find it was the *episkopoi*, when this term had begun to be restricted to the heads of the local churches. Though, as we noted earlier, neither this nor any of the words chosen for Christian ministers were priestly, it was inevitable that the priestly and sacrificial character latent in the eucharist would come to be expressed by a direct use of priesthood language. We find this clearly developing already in Ignatius of Antioch.[17]

The earliest explicit application of priesthood language to the eucharist (though this must not be misunderstood as though it were 'proving' a modern controversial thesis) is by referring to it the prophecy of Mal. 1:12, 'For from the rising of the sun to its setting my name is great among the gentiles, and in every place incense is offered to my name and a pure offering'. The *Didache* (which if not certainly of the first century, surely contains much material from the apostolic period) in ch. 14 applies this text to the eucharist and calls it 'your sacrifice' (*thüsia*). Similarly Justin in the mid-second century says the Malachi text is fulfilled by the eucharist, which has replaced the old sacrifices and 'is offered in every place by the Christians', who are 'the true high-priestly race of God'.[18] Irenaeus uses the same text and calls the eucharist the 'sacrifice of the New Covenant'.[19] Without doubt, this language is all still like that of Heb. 13, essentially figurative (once again, I do not mean that it does not express a reality, but that it is not a matter of simple objective statements that a sacrificial rite is being performed); what these instances show is the Church's awareness that sacrificial language is appropriate not only to Christian life in general but to the eucharist in particular. As this view of the eucharist became explicit, it became important to find the right way to express the priestly character now seen as latent in the apostolic ministry; the problem was particularly acute because of the painful confrontation of the Church with the Jews, who still stood for the continuing value of the old priesthood and cult, even if it was necessarily in abeyance.

[17] Consider the implications of *Magn.* 7, *Trall.* 7 and *Philad.* 4.
[18] *Dial.* 116–17.   [19] A.H. IV, 29, 5ff. (Harvey II, pp. 199–200).

A False Trail: the Attempt to give Christian Ministry a Levitical Pedigree

The earliest instances of priesthood language applied to Christian ministers are difficult to interpret. In the *Didache* (13:3), *archiereus* is applied not to apostles or *episkopoi* but to prophets, as a reason why they should receive firstfruits. The easy way out is to say that prophets are regarded as deserving honour like that formerly given to the high priest, but it has been argued that the application is deliberate and in the proper sense, reflecting a view of prophecy as authentically priestly.[20] Certainly, even in the New Testament the 'priestly' word *leitourgein* is used of the activity of prophets.[21] If the language is meant in the proper sense, however, it looks as if the notion of priesthood here has been radically revalued in the light of the gift of the Spirit, and therefore is not much out of line with the main trend of New Testament thought.

Still more difficult is 1 Clem. (generally dated about 90 A.D.), chs. 40–4. The context in which Clement speaks of the ministry is an exhortation to orderliness and acceptance of ranks and ceremonies as commanded by God. God, says Clement, commanded all to be done in order, with sacrifices performed at due times by the high priest, priests and levites; Christians ought to observe a like order. The new ranks of ministry, it is implied, are like the old. The apostles were appointed by Christ who was sent by God; they in their turn appointed *episkopoi* and *diakonoi* in various places. Then Clement commends Moses' way of appointing Aaron, to discourage ambition for prelacy. The apostolic ministry is described as having the function of cult (*leitourgein*) and of 'offering gifts'. Once again, the easy way out is to say that Aaron's priesthood and its activities are regarded as *types* of the apostolic ministry, but it is very strange that the activities of the levitical priesthood (ch. 40:1–5) and the restriction of sacrifice to Jerusalem (ch. 41:2) are spoken of in the present tense and with no suggestion either that they came to an end twenty years

[20] Cf. J. ARMITAGE ROBINSON, 'The Problem of the Didache', in *JTS* XIII (1912), pp. 352–4.

[21] The prophets and teachers in the church of Antioch are described thus in Acts 13:1–2.

previously or that the writer rejects them.[22] To say the least, Clement here shows a stronger sense of continuity than most early Christian writers. At many points he reflects liturgical phraseology of a markedly 'Judaeo-Christian' character which must be already traditional in ordination prayers, and which will be still echoed over a century later by Hippolytus.[23] This suggests a picture of the (local) church of Rome only gradually developing out of a thoroughly Jewish Christianity. But does Clement not imply even the claim that the new ministry has inherited a true priestly character from the old priesthood?

If this idea seems far-fetched, it is only because we have read the Fathers through too modern eyes. In sections 36, 61 and 64 Clement follows Hebrews in seeing Christ as high priest, but not in rejecting the Aaronic priesthood. In fact, the claim to continuity was made in Judaeo-Christian circles, while in early Syriac tradition it was standard doctrine. Eusebius preserves some very curious second-century stories which reflect ideas of this kind. He quotes Hegesippus about James 'the brother of the Lord' (that enigmatic figure who seems to have dominated the early Jerusalem church with its apparent attempt to maintain a sort of caliphate).[24] James, he said, was a 'nazirite', and 'he alone was permitted to enter the holy place, for his garments were not of wool but of linen; he used to enter the sanctuary alone', and made his knees as hard as a camel's by his constant kneeling in intercession.[25] Even if this activity were private, James seems to be regarded as entitled to enter by right into the sanctuary of the former temple, correctly vested as a priest. Likewise, Eusebius records Polycrates of Ephesus' letter to Pope Victor in defence of the Asian Quarto-decimans, in which he appealed to 'John, who

[22] For the tense, cf. Heb. 5 and 9. The author may be looking at the institutions in abstraction from time; or one may suppose, with some scholars, that Hebrews shows signs of being an early homily to Jews, later re-worked in an attempt to make it fit a somewhat different situation.

[23] See Appendix, and cf. A. JAUBERT, 'Thèmes lévitiques dans la Prima Clementis', in *Vigiliae Christianae* 18 (1964, pp. 193–203). She shows, in particular, how Clement's stress on order (*taxis*) closely reflects post-biblical Jewish literature, both orthodox and sectarian (Qumran).

[24] On this theory cf. O. KARRER, *Peter and the Church* (Freiburg–London 1963), p. 57.

[25] *Hist. Eccl.* II, 23, 4 (tr. G. A. Williamson, Penguin Classics, p. 100).

leant back on the Lord's breast, and who was a priest (*hiereus*), wearing the gold plate (cf. Exod. 28:36), a martyr and teacher (*didaskalos*).'[26] This is a problematic story for a number of reasons, but at least it shows a strong interest in continuity.

In fact, the Judaeo-Christians asserted that the line of lawful priesthood came through to the Church, and explained their claim in two ways; either they gave Jesus a levitical descent, or they said that he was 'ordained' by John the Baptist, whose father of course was a priest. The former idea may be linked with that current in the Qumran sect, who expected a 'messiah of Aaron' as well as one of Israel (the latter, presumably, being the familiar Davidic messiah).[27] The Testaments of the Twelve Patriarchs, on the other hand, seem to reflect a conflict between these two messianic conceptions; R. H. Charles judges that in the original version the messiah was purely priestly, but in the first-century re-working the messiah from Judah reappears, sometimes fused with the other.[28] This fusion appears in Christian tradition in a fragment ascribed to Irenaeus, 'He was born, according to the flesh, from Levi and Judah, as king and priest'.[29] This makes it very possible that 1 Clem. is hinting at the same when in 32:2 he speaks of the tribes of Levi and Judah as descended from Jacob, and between them mentions Jesus. The tradition is explicit in Hippolytus, and is known to Ambrose and Augustine.[30] On this theory, of course, the succession could not go beyond Jesus by generation, but his levitical descent could be regarded as entitling him legally to found a new priesthood.

The other tradition of this type sees Jesus as having been ordained priest by John the Baptist at his baptism, and as having then passed on the ancient order of priesthood to the apostles. This view is characteristic of the Syriac Fathers, who in this as in many respects are heirs to Judaeo-Christian tradition. Aphrahat, writing in Persia in 336–45, attests the doctrine several times, saying (for example): 'Jesus was anointed by John to be high

[26] *Hist. Eccl.* III, 24, 3 (tr. ibid., p. 231).
[27] E.g. 1QS 9, 11; cf. G. VERMES, *The Dead Sea Scrolls in English* (Pelican Books 1962), pp. 48–9.
[28] R. H. CHARLES, *Apocrypha and Pseudepigrapha*, II, p. 294.
[29] Frag. 17, Harvey II, p. 487.
[30] References in J. LÉCUYER, *Le Sacerdoce* . . ., pp. 82–6.

priest in place of the priests who transgressed the law.'[31] Aphrahat's contemporary St Ephrem has the same doctrine both in his prose works and in his hymns, from which the following example is translated:

> The Most High descended on Mount Sinai
>   and stretched forth his hand over Moses.
> Moses laid it on Aaron,
>   and so it continued till John.
> Therefore did our Lord say to him
> 'It is right that I be baptised by you,
>   that the Order may not perish.'
> Our Lord gave it to the apostles,
>   and behold, in our Church is its handing-on.
> Blessed be he who gave us his Order![32]

One cannot read of these traditions without feeling how misguided they were compared with the theology of Hebrews. Yet this anxiety to give a 'legal' pedigree to the apostolic ministry seems not far from the mind of Clement of Rome, the immediate associate of St Peter and St Paul, and indeed 1 Pet. reveals at least a shadow of this sort of thinking. On this, as on Christology, justification and other crucial topics, it cannot be said that even in the inspired writings of the New Testament there is only one theology. (This thought should give a salutary incentive to mutual tolerance between representatives of differing theological tastes!) Nevertheless, the main stream of Christian tradition witnesses clearly to the conviction that the apostolic ministry does not need or want this sort of foundation. The levitical dispensation can be viewed as a type; we recognise a certain continuity in God's ordinances but regard the new ministry as founded by a new intervention of the same God through Jesus his Son. The true basis of Christian ministry is not conformity to the old law but participation in Christ's ministry, with its twofold aspect of priesthood and service. Like the whole dispensation

---

[31] *Demonstration* XXI (*Patr. Syr.* I, 964. 14ff. and 25ff.).

[32] *Hymns against the Heresies*, 22, 19 (CSCO 169, Series Syr. 76, p. 84, my translation). Both Ephrem and Aphrahat have several other instances. The theme is treated in full in a study I hope to publish soon on the symbolism of the Church in the early Syriac Fathers.

which began with the Incarnation, Christian ministry is sacramental, or a means of making God's saving action present for men to enter into it both in worship and in pastoral service. The true basis is thus expressed by Theodore of Mopsuestia in the early fifth century:

> The priest makes a sort of 'icon' of the liturgy in heaven, because it would not have been possible for us to be priests (we who exercise our priesthood outside of the law) if we had not the 'icon' of the heavenly things.[33]

Priesthood by the gift of the Spirit

Levitical descent or succession was tried as a theory of Christian priesthood, just as in times to come there was to be an equally misguided harking-back to levitical regulations (which has left its traces in some details of canon law), but as a matter of historical fact the main stream of tradition knew that the central emphasis must be elsewhere, namely on the holy Spirit. After all, the scene in the gospels which looks most like 'ordination' is John 20:21-2, where Jesus breathed on the apostles and said 'receive the holy Spirit'.[34] It was at Pentecost that they began to exercise their ministry, as if they only then received the completion of their 'ordination'. The Fathers see every level of participation in Christ's priesthood – by baptism, confirmation and finally ordination – as a gift of the Spirit. This remains true, and determining, even when priesthood language has been definitely accepted, as we find in the prayer of consecration of a bishop in Hippolytus' *Apostolic Tradition*, a collection of sacramental prayers and rites which represents the usage in the church of Rome a century after Clement. The text of the consecration prayer in translation, is given in the appendix, side-by-side with a summary of 1 Clem. 40-4 which, though a passage of exhortation and not a liturgical text, shows some interesting similarities.

In the 'Hippolytan' prayer, as in 1 Clem., the former priesthood is regarded as the antecedent of the new; both are set up by God's

---

[33] *Hom. Cat.* 15, 15 (R. M. Tonneau O.P. (ed.), *Studi e Testi* 145, p. 485).

[34] Some Judaeo-Christian circles felt the need to improve on this and say that Jesus laid his hands on the Apostles; cf. *Acts of Peter* 10 (tr. M. R. James, *The Apocryphal N.T.*, p. 314) and a tradition about James in Chrysostom, PG 61, 327.

ordinance, and are presented in fairly close parallelism. But the centre of the prayer is the petition for the 'ruling spirit' or 'spirit of leadership' (*hēgemonikon pneuma*, Latin *spiritus principalis*). This phrase, taken from the *Miserere* (Ps. 51 [50]:14) means, in the Hebrew, a noble or generous spirit. In its translated form it has an interesting history.[35] Clement of Alexandria, as a Christian philosopher (contemporary with Hippolytus in the early third century), almost naturally read the phrase in the light of Stoic doctrine which called reason the 'ruling element' (*to hēgemonikon*) in man. A generation earlier, Irenaeus refers to the psalm phrase when speaking of the Spirit's work in the Church, in a passage which strikingly illuminates the Hippolytan prayer:

> This is the Spirit for which David asked on behalf of the human race when he said 'and strengthen me with the ruling spirit'. Luke says that this Spirit came down, after the Lord's ascension, on the disciples at Pentecost, having power over all nations to let them enter into life, and to open the new covenant. Thus in all languages they agreed together in a hymn to God, as the Spirit brought separated peoples together into unity and offered the firstfruits of all nations to the Father.[36]

In the Hippolytan prayer, as in Irenaeus, the psalm phrase is understood as that gift of the Spirit which gives a man leadership in succession to the apostles. The movement of the prayer suggests that the 'spirit of leadership' is paralleled by the 'high-priestly spirit' (*archieratikon pneuma*), which is connected not with sacrifice but with forgiving sins, and, at least in our Greek text, with appointing ministers (literally, giving out lots, *didonai klērous*) – that is, with apostolic functions as we know them from the New Testament. In between these passages comes the mention

---

[35] In this section I follow J. LÉCUYER, 'Épiscopat et presbyterat dans les écrits d'Hippolyte de Rome', in RSR 41 (1953), pp. 31–40; cf. his *Le Sacerdoce* . . ., pp. 354–9, and a brief summary in English in his contribution to the symposium *The Sacrament of Holy Order* (Collegeville, Minn. 1957), pp. 131–5.

[36] A.H. III, 17, 2 (Harvey II, p. 92). This rich and suggestive passage shows awareness, not common in the Fathers, that Pentecost was first the feast of harvest first-fruits (Lev. 23 : 15–21), and then the feast of the covenant (cf. H. J. KRAUS, *Worship in Israel* (Oxford 1966), pp. 58–61), the ideally appropriate time for the public inauguration of the new covenant. For a fuller treatment of this theme, see J. LÉCUYER, *Le Sacrifice de la nouvelle alliance* (Le Puy-Lyon 1962), pp. 35–51, 155–60.

of sacrificial and propitiatory functions, ascribed to the apostolic ministry but in the language of Old Testament priesthood. The 'offering of gifts' (a phrase common in late Jewish and Judaeo-Christian literature, and found in 1 Clem. 44) undoubtedly refers to the eucharist, as it clearly does in Irenaeus.[37] My purpose in setting out the Hippolytan prayer side-by-side with a summary of the passage in 1 Clem. is to suggest that this prayer, both in its consecrated phrases and in its general pattern, is indeed 'apostolic tradition', representing a developed form of a very primitive prayer of ordination, couched in typically 'Judaeo-Christian' language which is also reflected in 1 Clem. a century earlier. If, as regards the adoption of Old Testament priestly language, most of the New Testament writers and the main stream of expository tradition tend clearly to the side represented by Hebrews, it may well be that the liturgical tradition from the beginning stressed the continuity between the former dispensation and the apostolic ministry, and 1 Pet. may reflect the beginnings of this attitude. What is certain is that by about 200 A.D. 'priesthood language' was fully adopted in the proper sense, and yet the different character of Christian priesthood was safeguarded by putting the central stress on the holy Spirit's action rather than on the elevation of a person to sacral status.[38]

The Priesthood of Presbyters

It remains to review the process by which priesthood language becomes accepted in speaking of presbyters. Our extant documents, at least, show this becoming explicit only later than in the case of bishops. The reason is doubtless the nature of ordination prayers, as exemplified by the 'Hippolytan' prayer (and, indeed, by the pre-medieval parts of the current Roman form); sacrificial functions are not mentioned explicitly, but the prayer asks that the candidate may receive 'the spirit of grace and counsel, that he

---

[37] E.g. A.H. IV, 30-3, passim.

[38] This could be illustrated even more vividly from the *Didascalia* (a Syrian 'Church Order' of the early third century). Chapter IX (Connolly, pp. 85-101) develops what could almost be called a theology of priesthood, both of the people (p. 86) and of the various ministers. There is great stress on the dignity and mediatorial status of the bishop, but the basis of this is that he is empowered to 'act for God' especially by conferring the holy Spirit (pp. 93-4).

may share in the presbyterate and govern thy people with a pure heart'. Then comes the example of Moses' council of seventy elders (Num. 11:16ff.), as in Serapion and still in the Roman rite.[39] Thus the presbyterate is declared to be what it always was, a council of elders in the local church to help apostles and their successors; the Old Testament type adopted, until the middle ages, is not the levitical priesthood but the elders to whom Moses gave a share of his spirit.

The presbyterate is certainly regarded in priestly terms in the Hippolytan *Apostolic Tradition* and from then on, as we need not prove; but it is so regarded because presbyters receive a share in the 'ruling spirit' of the bishops.[40] In the Roman liturgy as described by Hippolytus the presbyters apparently concelebrate with the bishop (*Ap. Trad.* 4:2) and are ministers of baptism (ibid. 21), but they have not the power of ordaining. They impose hands at ordination as a sign of communion with the bishop in the same Spirit, but the central tradition has never seen this as sufficient for ordination in the absence of a bishop.

There are no certain cases of presbyters being called 'priest' (*hiereus* or *sacerdos*) till the later third century, though Cyprian probably provides examples. Likewise we have no explicit early evidence that presbyters acted as main celebrants of the eucharist, though already Ignatius probably implies it where he says that a valid eucharist must be celebrated 'by the bishop himself, or by some person authorised by him';[41] we may, surely, presume that the celebrant was often a presbyter.

With this, our sketch can be regarded as completed, though much filling-out would be desirable. The application of priesthood language to the Christian ministry has involved a whole sacramental theology of worship and a mystique of priestly consecration, for the classical statements of which we would need to go forward to the late fourth century, to St John Chrysostom and Theodore of Mopsuestia. But the essentials have been re-

[39] *Apostolic Tradition*, G. Dix and H. Chadwick (eds.) (London 1968), pp. 13–14. For a version of Serapion's prayer, cf. L. DEISS, C.S.SP., *Early Sources of the Liturgy* (London 1967), p. 130.

[40] Likewise in the *Didascalia* presbyters are described as the 'councillors' of the bishop (Connolly, p. 90).

[41] *Smyrn.* 8:1.

viewed, according to the limited scope of this paper. During the period under review it was not forgotten that priesthood is predicated more properly of the Church as a whole, the 'royal priesthood';[42] it was only later, as the pre-Christian idea of hierarchical caste re-asserted itself, that the non-ordained members of Christ's priestly *laos* increasingly abdicated their claim to their true dignity in favour of those who were masters of the ritual and had access to the dread world beyond the iconostasis or the rood-screen.[43] But this is another chapter in the story.

The process we have tried to trace appears complex and perhaps 'dialectical' rather than the development of a single tradition. But perhaps all Christian theology has to be like that, precisely because it is the exercise of self-understanding by the Church, the gathering of human beings who respond to the Gospel of Jesus and to the challenge of the Spirit, but always with human capacities, human understanding and human misunderstanding. The above study will serve a useful purpose if it stimulates reflection especially in two directions; the perils for theology if it forgets the essentially symbolic character of discourse with which it operates (in a word, if we forget our Jewish origins), and the perils for Christian ministry if it forgets that it is, primarily and essentially, a charism of the Spirit who cannot be imprisoned by human legislation.

[42] Cf. R. DABIN S.J., *Le Sacerdoce royal des fidèles dans la tradition ancienne et moderne* (Brussels–Paris 1950).
[43] Cf. Y. CONGAR, O.P., *Lay People in the Church* (2nd edn., London 1965), esp. pp. 1–27.

APPENDIX

PRAYER FOR CONSECRATION OF A BISHOP

(Hippolytus, *Trad. Ap. 3*)

(1) O God and Father of our Lord Jesus Christ,
    Father of mercies and God of all comfort,
    who dwellest on high yet hast regard to the lowly,
    who knowest all things before they happen,

(2) who gavest ordinances (*horous*) to thy Church
      by the word of thy grace,
    who from the beginning didst foreordain (*proörisas*)
      the race of the righteous from Abraham,
    instituting princes and priests
      and not leaving thy sanctuary without ministers
        (*aleitourgēton*);
    who from the foundation of the world
      hast been pleased to be glorified
      in those whom thou hast chosen,

(3) And[1] now pour forth that power [which comes] from thee,
    the 'princely spirit' (*hēgemonikon pneuma*)
    which thou gavest to thy beloved Child-Servant (*pais*)[2]
      Jesus Christ,
    and he bestowed on the holy apostles,[3]
      who established (*kathidrusan*) the Church
      in every place (*kata topon*)
    for thy sanctification,
      for the unceasing glory and praise of thy name.

(4) Father, who knowest the hearts of all,
    give [charge] upon[4] this thy servant
      whom thou hast chosen (*exelexō*) for pastoral charge (*episkopē*),
    to shepherd thy holy flock (*poimnē*)
      and to serve thee as high priest (*archierateuein*)
    blamelessly (*amemptōs*)[5] ministering (*leitourgounta*)
      by night and day,
    to propitiate thy face unceasingly
      and to offer thee the gifts (*prospherein soi ta dōra*)
      of thy holy Church.

(continued on page 42)

I CLEMENT, 40-44
(select summary for comparison)

40 All things should be done in due
order, just as God commanded

the temple services to be performed
not anyhow or without order but
at fixed times (*hōrismenois kairois*),[7]
and by his supreme will determined
(*hōrisen*) when and by whom service
should be rendered . . .
To the high priest are assigned
his proper functions (*leitourgiai*);
likewise to the priests, levites, laity.

41 We should behave likewise . . .

42 Christ received his commission from God,
and the apostles from Christ.
They set out with the fulness
(*plērophoria*) of the Holy Spirit.
As they went through various places
(*kata chōras*), they established
(*kathistanon*) their first-fruits (*aparchas*)[8]
to be episkopoi and diakonoi.

43 As Moses averted ambitious dissension in
choosing Aaron, by the sign of the staff
flowering to show whom God has chosen
(*eklelektai*) to serve him as priest
(*hierateuein*) and to minister
(*leitourgein*) to him,

44 So the apostles forestalled dissension
by arranging successors. Therefore you
ought not to eject those who have been
ministering blamelessly (*leitourgēsantas
amemptōs*) for the flock (*poimnion*) of Christ,
who have been blamelessly and devotedly
offering the gifts (*prosenenkotas ta dōra*)
of their pastoral charge (*episkopē*).

(Hippolytus, *Trad. Ap. 3* continued)

(5) And that by the high-priestly Spirit
  he may have authority to forgive sins, according to thy command
 to assign lots (*klērous*) according to thy ordinance,[6]
  to loose every bond according to the authority
  thou gavest to thy apostles,
 [and] to please thee in meekness and a pure heart,
  offering thee a sweet-smelling savour,
(6) Through thy Child/Servant Jesus Christ our Lord,
  through whom to thee be glory, might and praise,
 with the Holy Spirit, now and always
  and world without end, Amen.

Note on the Appendix

The best critical text of the consecration prayer is that of DOM BERNARD BOTTE in *La Tradition Apostolique de S. Hippolyte, Essai de réconstruction* (Münster 1963), pp. 6–10; cf. the edition of Dix-Chadwick, pp. 4–6. My version is slightly adapted from Dix's. A good recent study of the Hippolytan ordination prayers is given by D. N. POWER, *Ministers of Christ and his Church* (London 1969), ch. 11, pp. 30–52. The first epistle of St Clement is found in any edition of the Apostolic Fathers; a translation is in M. STANIFORTH, *Early Christian Writings* (Penguin Classics), where this passage is on pp. 44–6. It is to be understood that the 'summary' given here is determined by the purpose of emphasising the similarities in expression, not that of giving the gist of Clement's own argument. On the language and its echoes of early Judaeo-Christian phraseology I am indebted to Father Harold Bumpus, S.J., who has been working on 1 Clement at Tübingen, for most valuable advice.

Notes to text

[1] This 'and', as alien to Greek prayer style as to English, is translated deliberately to draw attention to it as a striking semitism still remaining long after the prayer had become acclimatised in Rome.

[2] *Pais*, like 'boy', means either child (son) or servant. It is used in the LXX for the 'Servant of the Lord' in Isa. 42–53, and in N.T. allusions such as Matt. 12:18. In the early sections of Acts it is a regular title of Jesus (3:13, 26; 4:25, 27, 30). This is generally considered a primitive and typically Judaeo-Christian feature, rare outside works of Judaeo-Christian character. Consequently its persistence in this prayer is remarkable.

[3] So the Latin version, our oldest witness. The Greek form (presumed generally authentic, but preserved only in a later, dependent document, the epitome of the Apostolic Constitutions) has 'which through thy beloved *pais* thou didst bestow on thy holy apostles'.

[4] The expression is semitic rather than Greek.

⁵ The adverb *amemptōs* can be taken either with the preceding *archierateuein* (Botte) or the following *leitourgounta* (Dix). A more general comment on section 4 of the prayer and the 'parallel' passages in Clement is in place. The apparently striking number of verbal coincidences are all adequately, and in fact most plausibly, explained by a shared Judaeo-Christian background. In the LXX *hierateuein* and *leitourgein* both render *kahan* (to officiate as a priest). *Amemptos* is not in fact a LXX word (*amōmos* is preferred) but the idea is obviously essential to the Jewish priestly ideal. *Prospherein ta dōra* (offer gifts) is a technical expression for priestly cult in the LXX, in late Jewish and early Judaeo-Christian literature. Besides this background, similarities in style with Hellenistic court language have been observed by R. KNOPF, (*Die apostolischen Väter*, I, p. 119), a fact to which Fr Bumpus has kindly drawn my attention.

⁶ This line is only in the Greek; it refers to appointing presbyters.

⁷ For Clement's stress on order (*taxis*) and its Jewish and Judaeo-Christian background, cf. A. JAUBERT in *Vig. Christ.* 18 (1964), pp. 193–200.

⁸ For this allusion to the original context of Pentecost, cf. above, p. 36, note (36).

BIOGRAPHICAL NOTE

PAULINUS MILNER *is a Dominican. He studied for two years at the Institut Supérieur de Liturgie in Paris after taking his S.T.L. at Le Saulchoir. He is now engaged in teaching theology and liturgy at Blackfriars, Oxford, and St Catharine's Centre for Nuns in London. He is author of* The Worship of the Church, *and editor of a collection of essays,* The Ministry of the Word.

3 A Methodological Note occasioned by the Paper of Robert Murray

PAULINUS MILNER O.P.

TO SUPPOSE THAT THE APPLICATION OF SACERDOTAL AND sacrificial language to Christ and the paschal events must naturally have led to the application of this same language to the eucharist and its ministers is methodologically questionable. Such a process must be demonstrated and not supposed. In fact the documents seem to indicate that the application of sacrificial language to the eucharist antedates any attempt to justify it by such theological arguments: so far from being the cause of the linguistic change the theological arguments appear rather as an attempt to justify that change. The deduction from the sacrificial nature of Christ's sacrifice to the sacrificial nature of the Christian eucharist does not appear until St Cyprian in the middle of the third century. His usage goes beyond what can be justified by his argument, for not only does he say: *passio est enim Domini sacrificium quod offerimus* (Eph. 63:14), but he will not hesitate to apply the word *sacrificium* to the gifts which the faithful bring to the church, rebuking the woman *quae in dominicum sine sacrificio venis, quae partem de sacrificio quod pauper obtulit summis* (De op. et eleemos. c. 15, CSEL, vol. 3 pt.

1, p. 384. M.L. 4, 613A). Thus he seems to be trying to justify a usage already established. To discover how this usage came to be established we must leave aside the theological explanation and examine a different theme in the available documents.

In applying to Christ and the paschal events the sacrificial language of the Old Testament, the early Church was using sacral terminology for events which took place outside the cultic setting. The same is true when this same sacrificial terminology is applied to the activity of the Christian community. Thus the new temple is said to be constructed of living stones (1 Pet. 2:5) and St Paul uses sacrificial language of any activity which aids the building up of this temple (Eph. 2:21). His own preaching makes him the 'liturgist' (λειτουργὸν) of this new temple and its priestly minister (ἱερουργοῦντα); the lives of those who hear him – like that of Christ with whom they are one body – become a sacrificial offering (προσφορὰ) which is acceptable (εὐπρόσδεκτος) because it is sanctified by the holy Spirit (Rom. 15:15–16). His own martyrdom is seen as a libation poured out on the sacrificial offering (θυσία) of the Philippians' faith (Phil. 2:17). The Romans are told that the offering of their bodies, i.e. of their whole persons, is a living sacrifice, holy and acceptable to God and that this is their spiritual worship (Rom. 12:1f.). In all this St Paul seems to be saying that the cultic activity of the old law has been replaced, not by any new cultic activity, but by the very life of the Christians and all that they do for the building up of the new temple of God. Naturally among the works singled out for sacrificial description are the almsdeeds by which they contribute to each other's support (2 Cor. 9:12; Phil. 4:18f.).

If we may now jump to a text emanating from Syria a little before St Cyprian we can see how this tradition continues.

Hear these things, then, ye laymen also, the elect church of God. For the former people also was called a church; but you are the Catholic Church, the holy and perfect, a royal priesthood, a holy multitude, a people of inheritance, the great church, the bride adorned for the Lord God. Those things then which were said beforetime, hear thou also now. Set by part-offerings and tithes and firstfruits to Christ, the true high

Priest, and to his ministers, even tithes of salvation to him the beginning of whose name is the Decade. Hear, thou Catholic Church of God . . . instead of the sacrifices which then were, offer now prayers and petitions and thanksgivings. Then were firstfruits and tithes and part-offerings and gifts; but today the oblations which are offered through the bishops to the Lord God. For they are your high priests; but the priests and levites now are the presbyters and deacons, the orphans and widows: but the levite and high priest is the bishop. . . . And the orphans and widows shall be reckoned by you in the likeness of the altar. And as it was not lawful for a stranger, that is for one who was not a levite to draw near to the altar or to offer ought without the high priest, so you shall do nothing without the bishop. . . . Do you therefore present your offerings to the bishop, either you yourselves, or through the deacons; and when he has received he will distribute them justly. For the bishop is well acquainted with those who are in distress, and dispenses and gives to each one as is fitting for him; so that one may not receive often in the same day or the same week and another receive not even a little. For whom the priest and steward of God knows to be the more in distress, him he succours according as he requires. . . . Therefore love the bishop as a father, and fear him as a king and honour him as God. Your fruits and the works of your hands present to him that you may be blessed; your firstfruits and your tithes and your vows and your part-offerings give to him; for he has need of them that he may be sustained, and that he may dispense also to those who are in want, to each as is just for him. And so shall thine offering be acceptable to the Lord thy God. (*Didascalia Apostolorum*, R. H. Connolly (ed.), Oxford 1929, pp. 85–92.)

From this passage two things are clear. Firstly, just as in the writings of St Paul, the place of the ancient cultic sacrifices is taken by prayers, petitions and thanksgivings, that of tithes and firstfruits by the oblations which are offered through the bishop to God. Secondly the oblations in question (προσφορά) are alms in money or kind which are to be distributed to those in distress. These are offered by the bishop to the Lord. The whole point of the passage is that since these almsdeeds have a sacrificial aspect they must not be made privately but with the knowledge and under the control of the bishop who in this new cult takes the place of the priest. It seems likely that the phrase in the contemporary prayer for the consecration of a bishop of the *Apostolic Constitutions*, 'May he offer to thee the gifts of thy Church' (Dix-Chadwick [eds.] p. 5) refers to the same custom.

The connection between this system of almsgiving and the eucharist is not clear. The Didascalia attributes to the eucharist a sacrificial nature ('thanksgivings' above p. 47) and also says that it should be offered in the cemeteries for the dead (p. 252). It may be that the dedication to God of the oblations takes place at the eucharist or it may rather have taken place in the context of an evening agape.

The Didascalia throws an interesting light on the well known passage of the Apology of St Justin.

What soberminded man then, will not acknowledge that we are not atheists, worshipping as we do the maker of the universe, and declaring, as we have been taught, that he has no need of streams of blood and libations and incense; whom we praise to the utmost of our power by the exercises of prayer and thanksgiving for all things wherewith we are supplied, as we have been taught that the only honour that is worthy of him is not to consume by fire what he had brought into being for our sustenance, but to use it for ourselves and those in need, and with gratitude to him to offer thanks, by invocations and hymns for our creation and for all the means of health and for the various qualities of the different kinds of things and for the changes of the seasons and to present before him petitions for our existing again in incorruption through faith in him (1 Apol. 13).

I suggest that once we leave aside the kind of theological argument used by Cyprian, we can see evidence that the practice of applying sacrificial language to the eucharist grew from its being regarded as the pre-eminent thanksgiving and also from the fact that the almsdeeds of the community were associated with it. This is supported by the strange fact that none of the early eucharistic prayers contains any direct mention of the offering to God of the sacrifice of his son, while they are full of references to the sacrifice of praise, the unbloody sacrifice and the presentation of gifts and προσφορὰ It may well be that the eucharist attracted to itself the sacrificial language of the Old Testament, not immediately because of its connection with the paschal events, but because it was the focal point of the thanksgivings and almsdeeds of the community which themselves were seen as replacing the sacrifices of the old law.

PART TWO

INTRODUCTION

The first of the four historical papers read at the symposium again raises the question of the use of Old Testament levitical models as a guide to understanding the origins, nature and functions of the Christian ministry. Dom Jean Leclercq points out that in the middle ages the use of this model was part of a general assumption of the continuity between the world of the Old Testament and that of medieval Christendom. There was little attempt to justify this assumption, so the model of the Levite was accepted implicitly rather than explicitly; it was taken for granted that it provided the obvious key to the theological interpretation of the Christian priesthood.

Thus the contemporary crisis in the theology and practice of priesthood marks the ending of a situation which goes back to the fifth century. Since that time one particular model of Christian ministry has so dominated the scene that it has come to be seen almost as an immutable constituent of the gospel message. In the contemporary concern about priesthood it is important to be aware of the extent to which the formation of this model, at the time of the collapse of the western Roman empire, was determined by non-religious aspects of the situation. Sociological factors, and the influence of secular structures, rather than specifically theological considerations, led to the predominance of this model.

Once this is grasped, the current debate will be liberated from the restrictions of a model which, no matter how effective it may have proved in past situations, is no longer to be accepted without question. This means that there is far greater freedom in the reconsideration and restructuring of the ministry than has sometimes been supposed. It also means that we must have the realism, and the humility, to appreciate that our contemporary solutions to the problem of priesthood will not consist in the recovery of some mythically 'pure' notion of priesthood, but will also be affected by our current 'secular' needs and presuppositions.

BIOGRAPHICAL NOTE

JEAN LECLERCQ *was born at Avesnes (France) on 31 January 1911. He entered the benedictine abbey of Clervaux (Grand-Duché of Luxembourg) in 1928. He studied theology and history at Saint Anselm's in Rome, then in Paris where he attended the Institut Catholique, the Ecole des chartes, the Ecole Pratique des Hautes-Etudes (Section of historical sciences) and the Collège de France. He has become more and more committed to the cause of renewal of the monastic life, in Europe and North America, but also in the Third World. He has visited numerous monasteries in Asia, Africa and Latin America. He is Doctor honoris causa of the Catholic Universities of Milan and of Louvain, Corresponding Fellow of the British Academy, Professor at Lumen Vitae (Brussels) and at the Gregorian University. A complete bibliography up to August 1968 is to be found in* Studia monastica, *10 (1969), pp. 331–59. His main publications are:* The Love of Learning and the Desire for God, *2nd edn., New York 1962.* The Spirituality of the Middle Ages, *in collaboration with L. Bouyer-F. Vandenbroucke, London 1968.*

4 The Priesthood in the Patristic and Medieval Church

JEAN LECLERCQ

HAD I BEEN ASKED TO ELABORATE AN ORIGINAL SYNTHESIS or to expose new findings on this subject, I should have been faced with a difficult task for it would be hazardous to attempt to deal with fifteen centuries of history within the limits of one short paper. However, all I have been asked to do is to introduce a debate with a survey of the main problems concerning the priesthood in the ancient and medieval Church.

As far as I know, there exists no complete study on this subject, though there are many valuable preparatory studies. My main source of information will be *Priests Yesterday and Today*, a remarkable book published in 1954 in the series Unam Sanctam, under the direction of Father Congar. The contributors to this volume – Canon Bardy, Professors Laprat, Le Bras, Lemariginier, Fathers Vivaire and Henry – are all outstanding scholars and well-known Christians. To this principal source of information I shall add texts and gleanings from other works.

As is often the case for other topics, the major difficulty here arises from the fact that there exists relatively little information concerning the 'average priest'. Historical documents mention the extremes: they present the virtues of the holy priests for our imitation, and denounce the failings of the weaker brethren as something to be avoided. But there must also have been, between these two limits, a great deal of holiness as well as many failures among the mass of anonymous priests. However, our purpose here is not to judge consciences, but to examine to what extent their conduct was influenced by facts of milieu and institutions.

During the very long age of the so-called patristic and medieval Church, which extends from the 2nd to the 15th century, we must distinguish, for what concerns the west, two main periods separated by an ill-defined space of time which varies – to the extent of one or more generations – according to the different regions. We can say in general that the 5th century is the transition period and that the passage of the Church from the patristic to the medieval age was completed before the opening of the 6th century. Thus the medieval period of the Church covers nearly a thousand years and is considerably longer than that of the patristic Church. Although certain changes took place during the middle ages, none had the importance of those which occurred in the course of the 5th century: these were decisive steps which the Church took as she evolved from the patristic to the medieval age. Let it be said in passing that though this second period came to a close with the 15th century, it is not impossible that the third period of the Church's history began only in the middle of our own 20th century.

Let us now try to characterise the first two periods of the Church, with special reference to the problem of the priesthood which is our concern here.

BEFORE THE MIDDLE AGES

The first four centuries of the Church are generally blocked together under the title of 'patristic period'. It came to a close in the west with the gradual disappearance of the structures of the Roman empire; the disintegration of the political and administrative framework entailed important consequences in the cultural and religious fields. Two characteristic facts of this period stand out as being particularly relevant for the question in hand: (1) facilities for culture became equally accessible to laymen and to clerics; (2) both categories of the faithful enjoyed direct participation in the life of the Church.

History shows that *laymen* took an active part in all of the internal workings of the Church. They had an important role to play in the liturgy, which was still, at that time, a 'popular' liturgy, that is, a liturgy for the people. They had their word to say in the election of bishops, and the nomination of priests. They contributed to the drawing up of church laws and customs;[1] prepared some of the matter for discussion at the councils, and even took part in them. They administered church properties, and it was an accepted thing that they should be allowed to preach (*docere*),[2] the records show that they often did so.[3] In brief we may say that laymen were recognised as being full-time Christians and were given full shares in church affairs. There was no monopoly on the part of the *clerics*: they lived among the laymen, had the same way of life and manner of dress; they were urged to practise chastity, either within the married state or as celibates; they officiated at the altar and administered the sacrament of baptism.

Let us now examine in greater detail the way in which clerics were recruited, and the duties that were expected of them.

Recruitment. The only condition required was a certain standard of honest living. Though recruits were drawn from every social class – except that of slaves who were excluded on account of the rights which their masters had over them – they came mainly from the higher classes and as early on as the 4th century particularly towards the end, 'Bishops were important people able to live an easy life'.[4] There were even episcopal families in which the right to preside over the churches was passed down from generation to generation in either direct or collateral line.[5]

Duties. The office of preaching was generally assumed by the bishops;[6] thus priests were free to give themselves to other occupations, and could be satisfied with very little learning, as they

---

[1] Cf. Y. CONGAR, *Lay people in the Church*, London 1957, pp. 230–2.

[2] Cf. P. RICHÉ, *Education et culture dans l'occident barbare*, Paris 1962, p. 547.

[3] Cf. G. BARDY, 'Le sacerdoce chrétien du Ier au Ve siècle', in *Prêtres d'hier et d'aujourd'hui*, Paris 1954, p. 35.

[4] BARDY, loc. cit., p. 33.   [5] Ibid., p. 34.   [6] Ibid., p. 35.

very often were.[7] They served in the local churches as the immediate auxiliaries of the bishops. The work and mentality of priests was pastoral rather than missionary: they cared for existing Christian communities, but did not consider the evangelisation of the neighbouring heathens as coming within the scope of their ministerial functions:[8] 'The diocesan clergy has never been missionary and was not meant to be so.'[9] Due to the fact that the priests lived close to their bishops, they dwelt mainly in the towns, and rural areas were poorly served.

How, we may wonder, did these priests earn their living? It was generally supposed that they should support themselves on the offerings made by the faithful. In the third century a ruling had filtered into many parts of Europe from Africa by which priests were forbidden to pursue any secular occupation. This law was not universally in force, and even where it was many priests did fulfil secular functions which had nothing to do with the service of God and the faithful[10] and for which they received a certain pecuniary remuneration: some were appointed officers in the service of secular princes; others became salesmen, even travelling salesmen; others again set up in 'business', *usura*, as money-lenders and bankers, making profit on church wealth. Thus, by various ways and means, they supplemented the meagre income obtained from the offerings of their parishioners. Thus, too, arose those temptations peculiar to churchmen: lucre in all its disguises. It is not surprising then that the councils should have legislated about the work to be done by clerics: the fact of restricting the forms of work was not a censure of work itself, but only of certain occupations deemed incompatible with the clerical state.

THE MIDDLE AGES

The medieval period began after the barbarian invasions and the fall of the Empire in the west brought about by the disintegration of its political and administrative structure together with the cultural conditions which they had entailed. The real transition

[7] Ibid., p. 36.   [8] Ibid., p. 50.
[9] Ibid., p. 53.   [10] Ibid., p. 58.

period was, as has been said, the 5th century. The legislative basis
for this evolution can be traced back to 314 when Constantine
transferred the privileges of heathen priests to Christian bishops
and priests. However, the imperial changes did not come into
effect immediately. This may have been due to the fact that in the
years following the decree, the active personalities in the religious
and cultural evolution were not the priests themselves, but the
governors, prefects, procurators, praetors and other government
officials. Even in the east the legislation of Justinian may have
carried more weight than the Edict of Constantine. In the west,
it was only after the barbarian invasions, when all the administrative framework had disintegrated, that the functions held by
government officials passed into the hands of the Christian
bishops. It is this delay which explains that Christian priests took
over profane affairs in the Roman society and not what was
sacred or religious.

Though this change brought about no radical modification
within the Church, it had a profound influence upon its internal
structure and forms of life. These transformations came about
gradually: they were prepared, even to some extent anticipated,
and it is possible that they could not have been avoided. Not all
the elements of this slow evolution are to be explained by political
and sociological factors though these certainly had a decisive
influence.

Several scholars have carried out patient analytic research on
the mutations which took place in the western Church during that
period.[11] Authors such as Christopher Dawson, Father Congar,

[11] RICHÉ, op. cit.; s. MOCHI ONORY, *Vescovi e Città, Set. IV–VI*, Bologna, pp. 19–
33; J. GAUDEMET, in *L'Eglise dans l'Empire romain (IVe–Ve s.)*, (*Histoire du droit et
des institutions dans l'Eglise en Occident*, III), Paris 1958, has made a careful study of
the evolution which took place in the period 'from Sylvester to Gelasius', to use his
own words (pp. 711–12). He has examined at length, pp. 152–79, the following points:
*The status of clerics. The privilege of clerics. Habit. Celibacy. Chastity of married clerics.
Resources. Exemptions*; on pp. 315–20 he goes into the question of *honours: titles and
insignia. Juridical privileges. Social prestige*. His conclusion is that 'the organisation of
the Church bears the stamp of Rome. The care for structures, the importance of the
hierarchy, the development of legislation and the control of tribunals witness to a
taste for order. But the Church is too young, in a world that was once pagan, for
Christianity to have deeply penetrated into social life' (p. 712). We may add that
this will be the task of the middle ages. From all these works it becomes evident that
the western Church was marked not only by a time – the fourth to the sixth century

H. Marrou and D. Knowles[12] have made synthetic surveys of the state of the question. The evolution in the east followed slightly different trends[13] and all that we shall do here is to give a brief summary of the main facts concerning the west.

We can say that there were two major elements underlying the changes in the way of life of churchmen: (1) Laymen no longer enjoyed the same facilities for acquiring culture as did the clerics. (2) The political and social structures which had been in force were replaced by episcopal authority. This meant that new structures were progressively built up: there was constant strife between the laity – in the person of the princes – and the clerics; the laity strove to gain more and more control over them. But at the beginning of the middle ages it was the clergy – that is to say, mainly the bishops who were sometimes more numerous than the priests – which was invested with secular functions. Any priests that there were served merely as the immediate auxiliaries of the bishops. A further step in this evolution occurred when the bishops relegated most of their ministerial functions – preaching,

– but also by a place: Rome. We may lawfully wonder, simply from the point of view of history, whether this double mark has necessarily to be definitive.

[12] C. DAWSON, 'The Sociological Foundation of Medieval Christendom', in *Medieval Essays*, New York 1954, pp. 59–62; Y. CONGAR, 'The Historical Development of Authority in the Church. Points for Reflection', in *Problems of Authority in the Church*, edited by JOHN M. TODD, Baltimore–London 1962, pp. 125–35; H. MARROU in J. DANIÉLOU-H. MARROU, *Nouvelle histoire de l'Eglise*, I (1963), pp. 404–6: *Contrecoup des invasions barbares*, and pp. 494–503: *Émergence de la chrétienté médiévale*. D. KNOWLES, *Nouvelle histoire de l'Eglise, Le moyen âge*, 1968, p. 39. In *The Spirituality of the Middle Ages*, London 1968, in collaboration with F. VANDENBROUCKE, we have tried to characterise, for each period, the three milieu of clerics, laymen and monks and nuns, and the evolution of each of them.

[13] Cf. L.BRÉHIER, 'La vie chrétienne en Orient', in *Histoire de l'Eglise* (Fliche-Martin), t. IV, Paris 1937, pp. 539–42, 553–6. G. DAGON, 'Aux origines de la civilisation byzantine. Langue de culture et langue d'état', in *Revue historique*, 241 (1969), pp. 23–56, has shown that the linguistic difference between the eastern empire and the barbarian western world – which, at least in its elite, remained Latin and became even more so – is the symbol of a growing separation between these two parts of the political and religious world which grew out of the ancient Roman empire. In the eastern empire, hellenisation was accentuated, and there was a concomitant dissociation between State and culture: the Roman empire became the Byzantine empire (p. 55). In the west, there was no longer any Roman empire, and there set in a gradual association of Church and culture.

administration of baptisms, presiding over the eucharistic celebrations – to their priests while they busied themselves with
governing, administration and control. It was during the course
of the 5th and 6th centuries also that more and more priests began
to reside in rural areas. These different factors are sufficient to
explain the widening of the gap that took place between the laity
and the clerics. Not only were laymen looked down upon as
irresponsible children whose duty it was to venerate and obey the
priests, but they even came to accept this state of affairs as
normal.[14] This change of mentality was expressed, even symbolised, in certain material changes: for example, the altar was
pushed back to the end of the apse which signified that the
liturgy had become more and more of a ceremony, a strictly
clerical affair in which laymen had nothing to say. As O. Nussbaum puts it, 'No one took any notice of the congregation'.
During the 6th century there crept in the custom of saying masses
without a congregation: the 'private' mass, as it was called, the
missa sine populo, a mass-for-the-priest, or priests, was just one
more reason for ignoring those who were not there – the lay
people.[15]

The clergy formed a special category of Christians, an order set
apart and distinguished by its juridical privileges, its culture –
varying in degree according to the individual cases, but on the
whole more developed than that of the laity – the way of life
implying celibacy, and the work which they were allowed to do:
members of the clergy earned their living either 'from the altar' –
offerings, tithes, etc. – or from a benefice, in particular from the
revenue on lands owned by the church to which they were
attached. Those priests who were not able to live on these
sources of income were allowed to work, in agriculture or a craft
(*artificiolum*),[16] but were never allowed to trade.

[14] On this growing separation between the clerics and the laypeople see D.
KNOWLES, *Nouvelle Histoire de l'Eglise*, 2, pp. 316–18, who makes in particular this
remark: 'Soon, the words "Church" and "churchmen" came to apply to the clergy
alone as opposed to laymen.'

[15] O. NUSSBAUM, *Der Standoft des Liturgen am christlichem Altar vor dem Jahre 1000*,
Bonn 1965, pp. 414–19.

[16] B. LE BRAS, *Institutions ecclésiastiques de la chrétienté médiévale*, I, 1, Paris 1959, p.
165.

All this resulted in what G. Le Bras has called 'the exaltation of the clergy',[17] a phenomenon which has two main aspects: the progressive *clericalisation of the church*, which was manifested by a growing tendency to place all church affairs into the hands of the clergy; and, secondly, a concomitant modification of the life of the clerics; if we may make use of a recent French neologism, we could call this second process the *'clergification' of the clerics*. It had several consequences of which the first was that the clerical state of life became a reality of the sociological order, whereas at the beginning it was purely ecclesial and sacramental: from the merely ecclesiastical status which it had always been, it now became an officially recognised secular status. Henceforth clerics took up social functions, they became public officers such as registrars. Bishops were given higher rank than priests, but all were public men of social standing. Bishops were given the title of *'illustrii'* and ranked with the senators. This obliged them to keep up a certain standard of living in harmony with their social status and this to such an extent that 'bishops were practically obliged to live in luxury in order to please the higher classes of society'.[18] In short, clerics ($\chi\lambda\eta\rho\sigma\varsigma$) became 'clergie' in old French, and 'clergy' in English. The cleric became a clergyman, a member of one of the higher classes of society. He had originally been 'set apart' in view of his sacred functions, and he ended up by being 'separated' because of his profane functions. A second consequence of the process of 'clergification' was that the clergymen were unequal to their tasks: very few had received adequate preparation for assuming the dignity and privileges inherent to their newly acquired social status: they were, in general, lacking in the necessary personality and prestige. This lack is easy to explain when we consider the *recruitment* of clerics, the *formation* which they were given, and the *occupations* which they followed.

The manner of *recruiting* clerics had never been very satisfactory: many, even though they had no real calling to the priesthood, had been obliged by their families to enter the clerical state on account of the financial advantages implied; they were

[17] This is the title of a chapter, ibid., pp. 150-71, of which the two last parts are: *Speculum clericale* and *Esquisse des réalités*.
[18] G. BARDY, loc cit., p. 57.

what we should today call 'sociological vocations'. The *formation* too left much to be desired: very few clerics had received any solid or suitable instruction; their 'studies' were generally reduced to the minimum of schooling acquired during attendance, sometimes very short, at a monastery or parochial school; some had no more than the rudiments of learning dinned in by the parish priest. Very often clerics were not obliged to do any real *work*, for they gained sufficient income from church revenues. This meant that many led a life of indolence, and this to such an extent that councils were obliged to bring in regulations forbidding priests to frequent the inns, to hunt and to gamble.

It is not surprising then that though the 'clergy' was an institutional elite, a civil status, a social class of its own, it was far from being a professional elite known for its competence: 'clergy' came to signify a privilege rather than a service. Thus practically everything depended upon the virtue of individual priests, a fact which accounts for the contrast between theory and practice. There existed, side by side, a programme for the ideal high attainment and witnesses to the practical realisation of this programme of which, it must be said, they frequently fell short: there were, indeed, examples of virtue, even of great holiness among the clergy, but there was also much human frailty and many a failing.

The gradual evolution that took place was nothing less than the secularisation of the clergy. The word secular may have several meanings. Among other things it can signify 'of this age', of this *saeculum*; it can also mean profane, civil, temporal, belonging to this world and its affairs as distinct from the Church and religion; or again, it may mean 'worldly' and apply to the way of life lived in the world. It is easy to slither from 'civil', 'temporal', to 'worldly': the one opens up the way to the other and when, in the 11th century, diocesan priests were called for the first time 'secular' priests, the word conveyed a shade of disapproval, it implied that they were priests living a worldly life.

Another result of the 'exaltation of the clergy' and which we must also take into account was that 'for almost everyone at that time there was *no clear distinction between the spiritual and the temporal, or the political, order* . . . and the clergy came to be more and more penetrated by the barbarous world and ambient society, and to be caught up in the feudal system'.[19]

Having thus established the main characteristics of the transformation of the priesthood which took place with the passage from the patristic to the medieval age, I now wish first to give a brief account of the evolution which took place during the middle ages, and secondly, to illustrate the fact with two points in particular which will serve as symbols for all the rest.

Having sketched the state of affairs in the primitive and early medieval Church, we may briefly ask how things evolved in the middle ages.

THE DEVELOPMENT OF THE SOCIOLOGICAL STANDING OF THE CLERGY

As a general statement we may say that there was no decisive change until the end of the middle ages, and perhaps not even until our days: the sociological separation between the clergy and the laity did not lessen. There were only two changes that had any importance: the development of the basic structure and a series of reforms to palliate its inconveniences.

In this matter a distinction must be made between the bishops and the priests. With regard to the *bishops* we notice that the same process which had led to the widening of the gap between clerics and laity also had some part to play in separating the bishops from the priests.[20] More and more bishops came to be elected by the princes and lords or under their influence, and thus became their close auxiliaries and more and more involved in the feudal system. They were caught up in political and secular affairs, and were even sometimes obliged to do military service, a fact which explains how the warrior bishops, against whom St Bernard and many councils reacted, came into being. Bishops became richer and richer, and were obliged to keep more and more *familia*. The ministers of God and his people became prelates and pontiffs. Sometimes the priests were reduced – since the clergy was no

[19] G. LAPRAT, 'Le sacerdoce chrétien du VIe au IXe siècle', in *Prêtres d'hier* . . ., p. 97. On this mixing of profane, sacred political and religious function, see D. KNOWLES, *Nouvelle Histoire de l'Eglise*, 2, p. 61.

[20] Cf. LAPRAT, *Prêtres d'hier*, pp. 72-82.

longer the affair of the laity – to praying for the bishops, and not only *for* them, but even *against* them as is shown by the fact that certain missals contain a *missa contra episcopos male agentes*. These propers were copied in manuscripts, which seems to indicate that the opportunity of saying them was not absolutely rare.

Concerning the *priests*, documents show that the rural clergy became more numerous.[21] But since the villages (*villae*) belonged to the lords, it was not surprising that they had much to say in the appointment of the parish priests. The village churches were 'private churches', *Eigenkirchen*, the privately owned property of the lords who naturally chose the priests who best suited their own purposes and interests. Once a priest was appointed he had the right to remain in residence until the end of his life, and that heedless of any scandal which he might create; the only cause for which he could be deprived of his living was infidelity.

However, from the 12th century onwards, especially in urban areas, though the parish continued to be the official centre of church life, it was no longer the only one. There arose two new entities of religious vitality and ferment: the religious orders for non-diocesan clergy, and the corporations and confraternities for the lay people.[22] Changes in the structural organisation of the church led to the formation of diocesan chapter and curia which limited the power of the bishops. There was a gradual widening of the gap between the lay, and the clerics whose monopoly was rejected first in secular realms and later in church affairs too, though this was fully realised only after the 16th century reformations; furthermore it penetrated into the mind of the Catholic Church only *with* and *after* Vatican II. Parallel with this increasing separation of clergy and laity, there was – especially in the 13th century – a movement in favour of greater professional competence among clerics. Nevertheless the two principal and constant temptations of both bishops and priests continued to be the 'love of money and the abuse of authority'.[23]

To remedy the disorders engendered by this state of affairs, several reforms were brought in. In the Merovingian times there were the rulings of St Boniface and the councils of 743–4. In the

[21] Cf. LAPRAT, ibid., pp. 82–7.   [22] Cf. LE BRAS, *Prêtres d'hier*, pp. 153–83.
[23] LE BRAS, ibid., p. 177.

Carolingian age, at the close of the 8th century and the beginning
of the 9th, reforms were made again but they had no lasting effects.
The monk Hildebrand who became pope Gregory IX, had more
success; the gregorian reform, named after him, took place in the
11th century[24] and resulted in the abolition of some of the
major abuses among the clergy with an attempt at introducing the
'canonical life' and an effort to restore to the laity a more active
participation in church affairs – notable in the wars against the
non-Christians. However, far from modifying the structural
changes brought in and enforced by the Carolingian reform,
it led to an even more tightly compacted Roman centralisation
which actually coincided with and led to the epoch of the eastern
schism. From the 12th century onward the successive efforts at
reform on the part of many saints and some popes and councils
often resulted in spiritual revivals, but did nothing to modify the
basic structures. The process of 'clergification' became stronger
and stronger which meant that the clergy became more and more
isolated from the laity.

TWO SYMBOLIC PROBLEMS

Two points about clerical life may be selected to demonstrate the
growing isolation of the clergy: (1) clerical celibacy and (2) clerical
dress.

1. *Clerical celibacy*. As we have seen, the clergy have always had
a way of life separate and distinct from that common to laymen.
The first way in which they were separated was by living in
celibacy. In the *patristic Church* there existed no universal law by
which celibacy was imposed upon all priests.[25] From the 1st
century onwards there had been a sort of spontaneous praxis in
this matter; during the 4th century this voluntary celibacy tended
to become an institution – a fact which is probably to be explained

[24] Cf. J. F. LEMARTIGNIER, in *Prêtres d'hier*, pp. 114–52. Concerning the 'monastic'
character of the gregorian reform which was brought about by monks and tended
to 'monasticise' the clergy, see D. KNOWLES, *Nouvelle Histoire de l'Eglise*, 2, pp. 200–3.

[25] A valuable survey of this evolution in HEFELE-LECLERCQ, *Histoire des conciles*,
II, 2, Paris 1908, pp. 1321–48, with bibliography; a more recent bibliography is to be
found in G. LE BRAS, *Institutions*, p. 163.

by the esteem accorded to consecrated virginity and to the monastic life; it was not, however, universally considered as obligatory.[26] It was only during the 5th century in the west that celibacy was tied to the priesthood, and the law continued to be enforced in spite of – or maybe even on account of – its dangers and the many infringements. The reason brought forward during the first period in support of priestly celibacy was that continence was 'beautiful', becoming, 'to those who wished to minister'.[27]

In the *medieval Church*, though the law of celibacy was kept in force, periodically it was brought into question and even combatted – particularly in the 11th century – and in fact 'in no country does celibacy seem to have been rigorously observed'.[28] Many priests lived in concubinage, and many more priests were married than we would like to believe. The laity was well aware of this state of affairs, with the result that the married priest was despised and the celibate priest held in suspicion. Parishioners preferred to have an unmarried priest in order not to have to give financial support to his family; and yet, if he had no concubine, they had reason to fear for the peace of their own household. Thus, to all intents and purposes, 'the law of celibacy remained, in many places, a dead letter'.[29] Schillebeeckx has quoted and commented the advice which some bishops gave to their priests: '*si non caste, tamen caute*: if not chaste, at least be cautious'.[30]

However, in spite of the many instances when human frailty led to the violation of the law, priestly celibacy was always presented as the ideal, not only in the Church's legislation, but also in the writings of all those saints and spiritual masters who expressed her highest aspiration. The motives they brought forward were no longer mere reasons of convenience: they took the obligation for granted and sought to justify it first, and mainly, on grounds of personal asceticism, and secondly as a

---

[26] On the influence of monasticism see, E. SCHILLEBEECKX, *Autour du célibat du prêtre. Etude critique*, Paris 1967, pp. 27-32, and my book on *Vie religieuse et vie contemplative*, Paris-Gembloux 1967.

[27] Texts are quoted in HEFELE-LECLERCQ, op. cit., p. 1341.

[28] LE BRAS, *Prêtres d'hier*, p. 176.

[29] LE BRAS, *Institutions*, p. 168.

[30] *Autour du célibat*, p. 42. The fact that clerics were married, in more or less greater numbers, according to the periods, recurs constantly as a leit-motiv in D. KNOWLES, *Nouvelle Histoire de l'Eglise*, 2, pp. 53, 204, 206, 272, 283.

means among others of being freer for a more perfect exercising of the ministry. Later, celibacy was presented as being one of the elements inherent in the priest's total commitment to Christ. Thus, throughout the middle ages, though it was frequently contested in different quarters, celibacy continued to be considered as something 'beautiful', 'becoming'. Nevertheless the practice of it always remained difficult on account of the barbarous condition of many people in the middle ages. This explains, perhaps, why it has been more faithfully observed in recent times when men and manners have become more refined.

2. *Clerical dress.* Clerical dress was also a form and a symbol of the increasing separation between the clergy and the laity; it was introduced more and more from the 5th century onwards, as has been shown in various studies.[31] It is not so much the history of how the clerical dress came to be adopted which interests us here as its signification.

In the patristic Church, not only was there no distinct dress for clerics, but they were even forbidden to have one. The only injunctions they received in this matter were that they should avoid luxury and outward show, and that they were to wear clean clothes for liturgical functions. When as late as 428, Pope Celestin wrote to the bishops of Vienne and Narbonne, in the south of Gaul, urging them not to introduce a special dress which 'does not come from the Church'[32] he insisted that a bishop should be distinguishable from his flock 'by his teaching, not his dress'.[33]

[31] J. DESHUSSES in *Dictionnaire de droit canonique* 4 (1949), col. 701-10; bibliography in Y. CONGAR, *Pour une église servante et pauvre*, Paris 1963, p. 73, n. 37; P. SALMON, *Etude sur les insignes du Pontife dans le rite romain*, Rome 1955, pp. 19-28, has collected facts on the origin and evolution of the titles, functions, insignia and privileges by which, from the time of Constantine onward, bishops were assimilated with high ranking imperial officers. H. NORRIS, *Church Vestments*, London 1949, p. 166, has shown that the cassock dates from the fifth century. On this appearance of the long habit for clerics, see also J. CHELINI, *Histoire religieuse de l'Occident médiéval*, Paris 1968, pp. 47-8; D. KNOWLES, *Nouvelle Histoire de l'Eglise*, II (1968), p. 179.

[32] 'Contra ecclesiasticum morem faciunt qui in Ecclesia non creverunt, sed alio venientes itinere secum haec in Ecclesiam, quae in alia conversatione habuerunt, intulerunt,' text quoted and commented by H. LECLERCQ-H. MARROU, art. *Costume ecclésiastique, Diction. d'archéol. chrét. et de liturgie*, 15 (1953), col. 2 990. Cf. CONGAR, *The historical Development*, loc. cit., p. 135.

[33] 'Discernendi a plebe vel ceteris sumus doctrina, non veste,' ibid.

During the middle ages, a distinctive dress for clerics came to be the sign of their order, of their special social status; it was similar to that of the Roman officials whose place and office they had come to occupy. It was one more indication of the secularisation of an ecclesiastical function. Originally all that was required of priests was that they should not be secular, that is 'worldly', but now a step further was taken, ordinary neat clothes (*incessus*) were replaced by clerical dress (*habitus*) with the result that priests adopted the long robe instead of the short tunic which was the dress of ordinary people.[34] In the Gauls, priests were forbidden to wear the *sagum*, the popular dress, and it was even stipulated that they should not be dressed 'like laymen', *laicorum more*;[35] nor like seculars, *secularibus indumentis non utantur, nisi ut condecet, tunica sacerdotali . . .*[36] *Stolis utatur, que concesse sunt clericis . . .*[37] The new clerical dress was called *ornatus sacerdotalis*,[38] and in fact it actually did come to be more of an ornament than anything else. Whereas the ancient Church had always avoided the use of showy colours, some ecclesiastics now began to wear purple and red – a custom which has prevailed to our day. And of course, there always remained the danger of foppishness and eccentricity against which so many councils reacted.

By way of parenthesis it may be mentioned that the monks, who originally had kept to the peasant dress – the short *tunica* of which St Benedict says that it must not be too short, *non nimis curtae* – donned the long Roman robe of the clerics when they themselves were clericalised.

I am well aware of the fact that in this historical survey there are many generalisations and simplifications. I have insisted constantly on the fact of the influence of secular structures on the life of the clergy because it appears to me to have been decisive. This evolutionary process started, we have seen, with the fall of the Roman empire and the barbarian invasions which resulted in the setting up of new kingdoms and institutions. This latter element

[34] 'The talar was the dress worn by patricians . . . it was also the dress worn by priests . . .' Ibid., 2996.
[35] LAPRAT, in *Prêtres d'hier*, p. 83.
[36] Synod of 692, in *Decretum Gratiani*, c. 21, 9. 14, c. 2, ed. Friedberg, col. 858.
[37] Synod of 743, ibid., c. 3. 858.
[38] Synod of 826, ibid., c. 4. 858.

is proper to the west: the evolution of the eastern empire followed a different course.

The stress I have laid upon the influence of sociological data does not infer that there was no internal evolution of the clerical institution.[39] There certainly was one, and its determining factors were of the spiritual order. And we may even go so far as to say that it was just this internal change which allowed the clerical institution to withstand the menace of being completely wiped out by secular influences.

To conclude, let me quote a passage from G. Le Bras from whom I have already borrowed many of my facts: 'Since so many obstacles and adversities were not able to destroy Christianity, we may dare to suppose that there were many clerics who carried out their duties correctly'.[40]

The history of the clerical state in the early and medieval Church is a diptych whose panels are well illustrated by three texts which I recommend for your reading. The first paints the portrait of a *Model Parish Priest: St Gilbert of Sempringham* who lived in the early 12th century.[41] The second text is an extract from a 13th century author, Odo of Rigaud, on the *Habits of Priests in Normandy*.[42] The third text gives an account by Ordericus Vitalis of *An Attempt to Enforce Clerical Celibacy*[43] which took place in 1119. In this passage we read of priests contesting with the bishop about celibacy in a cathedral; he calls in the guard to restore order, to the great scandal of the 'old priests', the 'ecclesiastics of advanced age', who cannot understand what all the fuss is about.

PRIESTLY LITERATURE

Having recalled briefly the facts, it will now be interesting to see who among the great representatives of patristic and medieval

---

[39] This internal evolution has been illustrated for what concerns regards celibacy, by E. SCHILLEBEECKS, *Autour du célibat*, pp. 17–72.

[40] G. LE BRAS, *Institutions*.

[41] Text in J. B. ROSS and M. MCLAUGHLIN, *The Portable Medieval Reader*, New York 196A, pp. 73–5.

[42] Ibid., pp. 78–80.   [43] Ibid., pp. 75–8.

literature were the writers who have contributed most to the creation of the moral, ascetic and spiritual 'model' of the priest.

Could we say that St Jerome was one, he who is venerated under the title of *Hieronymus presbyter*? Possibly. Yet, on the other hand he had been ordained against his will, and he never forgave the bishop who had forced him to take orders: his desire for the monastic and solitary life made him fear being tied down to a post obliging him to assure the liturgical and pastoral service of a community which was also a presbyteral college.[44] Whenever he had the opportunity of writing to priests on this subject, it was nearly always in order to warn them against those abuses which were likely to creep in on account of them being obliged 'to live on the altar', and against those which could possibly arise by reason of fiscal and other privileges.[45] In particular he stated that 'ecclesiastical revenues were not to be spent on the profane education of sons of priests'.[46]

During the patristic period, the western doctor who most influenced the development of priestly institutions was St Augustine. This he did not only by his example and his teaching, but also because he encouraged a form of clerical life which, if not completely monastic, was at least canonical – with celibacy and the common life. It was this project which was the basic inspiration of future reforms of the clergy throughout the middle ages.[47]

During the middle ages the average priest, such as he really was from the 5th century onwards – that is, as he had come to be as a result of the evolution of history – based his life on a spirituality received from vast and varied writings which were largely pastoral in nature. Two great figures contributed to the moulding of the image of the medieval priest. The first is situated at the opening of the middle ages, in the 6th century: St Gregory the Great. He made his greatest contribution in his *Book of the Pastoral Rule*.

[44] In *Chances de la spiritualité occidentale*, Paris 1966, pp. 152–3, I have quoted texts and facts. On the lateness (eleventh century) of the accession to the priesthood of a fairly great number of priests, D. KNOWLES, *Nouvelle Histoire de l'Eglise*, 2, pp. 185 and 312.

[45] P. ANTIN gives some texts in his *Recueil sur S. Jérôme*, Bruxelles 1968, p. 469, at the word 'Prêtre'; following on the references is another word which sums up their contents: 'Anticléricalisme'.   [46] Ibid., p. 316, n. 36.

[47] This aspect of St Augustin's influence has been admirably exposed by G. LADNER, *The Idea of Reform*, Harvard University Press 1959.

The vocabulary which he uses is in itself revealing. He calls the members of the clergy neither 'ministers' nor 'servants', nor even priests; he speaks of 'pastors', 'preachers', 'doctors', and uses a vocabulary which implies that there is a certain superiority within the clerical state itself: he speaks of rectors, prelates, *praesules*, *praepositi*. And since they are to be occupied with so many affairs, his main care is to assure that, in spite of all their activity, they keep up a 'contemplative life'.[48] This book had enormous influence. The most ancient extant manuscript of it seems to have been taken to England very early on, perhaps even during Gregory's lifetime. King Alfred the Great (871–900) had it translated into Anglo-Saxon, and it has been said that 'in the middle ages, this book was for the secular clergy what the Rule of St Benedict was for the religious orders'.[49]

Six hundred years later, after the gregorian reform, St Bernard of Clairvaux rewrote St Gregory's *Pastoral Rule* for the clergy of his own times: I think I have shown that such was his intention when he composed the *De consideratione* where he insists on the necessity, for the pope and for all, of keeping up a life of prayer in the midst of 'excessive occupations'.[50] St Bernard gives the picture of a reformed clergy in three other writings; in two treatises, on the *Conduct and Functions of Bishops* and *To the Clergy, on Conversion*, he exposed the theory; in his *Life of St Malachy* he seized the opportunity afforded by the death of an Irish bishop, whom he had scarcely known, to sketch the portrait of the ideal bishop.[51] His entire effort was directed to combating the temptation constantly besetting the clergy of power and wealth – with all the consequences they imply – as a result of the often privileged situation they hold in society. This explains his special insistence on poverty.[52]

Unfortunately, in all the medieval priestly literature we find Old Testament texts concerning the levitical priesthood applied

---

[48] Cf. *The Spirituality of the Middle Ages*, p. 8.

[49] B. ALTANER, *Précis de patrologie*, Mulhouse 1961, p. 650.

[50] *Recueil d'études sur S. Bernard*, III, Rome 1969, pp. 98–100.

[51] Ibid., pp. 94–8.

[52] J. LECLERCQ, 'St Bernard on the Church', in *Downside Review*, 85 (1967), p. 283: 'The Reform of the Clergy'; p. 285: 'The Episcopate'; pp. 286–8: 'The Duties of a Priest'; pp. 288–90: 'The Virtues of a Priest'.

to bishops and priests as they then existed in the Church; even St Gregory and St Bernard fell into the trap. The transfer is constant throughout medieval times, but it comes to a climax in the 11th century with the gregorian reform and the vast polemic literature made up by the 'Books of the controversies between the popes and the emperors' *Libelli de lite*. This subject has been dealt with by Hackelsperger[53] and I myself have written about it in a study of which a part was printed in *Concilium* in 1966.[54,55] It is not necessary here to do more than simply recall the main facts:

1. *The intention* of the polemic literature of the 11th century was to affirm the superiority of one of the two authorities, civil or ecclesiastic, over the other. Thus they have nothing to do with theology; their sole concern is polemics. Scriptural quotations were used merely to show – and this is sometimes explicitly stated – that the arguments which bore most weight with the people, were those which came from the Bible – and sometimes it happened that they would accept no other argument.

2. *The method* was nothing more than pure literalism absolutely void of any sense of history and of evolution. There had been priests in the Old Covenant, there were some in the New Covenant, thus it was only normal to apply to the second what had been said about the first. Moreover, the use of biblical argument was often ambiguous; for example: those who advocated the marriage of priests called upon the Book of Numbers (12:12) which mentions the wives of the priests; or else they pointed out that St John the Baptist was the son of the priest Zachary. This use of scripture erred by excessive literalism: writers merely sought to discover in the Old Testament the ideas of their own times and milieu. Instead of examining the Bible objectively, they made a selection in order to support a cause – that of reform – and certain specific interests, which were those of the party to which one belonged and was defending.

[53] HACKELSPERGER, 'Bible und mittelalterlicher Kirshgedanken Studien und Beitrage zum Gevrauch der Bibel' in *Streit zwischen Kaiser und Papstum zur Seit der Salier*, Battrop-in-Westfalen 1934.

[54] *Bible and Gregorian Reform*, n. 17, 1966, English edition, pp. 34–41.

[55] Cf. J. LECLERCQ, 'The Exposition and Exegesis of Scripture from Gregory the Great to Saint Bernard, in *Cambridge History of the Bible. The West from the Fathers to the Reformation*, Cambridge 1969, pp. 183–97.

3. *The result* of this use, even this abuse, of scripture was most regrettable. Doubtless these books were written not with the intention of making theology progress, but in order to reply to concrete historical needs. Nevertheless, these ideas, illustrated as they were by biblical texts, were to be found in many a writing as well as the letters of the popes. They thus found their way into canonical collections, and by this means came to constitute an arsenal of texts serving as *'status quaestiones'* for many discussions in scholastic theology from the 12th century onwards. To a certain extent, even in our day this polemic still clutters up manuals of theology, liturgy and books of piety. Congar has helped to eliminate many of these unappropriate themes by his scholarly writings on their origins and their history. All that remains to be done now is to reject any scripture text as an argument in connection with the priesthood unless its use is scientifically sound.

The fact that monks became priests with no other function than that of solitary celebration of the eucharist crept in little by little, and rather slowly, throughout the middle ages and only became general towards the end of this period. It was explained by reasons of a practical, economical, or devotional nature.[56] But it has never been the object of a theological justification of any worth. The most recent, the author of which has avoided engaging his reputation, preferring to remain anonymous,[57] has been described as making use of a 'theology which calls largely upon reasons of *convenance*'.[58]

Lastly, the facts and ideas which have fashioned the model of the priest during ten centuries came to a climactic head – one which was neither exceptional nor rare – at the beginning of the 16th century with the theology of Josse Clichtove, a humanist whose work has recently been illustrated by a scholarly and beau-

[56] I have assembled texts and facts on this point in two long studies 'On Monastic Priesthood according to the Ancient Medieval Tradition', in *Studia Monastica*, 3 (1961), pp. 137–55, and 'Le sacerdoce des moines', in *Chances de la Spiritualité occidentale*, pp. 125–78.

[57] 'Contemplation et sacerdoce', in *Angelicum*, 42 (1965), pp. 463–88.

[58] P. C. in *Collectanea Cisterciensia*, 29 (1967), p. 28. Concerning what Paul VI has said on the subject in a speech in December 1966, an authorised interpretation has been given in the *Osservatore Romano* of December 14th 1944; a résumé of this speech is given in *Collectanea Cisterciensia*, 29 (1967), p. 27.

tiful book. For him 'The fullness of religion is reserved to a caste of professional and privileged people'. He sets priests in a state of radical separation, both inward and outward, with respect to other men.[59]

CONCLUSIONS

1. This paper had already been written when Y. Congar's *L'ecclésiologie du haut moyen âge* (Paris 1968) came into my hands. The views which have been expressed above concerning the transition from the patristic era to the middle ages are confirmed with authority and competence. The change which affected the priesthood at that time was itself a consequence of an even deeper change: one which affected ecclesiology as a whole. Mentalities passed from a conception of the 'Church, community of Christians' to one which accepted the 'distance between the lay people and the Church of the clerics'.[60] In the first state there was 'an organic union between pastors and faithful' in matters touching liturgical celebrations, councils and other activities of church life. In the second state the idea that predominates is that 'the whole Christian life and the religious state depend upon the priests, their fidelity, the purity of their life, and their learning'. The 'different stages of the progressive distancing which took place between the priest and the faithful' seem to have arisen from a definition of the Church as 'consisting mainly of priests'.[61]

2. And so it was that mentalities gradually became accustomed by facts and theory to accepting 'the doctrine in the 16th century which taught that the priest is one set apart to the detriment of the teaching that the priest is with his people'. The 17th century even went so far as to recognise this separation as being an essential characteristic of the priesthood, and what is more the priest was commonly defined as being someone set apart. As it is this

[59] J. P. MASSAUT, *Josse Clichtove. L'humanisme et la réforme du Clergé*, Paris 1968, t. II, pp. 185–6. The whole of the second volume is devoted to the episcopate and the priesthood, and merits attentive analysis.

[60] These are the titles of pages 95 and 97.

[61] Ibid., p. 98, 'Ecclesia quae in sacerdotibus maxime constat': this definition and others are quoted p. 98, n. 173.

conception of the priest which has prevailed until our times, is taken for traditional. But, far from being essential to the priesthood – no more than the law of ecclesiastical celibacy is intimately bound up with the idea of being set apart – this conception of the priest is neither traditional nor primitive in the history of the Church. On the contrary, it is recent: it is characteristic of the modern priest. . . . Thus, in favour of the 'get back to the sources' movement which for some years now has been creating so much stir in the Roman Church, this conception of the priest is beginning to be strongly contested.[62]

We have already seen that the priest was separated not only by the sacred character of his functions, but by the privileged sociological conditions in which he carried them out in cultural, economical, civil and political fields. This has been the state of affairs almost to the present day, as much in ancient Christian countries as a whole as in mission lands where the clergy was often protected by the colonising power. Father William Byron s.j., in a sub-title to an article on the *American Pastor and Social change* wrote recently: 'The pastor is in many ways a man of the middle ages . . .', and further on he writes, 'The pastor, by and large, is a man of the medieval town . . .'.[63] And he concludes: 'Without a bad conscience, people are rejecting a Church that has no servant clergy.'[64] One of the wonderful things about Catholicism today, one of the signs of its vitality, is that the faithful, and members of the clergy are rediscovering the meaning of the priesthood as a service, a *diaconia*, a ministry, in such a way that they are continuing across the age of history the mystery of the One who said he had 'come to serve' (Matt. 20:28). Therein lies great reason for hope.

However, it would be an illusion to think that we shall be able to restore a priestly ministry in what might be called its pure state, one which would realise the evangelical ideal of priestly service and mediation without any other determining factor than the Gospel itself. The priestly institution, like any other, has always

---

[62] J. P. MASSAUT, *Josse Clichtove*, II, p. 126, who quotes, in a footnote, contemporary witnesses on the life of priests as 'a life of contacts', of 'presence to the world', of sharing in the 'life of labour'.

[63] In *America*, March 1, 1969, pp. 246–7.

[64] Ibid., p. 249.

been stamped by the state of the society in which it existed: history gives us a lesson in relativity and, consequently, modesty. The important thing – and that is the meaning of the progress taking place – is that it should be stamped by the society of today and tomorrow, not that of the middle ages.

INTRODUCTION

In 1965 the Convocations of the Church of England and the Methodist Conference set up the Anglican-Methodist Unity Commission to make plans for the implementing of proposals for union between the two Churches. The scheme presented by the Commission failed to obtain the necessary majorities for implementation.

In the course of their report the Commission set out both the common ground and the divergent views in the two Churches about the Christian priesthood and ministry. The following extract from the report will be found on pages 23–6 of *Anglican-Methodist Unity; Report of the Anglican-Methodist Unity Commission*, 'Part 2: The Scheme', London 1968. The original numbering of the paragraphs has been retained.

5 A Joint Anglican and Methodist Statement about Priesthood and Ministry

Common Ground: Ordination and Jurisdiction

66 Our starting-point is the conviction, shared by both our Churches, that God wills his Church to have ministers of the Word and Sacraments who have been called and commissioned to their work of pastoral oversight by those to whom authority has been given in their Churches. This calling and commissioning is ordination. On the basis of this common conviction, both our Churches, in ordaining, commission men to the ministry of the Church universal, although in the nature of the case neither can confer jurisdiction (ministerial responsibility and status) beyond its own boundaries.* The Service of Reconciliation will, however, initiate an extension of jurisdiction for ministers of both Churches; hence, if for no other reason, it is right to include in it specific prayers for both ministries.

Liberty of Interpretation within Defined Limits

67 In the New Testament, ordained ministers of the Word and Sacraments are commonly called presbyters. It is asked: In what

* This sentence refers to the intentions of the two Churches in their ordinations.

sense, if any, are they priests? To this question, which continues to provoke ecumenical discussion, Anglican answers vary, as is well known. In 1953 the Methodist Church made it a condition of the proposed conversations that 'the same liberty of interpretation of the nature of episcopacy and priesthood would be accorded to the Methodist Church as prevails in the Church of England', and the Church of England accepted this condition. What it implies is that any views which fall within the limits set by the Anglican formularies may legitimately be held by Methodists, as by Anglicans. In both our Churches, different positions regarding ministerial priesthood have been developed within the bounds set by their respective formularies. The Commission is fully convinced that nothing in the scheme now proposed involves an adverse judgement on the theological soundness of any of these positions.

Common Ground: The Priesthood of Christ and of the Church

68 The 1963 Report sets out, and the Commission reaffirms, the common ground on this subject as follows:

(*a*) It is our common belief that, in the New Covenant of the Lord Jesus Christ, he alone is priest in his own right. He has offered the one perfect and final sacrifice which atones for the sins of the world, he intercedes eternally for the world, he is the one mediator between God and men; through him alone God reconciles the world to himself.

(*b*) By sharing in his priestly ministry, the Church corporately is a royal priesthood, a holy nation. In and under Christ it offers God's pardon and grace to the world, intercedes with God for the world, and offers itself and its worship as a living sacrifice to God.

(*c*) Within the corporate priesthood of the whole Church every individual believer has his own responsibility of worship, witness, and service, and his own privilege of direct personal access to God in Christ for pardon and grace.[1]

69 Different opinions are held as to the way in which the Church shares in Christ's priestly ministry, but none of these intends to call in question that the work of atoning for our sins is Christ's alone.

[1] Op. cit., p. 23.

Ministerial Priesthood: Divergent Views

70 Discussion since 1963 has shown that the points covered in Sections (4)–(6) on pp. 23f. of the 1963 Report call for further comment. It is acknowledged that there are differences of doctrine within both Churches on the matters involved. These differences may be set out as follows:

71 Some Anglicans hold (i) that ordination within the historic episcopal succession by prayer with laying on of hands confers, in addition to grace and authority, a unique and indelible priestly character; (ii) that the ministry of presbyters who have this character is, through Christ, priestly in the sense that (*a*) they represent the Body of Christ in offering to God the eucharist in which Christ's offering is made present, and (*b*) they represent Christ in declaring absolution to sinners, and in blessing; (iii) that non-episcopal ordinations, in that they have departed from the norm,[2] cannot be said with certainty to confer this character. These Anglicans believe their position to be supported by the Ordinal of 1662 and its Preface, and by the practice of the Church of England in confining to bishops and presbyters the celebration of the eucharist and the declaring of absolution, particularly when these documents and practices are seen in the context of the Anglican appeal to scripture and the undivided Church.*

72 Other Anglicans take a different view. They value episcopacy; they do not deny that God's call and the Church's authorisation to presbyteral ministry are both for life; they affirm that a sacrifice of praise and service, responsive to the atoning sacrifice of Christ, is indeed offered at Holy Communion. But they deny that any part of the presbyter's ministry of Word or Sacrament is priestly in any sense beyond that in which the whole Church's worship is priestly.

[2] *IS*, p. 27.
* Some have found this paragraph ambiguous. It should, therefore, be stated that: (*a*) the statement 'ordination within the historic episcopal succession . . . priestly character' presupposed that ordination is the act of the holy Spirit in response to the prayer of the Church, and that the gifts referred to are therefore conferred by God; (*b*) the term 'represent' was used in the same sense as it was used by Dr William Bright, Dr R. C. Moberly, and others, in relation to the ministerial priesthood. Cf. w. BRIGHT, *Some Aspects of Primitive Church Life* (London 1898), p. 58, n. 2.

With Anglican divines of the Reformation period,[3] they understand the word 'priest' as simply a synonym for 'presbyter'. They
cannot find any grounds in the theology or practice of the New
Testament for regarding presbyteral ministry as in any sense
sacerdotal or mediatorial, or for doubting the adequacy of non-
episcopal orders, or for relating the presence and grace of Christ
at the eucharist to a representative act of offering by the minister.
In support of their position they cite the teaching of the English
Reformers and their successors,* and the history of Anglican relations with non-episcopal Churches and their clergy during the
century after the Reformation.

73 These views of priesthood, and others lying between them,
exist in the Church of England in recognised tension and recognised liberty within the unity of a common practice.†

74 The Methodist Deed of Union (1932) states: 'Christ's ministers in the Church are stewards in the household of God and
shepherds of his flock. . . . The Methodist Church holds the
doctrine of the priesthood of all believers and consequently
believes that no priesthood exists which belongs exclusively to a
particular order or class of men, but in the exercise of its corporate
life and worship special qualifications for the discharge of special
duties are required and thus the principle of representative selection is recognised.'

75 In interpreting these words, some allow that a minister may
rightly be called a priest on grounds suggested by 72 above,
namely that, in administering the Holy Communion and leading
the worship of God's people, he is the representative of the priesthood of all believers, which is the Church. Others would not wish
to use the word 'priest' of a minister, lest it imply an exclusive
priesthood, though all would ascribe to the ordained ministry of
the Word and Sacraments a distinctive function within the Church.
Methodists agree in affirming the priesthood of all believers and

---

[3] E.g. WHITGIFT, *Works* (Parker Society), III, p. 351: 'The very word itself (sc.
"priest"), as it is used in our English tongue, soundeth the word presbyter.'

* After 'successors' the words 'the history of the Ordinal' should be added.

† 'Recognised' here means 'recognised *de facto*'. These paragraphs describe the
limits of actual divergence within our two Churches.

in asserting that a minister is called of God to be an ambassador on behalf of Christ and a representative of the whole people of God.

76 The Methodist Conference, in its function as interpreter of Methodist doctrine, in the course of its Statement of 1960 elucidated the Deed of Union as follows:

> In the office of a minister are brought together the manifold functions of the Church's ministry, and it is his privilege to exercise them as the servant of Christ and of his fellows in the Church as a whole, as the Church under the guidance of the Spirit shall appoint him. . . . The Methodist Church is committed to the view that the ordained minister does not possess any priesthood which he does not share with the whole company of Christ's faithful people. But the doctrine of the 'priesthood of all believers' is that we share, as believers, in the priesthood of our great high Priest, Jesus Christ himself. . . . Into that priesthood of Christ we are taken up by faith, and we, in our turn, and in self-identification with him, offer ourselves in utter humility, and obedience as a living sacrifice to God. We are 'priests unto God', and therefore 'take upon ourselves with joy the yoke of obedience', as we are enjoined in the Covenant Service. So the doctrine does not mean that every Christian has the right to exercise every function and administer both sacraments. For it is not an assertion of claims, but a declaration of our total obedience. A Methodist minister is a priest, in company with all Christ's faithful people; but not all priests are ministers [that is, as the context shows, 'not all members of the priesthood of all believers are ordained ministers']. Ordination is never repeated in the Methodist Church. A minister is Christ's ambassador and the representative of the whole people of God.

INTRODUCTION

Even without the current debate about the Christian ministry within the Anglican and Methodist communities, the Methodist experience is an important one, for Methodism originated in a situation of great frustration over the provision of a formal Christian ministry for people deprived of it by political and economic changes. But the current debate about the union of the two Churches means that the nature and position of the Christian ministry has been explored in great depth in our own times and our own social situation.

Dr Kent writes as a Methodist, but he looks at the Methodist position within the wider context of the Free Church tradition in Great Britain. It is significant of the urgency of the problems that have arisen that he questions the value of the New Testament as an authority for the nature of the priesthood. Once the historical context of the New Testament Christian community had changed, it has to be asked whether the ministry which was created to meet its first century needs is the right one to perpetuate when the needs have changed. If such a radical question can be asked of the New Testament, it can certainly be asked of the form of the ministry in any succeeding period. It is at least possible that the social basis of the episcopal model of the priesthood has been fatally undermined, and that we must recognise that the definitions which we make for either the ministry or the Church are historically relative. Each generation has to generate its own models.

BIOGRAPHICAL NOTE

JOHN KENT, PH.D., *was born in 1923. He read history at Emmanuel College, Cambridge, where he later taught. He worked for the B.B.C. before entering the Methodist ministry in 1950. Since then he has taught church history in the Methodist theological colleges in Leeds, Cambridge and Manchester. He moved to the Bristol University Theology Department in 1965, and was made Reader in Theology in 1969. Dr Kent, who has many connections with America, has published* Elizabeth Fry *(1962),* The Age of Disunity *(1966), an essay on the Nonconformist Conscience in* Essays on Modern Church History *(1966),* From Darwin to Blatchford, *the Dr Williams' Library Lecture (1966), and 'The Study of Modern Ecclesiastical History since 1930' in* The Pelican Guide to Modern Theology, *vol. 2 (1969).*

6 *Models of the British Non-Conformist Ministry*

J. H. S. KENT

THE QUALIFIED 'YES' TO PRIESTHOOD WHICH EMERGES from the papers of Bishop Robinson and Robert Murray depends upon the belief that the evidence about the nature of the Christian ministry to be found in the New Testament and in the history of the early Church may be used to construct a model of the priesthood binding upon succeeding generations. Both papers assume that a theology of the priesthood was included in the original revelation, whether this revelation is limited to the New Testament writings, or extended to include the writings of the first five Christian centuries, writings whose status seems to be insufficiently criticised by both theologians. Both men, of course, represent Churches which have normally asserted that a highly institutionalised form of episcopacy is of the *esse* of the Church.

The methodological question which is raised is important. In the past, Free Church theologians have often said that the New Testament evidence describes a Christian ministry as integral to the Church but does not prescribe an exclusive or invariable form. (This was, for example, the language of an official Methodist statement on the doctrine of ordination published as recently as 1960.) In the ecumenical theology of the moment there is an orthodox doctrine of the Church which comes very close to what we have already heard described, as may be seen in this passage from the 1963 Report of the Conversations between the Church of England and the Methodist Church:

'God in Christ by the Spirit takes the initiative in bringing into being a people which is his Church; in entrusting it, though not as its own property, with means of grace; and in evoking individual faith and nurturing the Christian life by these means in the Church. Such a community must have order, not merely in the sense of disciplinary rules such as any voluntary society needs, but as structure, so as to be itself and perform its proper functions. The essential structure of the Church is divinely determined, since it is Christ's Church, not ours. For this, as for the Christian faith in general, we look to the Bible to discover the given, i.e., what God has appointed. . . . What is given in Order includes worship, word, sacraments, ministry, pastoral care, discipline of members, and participation in regulating the common life. These are gifts of the one Spirit and should operate harmoniously. It is true that the New Testament provides no fixed and self-evident pattern in which these cohere, but some of the given elements help to shape other elements in Order. For example, the sacrament of Holy Communion involves the saying of certain words and the performing of certain actions and requires certain rules as to who shall say and perform them and who shall be admitted to it.' (op. cit., pp. 20–1.)

No doubt the Methodist representatives who accepted this statement had their own ways of understanding it: nothing is less certain than what is agreed in an agreed statement of this kind, and the qualification that 'the New Testament provides no fixed and self-evident pattern' was presumably intended as an escape clause from unwanted conclusions. Taken as a whole, however, the passage implied that the New Testament contained and revealed the self-evident pattern of a divinely determined church order, the outlines of which emerged quite clearly from the passage (and indeed from the whole tenor of the Anglican-Methodist negotiations), which resembled closely the structure of the existing Church of England, and which must be obligatory because the Church was not a voluntary society but a divinely instituted community, Christ's Church and not ours.

There are, of course, Methodist theologians who would deny that Methodism shared the ethos of the Free Church tradition. Certainly, it is possible from within the Free Church tradition to criticise all these ways of defining the proper nature of the Church and Ministry and to say that the question of church order cannot be finally decided (as the Anglican-Methodist Report, for example, regards it as decided), in terms of the New Testament evidence. It is true that if the scriptures are set aside altogether the historical continuity of Christianity is endangered, but the value of the New Testament references as an authority for the nature of the priesthood may well be questioned. Their ambiguity and indecisiveness apart (which there is not room here to demonstrate, but which could be demonstrated), they may be seen as reflecting the earliest attempt to solve the problem of the institutionalisation of Christianity in a particular historical context, an attempt no doubt made on a spiritual as well as a secular level, but yet having no universal validity once the historical context had drastically changed. We possess no neat dominical ecclesiological statement to use as a standard by which to judge what happened in later history, and to search the scriptures for an 'essence of Christianity', as a substitute for a precise text, is a game which, as Loisy showed in *The Gospel and the Church*, not only Harnack could play. It is probable that one may speak of Jesus as 'instituting' the eucharist, but it is by no means evident that what he did either involved laying down rules as to who should administer the developed liturgical institution, or made inevitable particular conclusions about who should attend the celebration. And if it is said that in the present state of New Testament studies we ought not to demand a dominical utterance because we know that the New Testament reaches us through the intermediary of the early Christian community, the obvious reply would seem to be that the more the New Testament is seen to be the product of the early Church the less its authority is bound to become; one cannot, that is, make selective use of the argument that the community was guided by the holy Spirit. One may accept Jesus in his life, death and resurrection as a moment of existence which is also a moment of God's self-revelation, a moment when God and the world converge in a unique degree upon Jesus who was the Christ. But the new community which sprang from him, and which found its unity in its relation to the moment of revelation which he embodied, was not thereby empowered to solve the problem of institutionalisation in perpetuity. It is by no means obvious, in fact, that in the case of the Church's structure in general and of the ministry in particular, we should look to the Bible to discover what *God* has appointed once and for all: it is more likely that what we see in the Bible is the kind of Church which it was historically possible for men inspired by Jesus to create in the first century of the new era. We are so familiar with the idea that ecclesiastical discontinuity is sinful that we do not see how remarkable the assertion is. To preserve absolute continuity with the ecclesiastical past was reasonable (though not obligatory) as long as the historical context of Christianity had not changed beyond a certain degree. What many students of western culture now begin to suspect, however, is that a breach of cultural continuity took place between 1700 and 1900 such as will compel all institutions to modify themselves if they wish to survive. Discontinuity has ceased to be a choice.

This does not mean that Christianity is impossible but that bibliolatry is improvident. The new life of the Christian community remains prior to the New Testament, which contains the first attempt at a description of it; this new life in Christ is constantly available to the community (though not inevitably appropriated by them) throughout Christian history. Revelation is not therefore a series of propositions defined once and immutably so that the presence or absence of certain nouns or verbs from the text of the Bible settles the doctrine of the priesthood once and for all. Revelation is the Christ-event: the New Testament is evidence about the initial response of the community to the event which brought it into existence. The New Testament may be interpreted as containing the first reactions of the primary Christian community to the idea of priesthood, but this is not the same as saying that any later response of the community to the Christ-event will entail the same judgement about the need for, or nature of, the priest.

The Roman, Orthodox and Anglican Churches have all recognised this in as much as they have traditionally extended the area from which significant evidence about the priesthood may be drawn to include the first five Christian centuries. There is no strong ground, however, for stopping at this point in time. If one appeals to history one must appeal to the whole of history, and accept the consequences. One must also admit the possibility of the falsification of one's arguments by a different use of the historical data. One may not rule out in advance the possibility that later experiments with the office of priesthood have developed from a valid response by the community to the act of revelation. Indeed, to hold the contrary point of view is to imply a certain provinciality in the main stream of tradition. The new life which the Christian community shares is a gift which has constantly to be responded to afresh in transformed historical circumstances: this may mean not only the reform, but even the abolition, of the priesthood as previously understood. I would take the unity, spirituality and reconciling power of the Christian community to be the significant standard which any ecclesiastical form must serve if it is to be justified. In some periods priesthoods of the type made traditional in the early Church may seem to be the best way of maintaining this standard, but at other times it may become necessary to dispense with a traditional form of priesthood altogether.

If one turns from the general to the particular one finds that the growth of the non-Anglican attitudes to the ministry in England illustrates this wide range of possibilities. Down to the sudden collapse of the Commonwealth, no non-Anglican model of the ministry had finally established itself because the ambition of the dominant Puritan group had been to master the Anglican structure and use it for new purposes. There was no one 'Reformation', of course: one should not be bludgeoned by Lutheran or Calvinist scholars into accepting their natural conviction that the Reformation must be defined in the terms which their hero used, all other views being treated (if even mentioned) as deviations. By the early 17th century the career of the Quaker leader, George Fox, already set out the extreme position – that a fulltime, paid, professional priesthood is not self-evidently, or in the light of the New Testament evidence, or even in terms of the quasi-sacred tradition of the institutions themselves, part of the *esse*, the indispensable ultimate or core, of the living Church. All the Friends were potential vehicles of the holy Spirit; if an *episkope* existed, it resided in the Meeting of the Brethren. One can hardly say that Fox was one of the creators of even the radical Protestant ministerial model, since he denied that such a ministry was necessary, but his example, and that of the continuing group he founded, always lay in the background of later developments. In the early 19th century, for example, Elizabeth Fry, who is still insufficiently recognised as the most remarkable leader of the movement to restore contact between the Society and its 17th century origins, refused to follow the general trend of her family into the Church of England because she firmly declined to believe in the necessity of a separated priesthood; she saw no additional meaning in the separate institution of the eucharist as a ministerial function, as distinct from the direct communion with the holy Spirit which she believed she enjoyed. On more than one occasion, having invited Anglican and Dissenting ministers to her home at Earlham, near Norwich, she waited until the servants had cleared away dinner and then led them herself in a kind of prayer-meeting in which she was quietly asserting her own right to 'minister' in the Friends' sense, to speak as one through whom the Spirit spoke. This would not seem as remarkable in the 20th century, but it is necessary to recall that even as late as 1860 Anglican Evangelical parsons still objected to Anglican laymen who themselves preached or evangelised in other ways.

If one returns to the 17th century, however, and to the less radical side of the non-Anglican tradition, one finds that Presbyterians, for example, emphasised the existence of a divinely instituted order of ministers, characterised by preaching. They combined this with the pastoral aspect of the old priesthood. Here Adam Martindale, the Presbyterian diarist, offers an instance. He lived in the Manchester area and began to preach – without ordination – in 1646 – when he was twenty-three and had been earning his living as a teacher. He was asked to preach by a Presbyterian minister because of the shortage of preaching in the district on account of the troubled conditions of the Civil War. His activities caused a congregation at Gorton, now part of

Manchester, to invite him to become their pastor; he gave up his work and prepared for ordination. He describes this: 'besides other matters touching the work of grace in his own soul, his ends in desiring the ministry, and his direct call to the place where he would officiate, etc., the expectant must give a satisfactory account of his skill in the Greek and Hebrew tongues, in logick, philosophy and divinity; and also exhibit a thesis upon a question given in Latin, and to defend it' (*Life*, Chetham Society, 1845, p. 66). Here is the ideal of the learned ministry, acquainted at least with the non-scientific culture of his own age, an ideal which survived into the 19th century, and which compelled Protestant ordinands to study Greek and Hebrew well into the 20th century. Martindale survived these ordeals, and was ordained by other Presbyterian ministers in London in 1649.

To be a learned minister, however, was not enough after the Restoration (when Martindale became a teacher of mathematics in order to make a living). One had also to become a new kind of preacher, a revivalist, able to stimulate in the children of the congregation the behaviour necessary to permit their being admitted as full members of the local Church. Here was a fundamental difference from the Anglican model as commonly understood (and one which was to have a back-effect on the Church of England in the 18th century when Anglican Evangelicals introduced a similar view to a limited extent into the Anglican tradition). Conversion was held to be the ground of admission into Church membership, and conversion came to be defined by outward and visible signs, or at least by verbal witness to inward, invisible experiences. This process consisted of conviction of sin followed by a Protestant equivalent of the dark night of the soul, from which the sinner emerged into salvation through justification by faith understood as a conscious experience of forgiveness and reconciliation. The ideal minister had experienced this process himself, and knew how to recognise and guide it in others, or how to stimulate it (this was where the revivalism came in) if it did not show itself. This was his professional equivalent of the confessional and of spiritual direction in the older sense. The *sermon* became the normal means of awakening these responses and remains so in the tradition of men like Billy Graham. Similar views of Christianity were held elsewhere but the Free Churches of the 16th and 17th centuries linked 'conversion' tightly with membership, and condemned other ways of looking at Christianity as corrupt.

The conditions of the Restoration enforced all this. The Non-conformist minister became the pastor, preacher and leader of a small, ingrown, sometimes persecuted local church. The lay members often felt tempted to make their peace with the society from which they separated, and if they decided to remain loyal to Dissent wanted their children to do the same. The minister had to bind this group together. He was less concerned about the single conscience – he rarely heard any equivalent of aural confession – than with keeping the members on good terms with each other as a socio-religious unit. His preaching had also to keep in view the end for which the congregation existed, in theological terms the preservation of pure religion in a world morally, ecclesiastically and intellectually corrupted – the same theme of the godly remnant will reappear in the sermons of Spurgeon, the 19th century Baptist preacher. If the children could not be kept loyal to the local church the congregation, which was rarely aggressive or expanding, would die out, as many did. It was only if the model pastor could build up and sustain a socially satisfying group that Dissent seemed really worth while. The increase in population came slowly between 1690 and 1790; in the 18th century the older Non-Conformity actually lost members to the new, rampant Wesleyan Methodists.

Of less importance in this period was the political leadership which the pastor gave the local church. His members belonged to a social group not automatically committed to the economic and political interests of the ruling classes; representatives of Dissent might at any time come out in opposition. The pastor reflected this critical position, whereas the Anglican parish priest normally felt committed to the political and social status quo, except in chaotic conditions like those under James II, when the theory of divine right was hastily abandoned because the policy of the Crown threatened the future of Anglicanism itself. The divine right of the '*pouvoir légitime*' has remained a central point of Roman

Catholic political attitudes down to the present day and still colours John XXIII's encyclical, *Mater et Magistra* (1961). Dissenting ministers, on the other hand, felt much less obliged to concede the total legitimacy of any British government.

If at this point one compares the Free Church model of the ministry with that of the 'episcopal' tradition one finds that

(*a*) the Dissenter is not, for instance, a sacrificing priest. The trend of Protestantism after 1600 was towards occasional celebration; this decline of the eucharist as the centre of the spiritual life affected 18th century Anglicanism as well, but less radically, less permanently. The Dissenter became a preaching and not a sacramental figure.

(*b*) in England the Dissenter had a 'gathered' not a parish Church. His meeting-house might be the focus of the faithful over a wide rural area or a whole town. His congregation was socially more homogeneous than that of the Anglican parish: this perhaps gave him less freedom from lay control. He was the choice of the congregation, not a priest sent in by a superior power (either the bishop or the landowner). His tenure was less certain than that of the Anglican. On the other hand the Dissenting minister of the 17th and 18th century was freer than his modern equivalent. The 20th-century heirs of 17th-century Non-Conformity in Britain and the United States belong to nationally organised Churches deeply committed to the existing political and cultural forms of society which they are therefore not free to criticise: this was the Anglican, rather than the Dissenting situation, in the 18th century.

(*c*) Positively, the Dissenting model was more that of the preacher than the Anglican: he had to concoct his own liturgy and had a stronger tendency to set up as an independent theologian.

The situation began to change in the 18th century, as Dissent slowly recovered from a low water-mark reached about 1730 and the Anglican Evangelical and Wesleyan Methodist revivals developed. Wesleyanism is no longer definable. In the Wesleyan idea of the itinerant minister, however, the element of divine call came into great prominence, at times acting almost as an alternative to conventional ordination. Joseph Entwisle, for example, started as a Wesleyan itinerant in 1787 when he was twenty-one.

He had previously twice declined to become a full-time preacher, but nevertheless went to the Manchester Conference of 1787. Hearing that Entwisle was momentarily free from employment, John Wesley, without asking his agreement, appointed him as a full-time preacher to the Oxfordshire circuit. The first time that Entwisle knew of this was when he met Wesley accidentally in Oldham Street.

> 'Still shrinking from the work, of the importance of which he had more affecting views than ever, he hesitated, when Mr Wesley, laying his hand upon his shoulder and fixing him with his piercing eye, said with his characteristic brevity and in a tone of authority, "Joseph, you *must* go". He went in the name of the Lord, deeply sensible of his own insufficiency and humbly depending upon the divine aid. He often reflected with satisfaction on the energetic manner and piercing look with which "you must go" was uttered by the venerable Founder of Methodism; and a recollection of the high human authority by which he was called to the ministry, combined with a persuasion of a divine call, often afforded him comfort in after-life in seasons of trial and discouragement' (*Memoir*, ed. by his son, 8th ed. 1862, p. 23).

The element of calling is very strong here, and although Entwisle technically served a four year probation (without any fixed training) before he was admitted into 'full Connexion', as the saying was, he was not, strictly speaking, ordained at all – any recognisable ordination was introduced into the Wesleyan system only in 1836. Nevertheless, his biography is entitled 'The Memoir of The Reverend Joseph Entwisle, fifty-four years a Wesleyan minister', which, incidentally, dated his ministry from his original appointment by Wesley in 1787 and not from his admission into the full itinerancy in 1791.

A serious account of the Christian ministry can hardly ignore the Wesleyan itinerancy, which laid the foundations of modern British and American Methodism; 19th-century Anglican comment, which rarely went further than underlining their lack of episcopal ordination, seems very unimaginative. John Wesley regarded his itinerants as 'extraordinary messengers'. He appealed from a legally constituted spiritual order (the Established Church), as the norm, to an order 'spiritually constituted', but not therefore properly illegal. His actions illustrate the actuality of a fresh beginning in the history of the ministry; they were certainly regarded by his contemporaries as a breach of continuity, and one need not take very seriously (as too many Methodist theologians have) his politically motivated efforts to show that his actions could be intellectually reconciled with the Establishment. Episcopal theologians sometimes speak of the possibility of God in the holy Spirit replacing a priesthood which had, for the sake of argument, been wiped out by disease: Wesley said that the holy Spirit had for the time being replaced the 'dead' Anglican clergy with a 'living' Wesleyan itinerancy. He not only expected his itinerants to work full-time as preachers, he also expected them to act as the pastors of the Wesleyan societies. Between 1740 and 1780 he refused to allow them to administer the eucharist; this refusal had an important effect in increasing the Dissenting tendency to identify the ministry with preaching and pastoral work. That he finally commissioned some of his itinerants to administer Holy Communion (whether he could 'ordain' them or not is a fascinating legal problem to which there is no solution unless one believes that the Order of the Church is both divinely given and humanly known) was an attempt to regularise the irregular by irregularity. The itinerants had no doubt themselves that they were ministers and once John Wesley had died in 1791 soon began to administer the sacraments on their own authority. Thus an autocratic Anglican parson greatly swelled the number of Non-Conformist ministers.

To preaching and a limited social leadership – at any rate the Wesleyan itinerants were always telling their members *not* to engage in politics – the system added a return to something more like the priest as the spiritual guide and confessor. The perfect Wesleyan was meant to live in the ordinary world without allowing his complete relation to God to be corrupted by civil society: he was to attain the goal of Christian holiness within the Wesleyan society, yet without abandoning the world in the style of the ascetic tradition. Wesley stood between the 17th century culture in which perfect Christianity could still be achieved only by renunciation of civil society, its goals and satisfactions, and the 20th century society in which Christian perfection can no longer be defined at all. The role of the Wesleyan minister – and this was where the return to the older model came in – was to provide pastoral, spiritual criticism of the society's members, which was needed if they were not to relapse into spiritual self-satisfaction. Such a pastoral role required authority – the right to demand obedience – and so between 1790 and 1850 the Wesleyan ministry demanded more social and religious obedience from their laity than was expected by other Protestant non-Anglican ministers at this time. A claim to absolute authority over men's souls lay at the root of the Wesleyan system, which declined steadily during the 19th century into something more like standard presbyterian Protestantism.

After 1800 the English Free Churches expanded rapidly as much because of the rise in population as because of their own efforts. The characteristic 19th century Free Church model of the minister became the so-called 'great preacher', the pulpit star. This passage from the Baptist preacher, Charles Spurgeon, illustrates something of his impact:

'There are some of you "children of the kingdom" [that is, children of church members] who can remember your mothers. . . . I can conceive of no one entering hell with a worse grace than the man who goes there with the drops of his mother's tears on his head and with his father's prayers following him at his heels. . . . "Children of the Kingdom", do not think that a pious mother can save you. . . . I can suppose some one standing at heaven's gate and demanding, "Let me in, let me in". "What for?" "Because my mother is in there." "Your mother has nothing to do with you. If she was holy, she was holy for herself; if she was evil, she was evil for herself." "But my grandfather prayed for me." "That is no use. Did you pray for yourself?" "No, I did not." "Then grandfather's prayers and grandmother's prayers, and father's and mother's prayers, may be piled on the top of one another till they reach the stars, but they can never make a ladder for you to go to heaven by." You must have vital experience of godliness in your heart, or else you are lost, even though all your friends are in heaven. That was a dreadful dream which a pious woman once had and told her children. She thought the judgement day was come. The great books were opened. They all stood before God. And Jesus Christ said, "Separate the wheat from the chaff. Put the goats on the left hand and the sheep on the right." The woman dreamed that she and her children were standing just in the middle of the great assembly. And the angel came and said, "I must take the mother, she is a sheep, she must go to the right hand. The children are goats, they must go to the left." She thought as she went her children clutched her and said, "Mother, must we part?" She then put her arms round them and seemed to say, "My children, I would, if possible, take you with me" but in a moment the angel touched her: her cheeks were dried, and now, overcoming natural affection, being rendered supernatural and sublime, resigned to God's will, she said, "My children, I taught you well, I trained you up, and you forsook the ways of God, and now all I have to say is, Amen to your condemnation." Thereupon they were snatched away, and she saw them in perpetual torment while she was in heaven' (*New Park Street Pulpit*, 1855, pp. 306–7).

This was Spurgeon remembering his duty to save the children of the Church. But Spurgeon, vulgar, outrageously confident that he had solved all theological problems, full of the assurance given him by the knowledge that he had preached to thousands last Sunday and would preach to thousands again on the Sunday to come, was really the exception. As such, he seemed the example of what had become a powerful Free Church ministerial model during the Evangelical Revival. He was an ordinary country boy; he had received no particular training for the work of preaching; he remained fiercely fundamentalist in the heyday of biblical criticism; he often paraded a jaunty British patriotism; he took good care never to seem too impressed by or courteous towards the possessing classes; yet no one could deny that he both formed and held for the whole of his life much the largest single congregation in London. This legend of the successful preacher dominated the minds of Free Church ministers at the turn of the century, especially because they saw this success as bringing political as well as ecclesiastical influence.

And then, very quietly, the floods came. The preaching and the pastoral work (though men like Spurgeon did very little of the latter) had chiefly been intended to keep in being the Free Church congregation of the local church. These local churches survived from the 17th century down to the middle of the 19th century. Then they began to fall apart. This happened because the social cohesion of Non-Conformity, which appeared invulnerable even in 1900 to many observers, disintegrated. The pull of the new urban, industrialised, educated, secularising society, a society which was now willing to accept Free Churchmen as ordinary people because Anglicanism had lost once and for all the power to dictate the religio-social tone of the country, drew the Non-Conformists out of their isolation. Just how social, and not religious, the local churches had been it is hard to say. But nothing that the ministers could do held back the dramatic change, the spiritual emigration of the heirs of Dissent. The accepted model of the ministry simply became irrelevant, because few people wanted to live within the kind of local religious community which it had grown up to serve, and even fewer were still prepared to see a worthwhile career in the ministry itself.

I have had a close acquaintance with many Free Church ordinands over the past twenty years. What kind of a model is theirs?

(a) The model, still, tragically, centres on the image of the alleged 'great preacher'. In their hearts this is what the majority of them would still wish to be.

(b) They sometimes combine this with political preaching. They still share the late 19th-century Non-Conformists' dream of political influence without responsibility. They resemble the late Victorian 'political preacher' all the more because instead of any coherent theory of social renewal they have retreated to a variety of the 'Social Gospel', a programme which tried to reduce political to ethical decisions in order to avoid serious political division inside the local Churches. The late Victorians concentrated on sex, alcohol and gambling, their successors on sex and race. The collapse of serious Christian political thinking corresponds, in the Free Churches, to the recognition of the decline of the Church's political influence. Hence the fresh emphasis on financial benevolence (Oxfam etc.). What distresses the Free Church ministry here is that lay Christian activism does not really want clerical leadership.

(c) The model has no strong theological content. Free Church ordinands feel the intense pressure of competing professions: teaching, medicine, the civil services. When they withdraw from the ordained ministry they often turn to one of these forms of service. As ministers, however, their reaction is to compete by imitating, however inefficiently, those who work in these fields; they rarely try to compete *as theologians*. (This arises perhaps because they have little confidence in modern *orthodox* theology: great sophistication has been shown in finding new ways of presenting the traditional picture of man as fatally flawed by sin and unable in his works to please God, but few groups in 20th century society accept this account; 'radical' theology, on the other hand, has produced a layman's theology rather than a clerical one.)

Finally, present-day Free Church ordinands find that they can draw little strength from their Free Church past. Its revivalist element, for example, means nothing to most of them, or becomes a defiant mannerism for those who cling to fundamentalism as a simplification of their situation (and who therefore find it hard to accept the authority of the more critical biblical instruction which they receive in the typical seminary). They derive no advantage from the Free Church ministerial tradition of comparative poverty – they are aware that society no longer admires deliberate asceticism. At the same time, however, they cannot, in the style of their 19th century predecessors, take their economic position for granted: it has become a social problem for them. Their experience of life, moreover, is limited, not enhanced, by their Free Church background; they come from areas of society still protected to some extent from the strains of the modern world. They therefore often welcome the ecumenical movement as a socially transforming opportunity (the hostile reaction of clerical reviewers to this aspect of Bryan Wilson's criticism of the ecumenical movement in *Religion in a Secular Society* must have amused the author and confirmed him in his conviction that ecumenicity was largely a matter of improving the clerical image).

Granted, however, that the ecumenical movement will not absorb the non-episcopal bodies altogether, one sees at least two possibilities of revising the Free Church ministerial model. The first would involve the reversal of the past in a return to frequent celebration of the eucharist with the pastor liturgically identified as the visible centre of the local church. Two problems arise immediately. First, that the Free Churches have never possessed a theological justification of frequent communion; second, the countervailing force of lay attitudes which I have here associated with the name of Elizabeth Fry. This might equally be called the ecumenical alternative, however, because the long-term result of such a course would be the absorption of most of the Free Churches into the episcopal society.

This might seem attractive, until one realises that the social basis of the episcopal model of the priesthood is just as fatally undermined as that of the Free Church model, so that the ecumenical programme is now much less viable than it formerly appeared to be. There has even been a recent renewal of ecclesiological scepticism, a return to the view that institutionalised Churches perpetually threaten the Christianity of their members. This is a familiar idea in Protestantism (its most brilliant modern advocate was the Lutheran Soeren Kierkegaard) and has a long history in English non-episcopal Protestantism. There are, of course, other contemporary reasons for this renewal of doubt: a quickened sense of the degree to which the official Churches have become a consenting part of a dying stage in the development of western society; a theological reaction against the ecumenical emphasis on a corporate theology, on a social programme of western good works (mid-Victorian in ethos), and on a hierarchical ministry. Above all, there seems a grave danger that national or global religious institutions can survive in a thoroughly secularised west only if they secularise their religious functions. In any case, there is little unbiased evidence that people in western culture want to live in small organic communities, religious or secular.

Such a diagnosis fills one with ecclesiastical despair only if one feels that the New Testament contains and reveals the self-evident pattern of a divinely determined church order whose absolute continuity is a theological and moral necessity. The Free Church ordinand – and this is his second alternative – need not feel so bound. He may argue that the Church need not always be conceived of as a hierarchical structure, so that the goal of the ecumenical movement, for example, becomes little more than the setting up of a modified papacy at the head of a more broadly based Catholicism. For the immediate future, in fact, one may envisage the priesthood as no longer corporate but individual, as a calling, with or without official ordination, for which the one called has to find his own meaning because he cannot wholly believe in the corporate, hierarchical definition produced in the past under very different historical circumstances. One may see the collapse of the existing ecclesiastical order as inevitable if Christianity is to survive the secularisation of society. It is the point made, as far as Protestantism is concerned, by Martin Luther, and in the Free Church tradition by George Fox and John Wesley, that in extreme circumstances continuity, the view that Order is already given, is not of absolute importance where the model of the ministry is concerned.

However, the dialectic between the two positions which are here involved seems to me to be a clue to the proper understanding of both Church and ministry. Essentially, the minister is simply one whom God has called to concentrate his attention on the relation between God and man. He has no other absolute vocation. In periods of social stability and very slow social change, in a Europe still dominated by the religious circumstances of its genesis, he can form a milieu in which to express this vocation as sacrificing priest or preacher of the Word or pastor of souls. In periods of rapid change and instability, when western culture is moving from a religious to a non-religious basis, he may find it impossible to form any such milieu and therefore impossible to see himself in any of these roles. In such a society the temptation of those ministers who believe in Order and continuity is to impose the known roles regardless of the consequences – this kind of rigidity was one cause of the explosiveness of the 16th century Reformation when it finally occurred. The temptation of those who believe in freedom and adaptation is to exaggerate the possibilities of freedom, to indulge in their own brand of triumphalism, in fact, and then to despair because the secularising process is barely touched by individual dissent. What emerges is the historically relative nature of the definitions which we can make for either the ministry or the Church. At any moment the Church may be described as a structure of tensions, tensions which do not inevitably exist in equilibrium or tend towards some resolution. The model of the ministry cannot be set up purely in terms of the New Testament, or for that matter in terms of some specially favoured later period, such as that of the Counter-Reformation, or the early Victorian period seen from the angle of either the Anglo-Catholic or the Free Churchman. The model of the ministry is always a present problem to which each generation gives some answer. What one fears at the moment in Britain is that the answer of the inter-war generation which produced the ecumenical movement is now being imposed upon a transformed set of historical circumstances.

INTRODUCTION

The Orthodox Church's experience of applying the Christian life to the needs and political situations of Russia and the eastern Mediterranean countries has provided a range of problems and solutions which the west has never fully appreciated. Yet this stream of the Christian tradition can contribute insights which are directly relevant to the situation in the west. It is particularly important to have this experience and point of view available when apostolic Jerusalem is thought to provide the common starting point for discussion, and when the struggles to define the Christian faith during the ensuing centuries were largely carried on in the east.

The eastern Church experienced all the strains and tensions between the Church's formal structure of government and responsibility on the one hand, created to provide for the pastoral needs of the people but slow to change as the conditions and needs of the people changed, and the prophetic element in the Christian community on the other hand. The clash gave rise to a wide range of sects, which emerged to express aspects of the Christian life which the official organisation was ignoring, and a laicising movement which emphasised the priesthood of the whole people of God.

Fr Mélia suggests that any solution to the problems for priesthood created by this situation must be in terms of a harmonious cooperation which recognises the diversity of the Christian life and seeks to express this diversity within the union provided by the authority and pastoral responsibility of the bishops. (*Fr Mélia's article was translated from the French by Sister Mary Speakman* s.n.d.)

BIOGRAPHICAL NOTE

ELIE MÉLIA *is a member of St Sergius Orthodox Theological Academy in Paris, where he is also the pastor of the Georgian parish of St Nina.*

7 The Priesthood in our time: an Orthodox Point of View

ELIE MÉLIA

The Church of the Apostles

The different kinds of ministry which work together to unify and to rule the Church, the people of God and the body of Christ, are varied in their nature, and the balance between these different elements has been determined in the course of history. The present position is a development from the beginning of the apostolic age in Jerusalem, which is the original and the model of all local churches.

The apostles possessed, if this word may be used, the fullness of authority and power in the Church founded by Jesus Christ; they were responsible for the different ministries according to the charisms of the holy Spirit. The first movement towards specialisation took place with the institution of the seven deacons (Acts 6). Later, after the dispersal of the Twelve from the holy city, we find the Church at Jerusalem governed by James, the brother of the Lord, who was not a member of the College of Apostles. James was helped by the 'Elders', who were assistants like the 'zeqenim' of Jewish groups. Acts 14:23 shows that Paul and Barnabas established elders in every town in which they preached the Gospel.

When a serious ideological dispute arose, we see the collegial character of the Church, for the point was discussed and then decided by a meeting of the whole community (Acts 15:22, 23, 25), but the actual discussion was confined to the apostles and elders (Acts 15:2, 6). This 'council of Jerusalem' reveals a Church well organised into different ministries exercised according to rank, the different persons working harmoniously in accordance with collegiality.

In 1 Cor. 12 St Paul gives us a list, which appears to be precise, of the different kinds of Christian ministries. Yet the apostle is not here speaking generally and exhaustively, but with reference to differences of opinion which had arisen between small groups in the church at Corinth. The enumeration: first, second, third, does not here indicate a canonical order, but merely a list of different gifts which were well-known to his readers, the final criterion suggested by Paul being charity (ch. 13). St Paul's point of view is charismatic rather than canonical, and for this reason prophets and teachers are mentioned before those who exercised the charisms of 'helping' and of government. The only rank on which St Paul insists is that of the apostolate, for he refers to it to assert the supreme authority which every one acknowledged in the apostolic college in consequence of the unique divine vocation.

Moreover, at the period of the foundation of the Church, the inspired spoken witness to the gospel could not but take first place. This pre-eminence of the ministry of the word is confirmed by St Paul when he points out to his readers that he does not baptise but devotes himself exclusively to preaching (1 Cor. 1:17). The charity which is put forward as the supreme criterion is by no means a mere feeling; its touch-stone is the harmony that reigns, the real unity of the ecclesial community. It is in view of charity that prophecy is distinguished from the gift of tongues and is clearly much more highly valued (ch. 14). It is interesting to remark that at that time 'prophets' celebrated the eucharist (Acts 12:1–3) and this practice survived the time of the apostles, at least in some places; the *Didache* mentions it as occurring in Syria.

The Successors of the Apostles

The apostles were followed by a large number of bishops, the heads of the local communities. They were linked to the apostles by the *eulogimenoi andres*, such as Titus, Timothy, Clement of Rome, Ignatius of Antioch. It is important to explain exactly the limits and nature of this succession to the apostles.

The two chief ministries of the Church are found in different historical periods. The time of the apostles is the time of the foundation of the Church (Matt. 16:18; 19:28; Apoc. 21:14). The unique character of the apostolate could not be passed on to others, but the apostles were not concerned with that; obviously they had to make sure that the true character of what they had founded should be passed on to those who followed them. The permanent survival of the Church as originally founded demanded complete identity between the nature of its foundation and that of the ensuing ages.

The period of the bishops is the time of the development of the Church as founded by the apostles, but, *at the actual moment*, the function of the bishops was analogous to that of the apostles. The chief characteristic of this ministry, shared with the apostles, an intermediate ministry, is the fullness of the pastoral authority according to the promises made by our Lord to Peter and the Twelve; the bishops had to concentrate their efforts on and to supervise (*episcope* – superintend) the direction of the people of God in the various forms of services and charisms.

The apostolate is essentially the office of a vicar (*shaliah* – ambassador, agent) of Christ: 'As my Father sent me, so am I sending you' (John 20:21). Now Christ had three messianic powers: he was king, prophet and priest (cf. 1 Cor. 12:4–6), and all Christians share in this threefold ministry for the salvation of the world (1 Pet. 2:9), but they share it as a body, that is to say, in an orderly way, each in his own place. The three messianic powers are united and made effective in the pastoral office: the *shepherd of Israel* was at one and the same time he who gathered together the people of God and he who led it to the eschatological consummation.

In the episcopate, as in the apostolate, the three types of ministry are united in one person; in the Jewish religion they were divided among several persons, except, significantly, in the concept of the Messiah. Yet, owing to the circumstances of the new people of God, the duties of the priesthood were destined to carry privileges. The fundamental reason for this is the unique place held from the beginning by the eucharist, the sacrament of unity, the gift which moulded the body of Christ, the Church. The Jews had only one temple, at Jerusalem, to the exclusion of any other place of sacrifice; and sacrifice was considered the highest form of worship, as being the worship of the whole people of God. In the diaspora, as well as in Palestine, the Jewish communities gathered together in places of an inferior worship, the synagogues, in which prayer said in common, formally expressed but non-sacrificial, was entrusted to laymen. As they were separated by their race from the surrounding people, these communities felt that it was unnecessary to assert their individuality in any other way.

The position of the Christian communities was completely different. They were open to all comers who professed the Faith and they had a strong urge towards universality; their only bond of union was the eucharistic assembly, and the authority of the bishop, who presided at it, was proportionally strengthened. Each community from its experience of the eucharist derived the conviction that it was the Body of Christ, according to the doctrine about the Church taught by St Paul in his epistles. In the eucharistic assembly the pastoral office of the bishop was visible in its greatest power and splendour.

But tensions were not slow to appear at different levels of the organisation of the Church as it spread over the world.

Priesthood and Hierarchy in post-Apostolic History

From a period even before the time of Constantine, the harmonious balance of the ministries, maintained from the time of the apostles themselves, as their epistles bear witness, was to suffer attacks. The threat became definite by reason of the ideas of the 'spirituals', who claimed a special prophetic authority. The bishops, while emphasising the divine origin of their authority, as St Clement of Rome does in his letter to the Corinthians, took care to support their position by relying on the whole community, the collegiality of the people of God. Actually the bishops were far from aiming at taking to themselves all the powers, and abolishing subordinate officials; they had to strive against particularism or individualism which tended to division, the besetting sin of prophets everywhere.

About 107 St Ignatius of Antioch was moved to emphasise the authority of the monarchical episcopate. Historians have wondered what could be the reason for this protest. They have suggested as a hypothesis that there existed in those lands, side by side with the main communities, communities of Jewish-Christians who refused to share a common table with the uncircumcised. These peripheral communities probably had no bishops to lead them, but only elders. This, among other reasons, explains the marked preference of St Ignatius for deacons. For deacons were directly attached to the service of the bishop, while priests organised collegially could aspire to a certain autonomy on the priestly and hierarchical level.

At the end of the second century, Montanism, which the great Latin doctor Tertullian joined about 207-8, gave more honour to the office of prophets, whom these sectaries considered superior in rank to the bishops. Moreover the Catholic hierarchy, that is, the hierarchy of the greater part of the Church widespread in the Roman empire, was declared to be corrupted by the easy going customs of a lax episcopate. It is true that the bishops were more and more inclined to lower their standards, especially in the matter of penance.

In the face of the growth of the cruel persecution suffered from the power of Rome by the infant Church, we see the growth of the authority of martyrs and confessors. In the middle of the 3rd century at Carthage (Novat), and at Rome (Novatian) the confessors assumed great importance, going so far, in some cases, as to oppose the bishops. The Novatian schism, supported by considerable numbers, lasted for centuries, to merge at last into the (pure) Catharist movement. These heretics preached a Christianity reduced to a spiritual aristocracy, setting aside the majority, the 'ordinary' Christians. Although Novatian had had himself consecrated a bishop, the rejection of the Catholic hierarchy could not but weaken, among these schismatics, the very principle of hierarchical authority.

Monasticism and the Growth of Spiritual Direction

From the 4th century, monasticism, a perfectly orthodox move-ment which has always been the glory of the Church, nevertheless caused tensions in the structure of the Church, which had become characteristically hierarchical. Monasticism, on certain occasions and much to its credit, opposed the hierarchy, which had allowed itself to become too secular, too submissive to the ever-encroach-ing omnipotence of the state, as well as to sociological pressures. It was a layman's development, having no part in the hierarchy, except occasionally: it acquired a real independence in the very heart of the Christian people, by reason of its organisation in communities in monasteries and of the opportunities arising from that – opportunities in both the spiritual and the material field. But the prestige of monasticism increased especially through its essential values: insistence on eschatological standards and on the precepts of the Gospel, the defence of spiritual liberty, the effort to attain moral perfection, by prayer, ascetic practices, and the freeing of the spirit of man. All this greatly appealed to the people of God, who were thus exalted and maintained in a state of prophetic and eschatological enthusiasm, especially by the fuller use of the sacrament of penance. Formerly people resorted to the practice of penance only occasionally, according to the gravity of the sins and the scandal which they caused in the Christian community. The monks began the practice of regular private confession, and, in a more general way, the use of spiritual direction or the care of souls.

In this way, a prophetic ministry grew up in a sort of independ-ence of the ruling hierarchy. It is well-known that monks who had not received holy orders took upon themselves the direction of consciences in monasteries, even hearing the confessions of monks, as, for example, St Simeon the New Theologian in the 10th century.

This extraordinary state of affairs soon came to an end and penance was soon completely in the hands of the hierarchy. But this cannot be attributed to an unjust seizure of a monopoly of spiritual power by the hierarchy. It was required by the absolute necessity of unity which is as essential to the Church as the prophetic gift.

Enlargement of the Sphere of Authority in Teaching Doctrine

The Byzantine world in the middle ages was characterised by the struggle against heresies about the Trinity and the Incarnation. In this sphere too, side by side with the action of the hierarchy, there was a blossoming of creative theological thought. Many Fathers of the Church and numbers of heresiarchs were bishops, but there were also many eminent theologians who did not belong to the hierarchy.

As early as the 3rd century Origen, while still a young layman, was made the head of the catechetical school at Alexandria in succession to St Clement, a bishop. Origen was invited to preach at Caesarea and as his bishop, Demetrius of Alexandria, protested, he caused himself to be ordained priest at Caesarea so that he might continue in the ministry of preaching. Having been condemned at Alexandria for this second offence against canon law, Origen decided to stay permanently in Caesarea.

So, side by side with the formal teaching of doctrine (catechesis, decisions on dogma and canon law), established by the heads of the hierarchy, a wider and freer teaching was developed by the theologians. In the eastern Church, laymen could lecture even in the schools of theology, in spite of the prohibition of the Quini-Sexte council (692).

The Problem of the Fragmentation of Authority and of Hostility between the Priesthood and the Laity

A strain was thus created between the pastoral ministry providing for the guidance of the Church from above and the prophetic movement existing in the Christian community according to the free spontaneous action of the holy Spirit. This had serious results for the history of the Church and for its constitution. Movements of renewal and reform often showed a spirit of opposition to the hierarchy. The hierarchy guarded its authority with jealous care and often distrusted every influence which endangered the equilibrium of ecclesiastical law and order, for which the bishops are responsible. The small measure of the prophetic gift in the hierarchy gave rise to numerous sects embittered by lack of spiritual nourishment: faith-healing sects, sects claiming the gift of tongues, sects advocating absolute poverty, preaching sects hostile to the Sacramental system. At the very heart of the Church there arose a lay movement, or rather a laicising movement, instinctively hostile to the hierarchy and hotly defending their claim to the priestly dignity which belongs to the entire people of God.

The movement called 'secular' is completely modern, but its roots go far back to the middle ages which began with Constantine. The leaders were first of all politicians: the Byzantine emperors and the highly-placed officials of the Empire, anxious to exempt the state from the power of the Church, and, in the issue, to secure the supremacy of the state over the Church. The lawyers, as is natural, espoused the cause of the state. Another class of society followed the same course – the poor, who were often oppressed by the feudal bishops and by the monasteries which owned the land on which the poor depended. Finally the Renaissance: men of letters, artists, the learned, from the depths of their newly-acquired creative experience, demanded liberty of thought and speech from an authority too often distrustful and sunk in a barren legalism.

It is only fair to point out that at every stage the faults and failings of the hierarchy reflected the spiritual and intellectual state typical of the period.

The key to the problem is not to be found in a naïve hostility, too often called dialectic, between the hierarchical system and the prophetical strain. Some people go so far as to assert that this hostility is to the death, and declare that the hierarchy is fundamentally incapable of fulfilling the prophetical office. They identify those holding office in the Church with the rich who, our Lord said, would find it more difficult to enter the kingdom than for a camel to pass through the eye of a needle.

The problem is to seek a re-union, a new coming together, enriched by the experience of a Christian people which has renewed its spiritual maturity; this is true at least of a large élite; but this re-union is to be expected in the future rather than actually present.

Harmonious co-operation between the different ministries and charisms in a world falling under the control of man and subject to the swift course of history calls urgently for union under the aegis of the pastoral service of the bishops, re-orientated in its natural tendency towards unity – a tendency itself possessing the prophetic quality.

The discharge by seculars of the ever-growing spiritual responsibilities is not inimical to the authority of the bishops, but strengthens it and gives it richer, more fruitful elements.

But I realise that this suggestion is easier to bring forward than to put into practice in our time.

'Dialogue', so much extolled nowadays, is contrary to dispute as well as to monologue, for both of these tend to the vice of unilateralism. Nothing worth while can be done in the Church of Christ without charity and humility.

Renewal in the Modern Orthodox Church

This seems to be the course of history in the modern Orthodox Church. I refer to the awakening in south-west Russia or the Ukraine in the 16th century; to the 'philocalic' renewal in the monasticism of the 18th century; to the renewal in preaching and in the interior life in Greece in the 19th century; to the return to the Church of the Russian intelligentsia at the beginning of our century; and finally to the Orthodox diaspora as it exists in western Europe and in America.

A splendid page in the history of Orthodoxy was written in the 18th century by the Orthodox peoples of Lithuania and Poland, when the two countries were united in one. An enterprise of Catholic proselytism called 'Unia' was begun on the principle of an amalgamation of the Byzantine *rite* and the Roman Catholic *doctrine*. At the time, four out of the six Orthodox bishops who exercised authority in these lands accepted the 'uniate' movement; the other two were imprisoned by the royal government. The Orthodox people, deprived of their hierarchy, quickly organised themselves into confraternities legally established, containing laymen and members of the lower clergy, who were married, and also monks. The first care of these confraternities was to ask for approval for their statutes from the highest Orthodox authority, the Patriarch of Constantinople. He gave his blessing and also succeeded in refounding a regular episcopate for the region concerned. The confraternities went on all the same, in full accord with the restored local episcopate. They were the leaders in a large-scale campaign to restore religious fervour among the people, building churches to replace those which had been confiscated or destroyed, opening schools and even seminaries, publishing and editing catechisms, prayer books, liturgical books, books on apologetics or polemics, distributing Bibles, organising public controversy, liturgical and para-liturgical services. The theological knowledge of the Church in Russia is the product of this movement, which spread to the Muscovite state; public education in Russia is also, to a great extent, derived from these confraternities and their schools.

In the 18th century Mount Athos was the cradle of a spiritual renewal which spread throughout the whole of Orthodox monasticism and left a lasting effect on Orthodox piety in general. The originator was the metropolitan Macarius Notaras of Corinth who inspired and guided the monk Nicodemus. The latter published a collection of sayings of the Fathers of the Church and of masters of the spiritual life. The collection, which was called '*Philocalie* (love of Beauty) *des Saints Jeuneurs*' became incredibly popular; it is still the standard book of Orthodox spirituality. For example, a simple Russian peasant hardly able to read adopted the practice of continual prayer, carrying in his knapsack, a Bible and a copy of the *Philocalie* translated into Russian. This spontaneous popularity of a truly spiritual movement is a suitable subject for meditation for those who at present are trying to reform the liturgy and the whole Christian message, the language in which it is actually couched being supposed to be incapable of comprehension by the average members of the Church.

The 'philocalic' movement was continued to the end of the 19th century by the 'Colyvites' who also started from Mt Athos and spread in Greek-speaking countries; they enjoined a strict observance of liturgical rules and, in the tradition of St Nicodemus the Hagiorite, frequent communion. The Church in Greece experienced in the second half of the 19th century a renewal of preaching and personal holiness among the people, under the philosopher Apostolos Macrakis and the priest-monk Eusebius Matthopoulos. From this renewal came the missionary activity in contemporary Greece, like those of Zoë and others.

Between the two world wars the Church in Serbia experienced under the influence of Bishop Nicolas of Okhrida a widespread movement of spiritual vision and witness, the movement of the Bogomoltsy (the pious people or the people who pray to God); with fidelity to holy scripture and in the Orthodox spiritual tradition, ordinary people bore witness to their experience of the Faith in their daily life. The Metropolitan Nicolas himself was celebrated for his *Missionary Letters* which had a very large circulation.

In Roumania the Church attempted a revival of monasticism by reforming the monasteries and the monastic life, trying to adapt monasticism to the world of today. But the atheistic government prevented the development of this interesting effort.

In Russia the Church succeeded in attaining amazing fruits of holiness and spiritual effort, in spite of the organisation imposed upon her by Peter the Great – an organisation quite unsuitable to her traditional way of life. These fruits of holiness were especially evident in the monastic life, and, indirectly, in the episcopate owing to the fact that the bishops were always chosen from among the monks. But thanks to the four Religious Academies which fed both the monastic clergy and therefore the episcopate, and to the diocesan married clergy, the Church came to assume, to an extent not yet fully appreciated, its full responsibility in the most developed society in the world of Orthodoxy, in view of the decadence of the Orthodox countries subject to Turkey. It is impossible to omit the pastoral labour of a priest, Jean Serguev, the curé of Cronstadt, in the social sphere, in the working-class circles of that war-port, and in the direct spiritual sphere: he lived a life of prayer at a very high level recorded in his book *My Life in Christ*; he was granted a gift of healing known over the whole expanse of that vast country; he preached; his powerful words made it necessary to hold unique general confessions for the thousands of people who filled the cathedral of St Andrew; he was able to persuade the masses of ordinary people to practise frequent communion.

Another priest, Père Gapone, filled the masses with enthusiasm by his preaching on social subjects, but was accused by the revolutionaries of dealing with the police, and was murdered by them.

An abyss had opened between the Church and most of the educated. Pouchkine and St Seraphin of Sarov who were contemporaries did not know of the existence of each other. The slovophiles, and Gogol, Dostoevsky and even Tolstoy kept up interest in religion in literary spheres, but the greater number of the intelligentsia, especially in the universities, had joined the revolutionary movement and abandoned a Church closely associated with the tsarist state.

But, all at once, a number of university men and Marxist thinkers returned to the Church: Berdiaev, Bulgakov and others. They published a collection of essays, *From Marxism to Idealism* and began a review, *Vekhi* (landmarks). Similarly, societies of religious philosophy were formed and in them dialogue took place between the intelligentsia and the clergy.

The general interest of this movement arises from the fact that Russia was the only Orthodox country possessing any great industrial development, and accordingly, confronted by the social and technical problems which loom so large in the contemporary world. The converts from Marxism set before the conscience of Christians, from the heart of Christianity itself, not only the social problem, but the more general problem of culture and technique; they tried to discover a new Christian unifying theory of life, of a wholeness of life, a theory explaining also the universe – a vision similar in its aim to that of the Christianity of the middle ages.

The General Council of the Church of Russia, proposed by the tsarist government, but meeting only in 1917, reorganised the structure of the Church and re-established at every level the conciliar procedure, forbidden by Peter the Great. It was the completion of the effort for renewal in the Church, by the union of the traditional spirituality and the pressing problems of the modern world.

But the Bolshevist revolution of October 1917, over-riding the February revolution, set up a militant atheistic government. All creative religious activity was ended. A persecution of an atrocity unheard-of in the history of mankind fell upon the Church and every kind of religious life. A very great part of the intellectual élite was forced to emigrate: writers, university men, artists, the learned, military men, members of the higher ranks of the clergy.

The soviet government banished a number of religious thinkers who had survived the massacres and the famine and who by their banishment escaped from a religious persecution which was to be organised with increased savagery. The exiles formed a fine group of intellectuals; a number of them had been responsible for the renewal of which we spoke above. Moreover, a number of the bishops and some priests had left the country or had been expelled, or lived in lands independent of the former Russian empire. During the civil war and the first days of the emigration the authority and the sphere of action of the secular clergy had grown considerably owing to the disappearance of social and administrative structures. There is no doubt that, to an extent difficult to estimate, these witnesses, and often, these leaders of religious renewal have made a contribution to the renewal which has been visible in western Christianity, especially in Catholicism.

Among those religious thinkers who had left Russia and especially among the professors of the Institute of Orthodox Theology founded in Paris in 1924, the ecumenical movement found some of the principal participants in the theological dialogue.

The contribution of the Orthodox theologians of the diaspora is most apparent in the sphere of ecclesiology, and by this link we come back to our subject – the priesthood in our days. For ecclesiology tends to increase the esteem in which the pastoral office is held, in a way which is traditional but also creative and leading to renewal. Its effect is to give to this ministry a unity founded on the eucharist and developing a complementary theology of the holy Spirit.

INTRODUCTION

Fr Crichton's paper examines the main elements which have influenced the formation of the priesthood until the change of theological trends brought about by Vatican II. The threefold tension at Trent, created by the fear of conciliarism, interference from the new nation-states, and Roman fear of episcopal independence, prevented any clear ecclesiology from emerging. Yet the main problem was recognised: it was the need to distinguish between the divinely intended structure of the Church and the historical expressions and modifications it has received in the course of time, so as to give room for adaptation to meet the changing contemporary needs.

Trent met the needs of its time chiefly by the establishment of seminaries, and by reforms of the episcopate to emphasise its pastoral responsibilities; but it also laid the main emphasis on the priest as a cult minister, with the episcopate as an 'inflation of the presbyterate'. The consequences of these moves were influenced by Trent's simple rejection of the doctrine of the universal priesthood of the faithful, a failure which resulted in a silence which lasted until 1947.

The years which followed Trent saw a steady increase in the centralisation of the Church, with a growing emphasis on the juridical aspects of the Church's ministry. This was reinforced by Bellarmine's model of the 'pyramid' Church: a visible society with hierarchy and due subordination of its members in an ascending scale to the pope. The powers of the priesthood exercised within jurisdictional distinctions became the key to the Church's life, with strong emphasis on the *ex opere operato* aspect of the sacraments.

The ideals of the priesthood still commonly held by both priests and laity in our own day are the ones which emerged from such 17th century French thinkers as Condren and Olier, despite the Christocentric mystical approach of Bérulle which anticipated the views which are now becoming increasingly prevalent. This is at least partly due to the interruption of the work of Vatican I, which robbed the Church of the council's consideration of the *schema* on the constitution of the Church; this might well have anticipated the conclusions of Vatican II by nearly a hundred years. In the event, the theology of the Church's ministry remained all but static from medieval times until Vatican II. The severe criticism of the 'traditional' presentation of priesthood, and the problem of sacerdotal identity with which so many priests are now struggling, are direct consequences of these centuries of static theology.

Vatican II brought about a recovery of an older theological perspective. Within the priestly Church it is the episcopate which is the *primary* participation in the priesthood of Christ, with the bishop as chief shepherd of his flock rather than a mere administrator or liturgical functionary.

BIOGRAPHICAL NOTE

JAMES DUNLOP CRICHTON *was born 18 June 1907 and educated at Cotton College and then Oscott College. He was ordained in 1932, and has engaged in the pastoral ministry*

8 Church and Ministry from the Council of Trent to the First Vatican Council*

J. D. CRICHTON

MOST OF US, THAT IS THE NON-SPECIALISTS, ARE UNDER
the impression that the council of Trent invented the pyramid
Church and it is surprising to learn that it had no explicit ecclesiology at all. As a modern authority has written: 'Their (the
fathers of the council) constant guide was the principle of providing for various necessities from time to time, without ever
pretending to develop an integrated and complete plan which

* This paper obviously makes no pretence to be a complete investigation of the
whole doctrine of the period. It is a series of *sondages* that I hope are reasonably
representative. Apart from the short section on Febronius, there is nothing here
from the German theologians. The name of Sailer sticks in the mind but I could not
pursue that line. Nor regrettably is there anything about the Anglican ministry, an
area that certainly calls for a specialist and one hopes that someone will deal with it
some day at length and *sine odio theologico*.

since then. Since *1951* he has been editor of Liturgy (*now* Life and Worship). *He is
author of the following books:* The Church's Worship (*1964*); Changes in the
Liturgy (*1965*); The Mass and the People of God, ed. (*1966*). *He has contributed
to several other collections, and writes for* The Tablet. *He is a member of the National
Liturgical Commission; sometime consultor to liturgical* Consilium, Rome; *Roman
Catholic observer to the Church of England Liturgical Commission.*

would scarcely have been understood by those lacking – as was true of the overwhelming majority of the fathers – a clear concept of the Church'; and he goes on 'they avoided touching upon the problems concerning the structure of the Church'.[1] In fact the council was caught in a threefold tension. First there was the fear of the pope that the council would revive the conciliarism of the previous century. With this was connected the intervention of the new nation-states whose pressure on the council, as is well known, was severe, and finally there was a fear on the part of Rome of an episcopal independence that would restrict the activity of the papacy both for good and for ill. It is not then surprising after all that Trent came up with no worked-out ecclesiology and that it refused even to endorse the phrase of the council of Florence that the pope is the *Rector Universalis Ecclesiae*.[2]

It must be admitted that from the point of view of the ministry this was unfortunate. If sacraments are in different ways signs of the Church, that is, signs that manifest its nature, and if, as at Trent, there was no clear picture of the Church, the results are likely to be meagre. So far as I am able to discover, there was no radical re-thinking of the theology of the ministry at Trent, although, on the other hand, and for reasons that are not strictly theological, it would be untrue to say that the council merely reiterated medieval views. It did, in fact, clean up the clerical stable – a task of herculean proportions.

Inevitably, then, in giving an account of the Church and ministry at Trent, one can do no more than deal with particular features. An implied ecclesiology will only be discerned through such a treatment, on the supposition that it is possible to do so.

The Council of Trent

Trent, for both the Catholic and the non-Catholic mind, has become a myth. All sorts of things are associated with it that post-date it and most I think fail to distinguish the Church as it was when the council was sitting, and for some years afterwards, from

---

[1] G. ALBERIGO, 'The Council of Trent: New Views on the Occasion of its Fourth Centenary', *Concilium*, Sept. 1965 (Vol. 7, No. 1, pp. 40–1).
[2] See H. OUTRAM EVENETT, *The Spirit of the Counter-Reformation* (Cambridge 1968), p. 101.

the Church of the 19th century, which developed all the centralising and other tendencies that were present in the 16th century situation but only in germ. From the middle of the 16th century the papacy was slowly regaining the prestige it had had in the 12th and 13th centuries, and it was largely thanks to its energy in implementing the council that it began to do so. But the bishops at the council had grown up in a quite different world. Some of them were Renaissance humanists, almost all of them had been touched by the Renaissance and almost all of them were royal nominees. They had a fair conceit of their power and independence, at least vis-à-vis Rome. Most of them had no love for the Roman *curia* and were determined that it should be reformed. It was one of the points of tension between the bishops and the papacy. It is not surprising, then, that they held and insisted on a high doctrine of episcopacy – for all that some of them had never seen their bishoprics. There was in fact in the last session of the council an immense battle between what might be called the Roman view and that of the bishops. That the episcopate was of divine institution all were agreed and this was the conclusion that was eventually expressed in the canon (6).[3] But the question whether their powers were mediated by the papacy remained unresolved, as was the question whether residence in their sees was also part of the divine institution. This was an explosive question and the party that might be called the anti-curialists wanted to say that residence was of divine institution, mainly to prevent the innumerable exemptions from residence that the papacy so freely granted both to members of the *curia* and to others. They lost the battle of course but it was in connection with this whole matter that a particular, and perhaps a new, theological opinion came up.

It was put out by Lainez, the general of the Jesuits and one of the papal theologians to the council, not so much to fly a kite of his own but to attempt to resolve the differences between the two sides. It was an opinion destined to have a very long history and its influence can be discerned, I believe, in the debates of Vatican I.

In holy order he saw two powers: the *potestas ordinis* and the *potestas iurisdictionis*. For the priest and bishop the first is of divine institution and received by ordination directly from God. In this

[3] De Sacramento Ordinis, 6, Sess. XXXIII, Denz., 966 (ed. XVIIa).

respect they are the equals of the bishop of Rome. But they cannot exercise their ministry for a definite group of the faithful until they have received power in the concrete, i.e. *potestas iurisdictionis*. This is given by God immediately to the pope in the *plenitudo potestatis* which he receives through lawful succession in the see of Peter. It descends from the pope to each bishop who receives it 'by ecclesiastical law' (*droit*) from God mediately.[4]

There is much that could be said about it. We note the terminology: holy order is spoken of in the terms of 'powers'. This is a juridical thing and not obviously a grace or a charism. Secondly, we are not surprised that Lainez can say that bishops and priests are in this respect equals, indeed the equals of the pope himself. Here we have the medieval theology of order which owed so much to Jerome and the pseudo-Jerominian texts that bedevilled that whole theology. Finally, one is tempted to say that Lainez's view was a rationalisation of western practice. Apart from the abuse of provisions and other devices to keep the gift of bishoprics and even other benefices in the hands of the pope, an earlier and sounder tradition required no more than papal confirmation of any election to a see. But even this never applied in the east. Patriarchs and popes exchanged letters of communion, there were occasionally interventions on the part of Rome in disputed elections – not always with happy results – but I do not see in what sense the patriarch of Antioch or of Alexandria could be said to have received his jurisdiction mediately from the pope.

However, there is another aspect of the business that is of considerable theological interest. As a modern historian has observed, (Lainez's) 'underlying motive . . . was clearly to reduce as far as possible the limits within which the structure of the Church could be considered as divinely ordained, and so to make room for a degree of flexibility which would give the widest scope for exercising human initiative in a variable world. The lines of his argument will sound oddly familiar to historians of the Church of England. He held that nothing which did not depend on the direct word of God or on its immediate and rigorous consequences, no act or institution in which the intervention of generally human or specifically ecclesiastical creativity could be dis-

[4] For all this see L. WILLAERT S.J., *La Restauration Catholique* (Paris 1960), p. 338.

cerned, ought to be considered of divine ordinance'. Bishops are indeed of divine institution but their general and particular powers are ecclesiastical creations. The same writer remarks that Lainez's argument 'brought him in the end to what may be described as a papalist presbyterianism' – which is elucidated by one of Manning's unexpected epigrams that 'the pope is the only plank between a Jesuit and a Presbyterian'. It is not surprising that Lainez's theory was 'extremely displeasing' to the bishops of the council.[5]

Trent of course did not determine the matter but if Lainez's intention was to 'reduce as far as possible the limits within which the structure of the Church could be considered as divinely ordained', he was stating a principle that in this as in other matters is seen to be of crucial importance nowadays. It is in fact essential to distinguish what is the divinely intended structure from the historical expressions and modalities it has received in the course of time. On these terms the question has to be asked: is even the allocation of a determined territory and the obligation of actual residence of divine institution or not? Mobile bishops, though one hopes not *extravagantes*, may be an interesting possibility for the future.

Yet the council of Trent was strongly episcopal and if the Church can be seen as expressing its nature – and so uttering a theology – in action, there is no doubt about the esteem the papacy and the council had for the episcopate. A recent historian has observed that if 'the Jesuits ... (were) the maids-of-all-work of the Counter-Reformation ... the bishops had everything thrust upon them. It was in the nature of their office', and he goes on to record that a modern canonist has counted two hundred and fifty reforms and changes they were required to introduce, as well as giving 'an example in dress, behaviour, charity, modesty – and no doubt, by implication, good temper.'[6] It may seem regrettable that many of these tasks were to be performed by papal delegation but in the first place this was done to reinforce the episcopal office

---

[5] JOHN BOSSY in *The Spirit of the Counter-Reformation* by H. OUTRAM EVENETT (Cambridge 1968), pp. 135–6.

[6] For the above see H. OUTRAM EVENETT, *The Spirit of the Counter-Reformation*, p. 99.

and in the second, there were so many vested interests so deeply
entrenched that if the work of reform was to be carried out, the
bishops needed this extra authority. As it was, battles with
chapters and other privileged bodies continued for decades.

In sum, we can say that the council reformed the episcopate,
turning it from a career back to the pastoral office that it is and if
one of the theological weaknesses of the council is that it failed to
produce a theology of the word – and thus failed to meet one of
the major challenges of the reformers – it did in practice insist that
the bishop has a ministry of the word.[7] He must preach and teach
– and all too few had done this in the middle ages – and two of the
two hundred and fifty reforms he had to bring about were the
founding of chairs of theology in his cathedral and of seminaries
for the training of priests. All told, he must once again be a pastor
although in many parts of Europe it took two or three centuries
until this was generally achieved.

When we examine the decree of the council reforming the presbyterate we find a similar picture. The presbyterate is still defined
in terms of cult and its relationship to the episcopate remains
ambiguous.[8] In fact, until Vatican II the general view was that
the presbyterate was the true priestly office, that no higher 'power'
could be given to man and that therefore apart from the 'power' of
ordination and confirmation (though there were and are exceptions for the latter), the priest was the equal of the bishop. The
episcopate was some strange sort of inflation of the presbyterate,
logically no more than a sacramental, for the priest had everything already. Even the thomistic theology of various participa-
tions in the priesthood of Christ seems to have fallen out of theological consciousness except among Dominicans and their
theological followers.

[7] A. DUVAL O.P., in 'Le Sacrement de l'Ordre au Concile de Trent' (*Etudes sur le
Sacrement de l'Ordre*, Paris 1957) reveals the extraordinary emphasis laid by the council
on the importance of preaching and instruction both for bishops and priests. For
the bishop it is the *praecipuum munus* but it is not theologically related to his priestly
office. The same is true of what the council says about priests but the foundation of
seminaries, so strongly urged by the council, did produce eventually a priesthood
that was able to exercise a ministry of the word.

[8] Cf. Cap. I, Sess. XXXIII, Denz. 957. The visible sacrifice (the eucharist)
demands a visible priesthood. There is no mention at all in the *capitula* and canons
of a ministry of the word.

Even so, the council was deeply concerned about the presby-terate and determined to raise its standards and to make priests worthy ministers of God. If the priest remained primarily a cult minister, the council refused to envisage the massing-priest as either typical or desirable. The council fathers cut swathes through a multitude of abuses, abolishing the saying of masses in holes and corners, clandestine marriages performed by stray priests anywhere and a host of other undesirable practices. The effect was to abolish the clerical proletariat that the fathers had complained of in the first years of the council. The pastoral nature of the priest's function was clearly set out and if the ideal that was set before him was unduly self-regarding and remained so until yesterday, it did in fact create a body of priests who were pious, conscientious, sufficiently instructed and often heroic in their self-denial and devotion to duty.

As with bishops, so with priests, although the council failed to relate the ministry of the word to the priestly office, it strongly urged the practice of preaching and teaching and the Roman Catechism, meant for the clergy and a document of some theo-logical merit, was compiled after the council to assist them in this essential task. The days still quite recent when the appearance in Roman pulpits of a simple priest clothed in cassock and cotta caused a shock to the people were numbered, though in the ensuing centuries the performance has been very variable. No more than for bishops did the council see preaching as a *priestly* function of the presbyter.

The signal defect of the council of Trent however was its failure to meet the reformers' challenge on the subject of the universal priesthood of the faithful. Granted that the reformers' view was incompatible with the tradition, the fathers of the council saw nothing positive in the doctrine, refused to explore it and when reference to it was made, simply rejected it with a questionable reference to 1 Cor. 12:29.[9] There in fact the matter remained for centuries and it was not, as far as I know, until the encyclical of Pius XII on worship in 1947 that the Church made any official and positive statement of the matter.

[9] See *Dictionnaire de Théologie Catholique*, t. xi, c. 1351, s.v. 'Ordre' and Session xxxiii, cap. 4, Denz. 960.

Summing up the teaching of the council of Trent the writer in the *Dictionnaire de Théologie Catholique* – the date of his article is 1931 – says that 'since the council of Trent the history of the theology of orders is without incident'.[10] This is true, except that there was a certain hardening of positions and with the steady centralisation of the Church, the juridical emphasis became ever greater and the growth of the pyramid Church ever more irresistible. These tendencies are already just discernible in one or two *obiter dicta* of the council. For instance, it was said that all the sacraments converge towards the eucharist – a thoroughly traditional statement – but to this was added the extraordinary consequence 'in such a way that after the model of the celestial hierarchy, the hierarchy of orders is constituted under the only supreme head, the Roman pontiff, the vicar of Christ'.[11] Nor was the military metaphor wanting: 'if anyone says that all are priests, enjoying an equal power, then you turn the constitution of the Church upside down, *for the Church is an army in battle array . . .*'.[12]

We cannot leave the council of Trent without at least mentioning its epoch-making decision to set up seminaries for the instruction and spiritual formation of the pastoral clergy. It was a practical measure to raise the spiritual and moral condition of the clergy, but along with the institution of various congregations of clerks regular to which we shall refer below, it did much to change the image and so affect the theology of the pastoral ministry. As the products of the seminaries began to exercise their office in the next three centuries (though the full effects were not felt until the 19th century), the presbyter became the 'priest' *tout court* and when theologians and others discussed the priesthood they took the presbyter quite naturally as their point of departure. It can be said with a fair degree of truth that whereas in the middle ages it was bishops (often very unpastoral) and religious who held the field and dominated the scene, after Trent it was the priest in his parish. Over the centuries his professional competence, his spiritual quality and his pastoral zeal steadily grew and, with whatever limitations, he became a preaching minister of the

---

[10] Ibid., c. 1378: 'Depuis le concile de Trente, la théologie de l'ordre est sans histoire mouvementée.' The writer was A. MICHEL.

[11] *D.T.C.*, ibid., c. 1351.   [12] *D.T.C.*, ibid.

Church. All this and indeed much more must be credited to the seminary system. If it had defects, an excessive withdrawal from the world (which was necessary in the 16th and 17th centuries), a rather inward-looking piety and a strong tendency, more marked in some countries than others, towards the formation of the professional clergyman, on balance it was a most fruitful system that brought great benefits to the Church. If it is breaking down now, it is because the world has changed and the seminary system is no longer meeting its needs.[13]

The Influence of Bellarmine

Bellarmine is usually accredited with, or accused of, producing the theology of the pyramid Church. Or perhaps it would be more accurate to call it an apologetic of the Church which was conditioned by the needs of the time and that led to the hardening of the view, already in existence, that the Church is essentially the ecclesiastical hierarchy. This in turn led to a theology of the Church that Congar has called a 'hierarchology'.[14] Bellarmine was a learned theologian, almost infinitely greater than the little men who plundered him for the next three centuries to write their manuals, and of course he was aware of the inner nature of the Church, but unhappily for posterity he insisted on the external, hierarchical aspect of the Church and refused to admit into his definition of it anything to do with its inner life.[15]

---

[13] I cannot resist the temptation to include in a note, necessarily long, the image of the Tridentine priest painted by a learned if pious-minded historian: 'We have seen the picture the council presents of the priest: a man whose bearing, gestures, words and whole life are indicative of an equilibrium of thought and manner. Above all, he is filled with the spirit of religion (*esprit religieux*). In the mind of the council the perfect priest is first and foremost the perfectly good (*honnête*) man, virtuous, judicious, serious and conscientious. But all these qualities are to be permeated, enlivened, warmed, elevated and supernaturalised by the religious spirit (*religion*) which fills his being. . . . It is the council of Trent that sketched the portrait of the good parish priest we have come to know. Of dignified and venerable aspect, dwelling in his modest and secluded presbytery, always (however?) available to the poor and unfortunate, uniquely occupied with the good of souls and the service of Jesus Christ, he is the veritable image on earth of benevolence and charity; all this enhanced by his serene and reverend countenance, crowned often by a halo of white hair' (L. CHRISTIANI, *Le Concile de Trente*, Paris 1948, p. 209). The perfect *bourgeois*, in fact, in a cassock!

[14] Y. CONGAR, *Lay People in the Church* (London, Eng. trans. revised 1965), p. 51.

[15] JEROME HAMER (*The Church is a Communion*, London 1964, pp. 84-7) draws

Bellarmine's concern was with the Church as a 'perfect society which could and must stand independent of the world, a society which was complete in itself since its end and the means to that end were in its entire possession.' Against the reformers he was concerned to show that it was a visible society, with hierarchy, due subordination of members in an ascending scale. For him the Church was 'the assembly of men united together by the profession of the same faith, participation in the same sacraments, under the authority of lawful pastors, *principally of the Roman pontiff*, the vicar of Christ'.[16] It is almost as if the bishops are short-circuited, as the minority fathers of Vatican I constantly feared and complained. In another passage, subordination is strongly insisted on: 'The Church is a visible society but also a hierarchical society with an organic subordination of the faithful to their immediate pastors (here the bishops come in) and of all to the supreme head, the bishop of Rome.'[17] Nor is the influence of current political ideas absent – it was the age of the absolute monarch – for Bellarmine is happy to describe the Church as a monarchy 'though tempered by an aristocratic element'.[18]

In a Church that is a society of this sort, jurisdiction is obviously of crucial importance and it is not surprising that the already traditional theology of priestly 'powers' now received a new impetus, the relationship between bishops and papacy became increasingly difficult and the distinction between priest and bishop more than ever regarded as one of jurisdiction. The situation was

---

attention to a passage cited by Bellarmine from a (spurious) writing of St Augustine which speaks of the Church as a living body 'in which is soul and body, the soul being the internal gifts of the holy Spirit, faith, hope and charity. . . .' But he thought that the definition of the Church as an external visible society was sufficient: 'Nevertheless, for anyone to be able to be declared a member of this *true Church, of which the Scriptures speak, we do not think that any inner virtue is required of him*' (emphasis Hamer's). And Bellarmine did not hesitate to liken membership of the Church to membership of a particular nation (p. 84). Hamer's critique follows on pp. 85–6. Among other things he points out that 'this organised society exists with a view to something else. Bellarmine omits from his definition what is the whole object of the teaching of the Pauline epistles and St John', namely, a 'union of Christians with Christ (which) is a union of life' (p. 85).

---

[16] *D.T.C.* s.v. 'Bellarmine', c. 589. Italics mine.
[17] *D.T.C.*., ibid.   [18] *D.T.C.*., ibid.

made all the more difficult by the creation by Sixtus the Fifth of the congregations that were indeed necessary for the administration of an ever-expanding Church, but which meant that bishops came to be directed by people who were not necessarily bishops. They indeed all through the 17th and 18th centuries fought a rearguard action, the final battle being fought out at Vatican I, and the result of all this was a serious distortion of the way people regarded holy orders.

Other factors came into play too, of course: the general theology of the sacraments in which the *ex opere operato* element was enormously emphasised; the view of the liturgy that emerged in the post-tridentine world which exaggerated the tendency to look upon the presbyter as above all the minister of cult; the self-regarding spiritualities of the time which, as far as the priesthood was concerned, gave the impression that the obligations of the pastoral office were no more than occasions of self-perfection. There was the prevalent paternalism which at times could take oddly harsh features. The injunctions of bishops and synods give the impression that the pious parish priest, who otherwise was so deeply engaged in prayer and mortification, rose from his knees only to rebuke, denounce and punish his recalcitrant flock – so unsheeplike – and one may add, for his part, so unshepherdlike. How far this was actually the practice is another matter but the image of the priest formed by the council of Trent and the bishops and spiritual writers who came after it, persisted almost until today and if there is a malaise among the pastoral clergy, it is because this image is disintegrating. The historico-sociological mould in which the ministry has been held must now be cracked and stripped off if we are to see what priesthood really is.

The French School

It is a relief to move away from the arid, juridical, church-perfect-society theology to Bérulle who for all that he was a near contemporary of Bellarmine lived in a different world. He was that rare being who was both a mystic and a theologian, or perhaps one should say, an intellectual, for he is probably not considered a professional theologian. Nor must one look to him for a complete theology of the Church or the ministry. Like so many of his kind, his mind circled round a number of central insights which were the fruits of mystical experience rather than the conclusions of syllogisms.

The first thing that is noteworthy about his thought is that he held in a very close synthesis the incarnation, the Church and the sacraments. He speaks a theological language that immediately sets up echoes in the modern mind. First, he sees the hierarchical structure of the Church as the external expression of the interior 'missions' of the holy Trinity. The mission of the Church, with all its priestly structure, is founded on the mission of the word and by 'structure' he does not mean simply an interior spiritual structure. He was near enough to the Reformation to know that visible structure was essential to the Church. All the more important then is the lesson he is said to have learnt from pseudo-Denis that 'the hierarchy of order exists not for itself but for the mystical hierarchy of souls: "We do not have authority just to have it but simply to convey love (*pour faire la charité*)".' All this is very remarkable language coming from the same epoch that could produce the pyramid Church. Here is a man who sees the Church as the sacrament of Christ and it is strange that it has taken theologians of our age much toil to rediscover this truth that was in the tradition all the time.[19] Of course his way of expressing that truth was different from what is now current, but it is none the less remarkable that he sees the hierarchy as in a sense a charismatic one: 'Jesus is sacramentally present to his Church both by his priests and the eucharist. It is he who rules it by the hierarchy he instituted and which he animates with his Spirit. It is he who gives life to his Church by his own deified body.' The union of Christ with his Church is very close. Moreover, according to Bérulle (and these are his actual words) it is by the ministry of his priests that 'he (Christ) is before our eyes until the end of the ages and (through it) that he inserts himself into our hearts and that, as often as we would have it so'.[20]

It is well known that Bérulle had an extremely high ideal of the priesthood and there is something of the hieratic as well as of the

[19] All the quotations that follow are from PAUL COCHOIS's excellent little book *Bérulle et l'école française* (Paris 1963), p. 125.

[20] COCHOIS, op. cit., p. 126, quoting BÉRULLE, *Opuscule de Piété*.

hierarchical in this thought. He was caught up in the 'mystical invasion' of his time and was indeed one of its principal promoters. But he also had a grasp of the social dimension of the Church and for him the mystical body of Christ was a subject of profound meditation. The Church is a priestly body but it is not at all clear how far he saw the laity as sharing in Christ's priesthood.

The priesthood is only understandable against the background of the Incarnation. The hypostatic union is the priestly consecration of Christ's human nature and he is the unique priest and as priest 'he is the centre both ontological and historical of the whole of creation which it is his intention to lead back to God his Father'.[21] The Church is at the centre of this process and it is by it and the eucharist that mankind is drawn into unity. By the sacrament of his body we are drawn into the fullness of divinity that dwells in him and we are bound to him, that is, to what Bérulle calls the 'deified humanity' of Christ, 'by the singular and efficacious power of the sacrament of his body. It is this that incorporates us into his sacred humanity and enables us to live in him and of his life as his members. It is through it that we are able to live with him in his Father'.[22] If Bérulle is Christocentric in all his teaching, he is never content until he has drawn the soul into union with the Father and it is in these emphases that constantly occur that we can discern his view that the Church is a sort of emanation of the Trinity. The Greek and especially Neoplatonic background is always apparent.

Bérulle's priest then is a minister of this mystical Church and he is totally dependent on the unique priestly Christ whom the priest must imitate not merely in any 'pious' or externalist way but precisely in the depths of his soul and life. He has to interiorise the whole vast priestly experience of Christ, reproducing in himself the 'states' of Christ, not merely psychologically but ontologically, for, as is well known, Bérulle's 'states' meant something much deeper than a psychological realisation.[23] And the 'states' involved not only annihilation, abasement, suffering and the rest

[21] COCHOIS, op. cit., p. 126.
[22] COCHOIS, op. cit., p. 128, quoting the same *Opuscule*.
[23] Bérulle seems to come closer to Odo Casel's views of mystery-presence than to the psychological mystics. It is a point that is perhaps worth investigating.

but predominantly praise and, above all, adoration which was an attitude (and a word) that so strongly marks Bérulle's life and writing. The priestly state of Christ is to become the very existence of the priest, he is to be moved by the Spirit, his office demands sanctity not merely morally, to make him a respectable minister for his own or the people's edification. Sanctity is an exigency that arises from the very nature of the priesthood. Everything in the priest's life becomes priestly and holy since Jesus who is always priest is also the holy One and has become his whole life. For Bérulle the priest is a consecrated person rather as Christ was consecrated in the Incarnation to take up the priestly task of redemption, but that consecration was not a cultic thing, nor was it merely for cult. It embraced the whole life of the priest. It is very interesting to observe that here the hiatus between function and sanctity is bridged. For Bérulle the thought of the priest *fonctionnaire* was abhorrent and he had plenty of examples of it before his eyes as he wrote and prayed.

No doubt the ideal is high, some would say impossibly so, and no doubt Bérulle exaggerated, but it is a pity that the council of Trent or theologians before and after it could not present some such ideal to the Reformers.

We may end with a critique that is very just:

'Thanks to the influence of Denis, Bérulle gave too much importance to what is more neoplatonic than Christian in the dionysian theory of hierarchical mediations. . . . His distinction between the power of orders and sanctity is insufficient, and maladroit developments of his disciples on the Virgin-Priest and their tendency to see in the (lay) Christian "no more than an imperfect priest, or rather an inchoative priest and in the priest the perfect and completed Christian" (Saint-Cyran) are due to what he borrowed from Denis. But with Bérulle himself, these were only marginal temptations and do not touch the heart of a doctrine that places us at the centre of the faith. Recognition of these limitations leaves us all the greater liberty to admire the incomparable greatness of his mystical Christocentrism.'[24]

[24] COCHOIS, op. cit., p. 133.

To this we may add that if Bérulle has moved away from the cult-functionary priest to what might be called the mystical priest, that is, the minister of the mystical-sacramental life of the Church, his conception of the Church remains narrow. His priest is a member of a little group, rather inward-looking, so very different from St Vincent de Paul and his priests, and in spite of the fact that there was close contact between Bérulle and Vincent. It is curious too that in spite of the prominent place that Christ the Word occupies in Bérulle's thought there does not seem to be any *theological* connection between this teaching and the ministry of the word. The Oratorians were in fact very busy preachers and produced some great ones, like Massillon, but nowhere is the function of preaching seen as a consequence of Bérulle's theology of the Word.[25]

However, it seems impossible to describe, much less define, the nature of the Church and its ministry in the terms of theologies, however comprehensive. The life of the Church is greater than any theology and to get an approximate picture of what the ministry meant to 17th century Christians, you have to add to Bérulle, St Francis of Sales, St Vincent de Paul, Olier, St John Eudes and many more. It is legitimate to think however that the failure to comprehend something at least of this overflowing life in a coherent scheme is a witness to the narrowness of the theology of the time.

It was a disciple of Bérulle's, the somewhat enigmatic Condren, who developed a strain in the former's thought that is more than a little disturbing and that was to have extraordinary results in the formation of the French clergy in the next two centuries. Condren was much taken up with the notion of sacrifice and it is on this that he puts all the emphasis in his consideration of Christ's priesthood. Christ's whole redeeming work is summed up in sacrifice and where Bérulle put the emphasis on the Incarnation and the 'consecration' that it involved, Condren put it on the cross. Not so catastrophic, one might say, but when we see that for Condren sacrifice meant destruction and indeed annihilation,

[25] This at any rate is the conclusion I draw from reading the whole of BREMOND's third volume on the French School of his *Histoire littéraire du Sentiment religieux en France*.

then we begin to get uncomfortable. When, applying Bérulle's famous 'states', Condren comes to say that this is what the priest must do, evacuate his humanity, suppress all that is sheerly human in himself,[26] then we have launched on its long pilgrimage all that unhappy dehumanisation of the priest that has played so big a part in his training, at least in some places. The professional clergyman, who has the 'right' priestly (i.e. clerical) sentiments about everything and in every situation, the 'right' attitudes, the 'right' dress and all the rest of it, is on the horizon. And we reflect that it was out of this deep desire to interiorise the 'states' of Christ that came something that has become a term of reproach to the clergy.[27]

Another disciple of the French Oratory and of Condren in particular was Jean Jacques Olier, a more congenial character though psychologically very puzzling.[28] He deserves extended treatment, not only on account of the enormous influence he exerted in France by the foundation of the company of St Sulpice but also in North America where the Sulpicians staffed seminaries from the 17th century onwards and there propagated the doctrines of the French school. His influence cannot be exaggerated but all we can say here is that consciously or not, he propagated a notion of the priesthood that, deeply rooted as it was in Christ, resulted in fact in the creation of a clerical caste. No doubt his intention was to form priests with a strong attachment to Christ and with a deep interior life. No doubt he wished to save his young levites from contamination by a world that was corrupt enough (for all that was the Grand Siècle). But the radical weakness of his notion came from a theological fault. For him 1 Pet. 2 was to be

[26] There was a positive side to all this of course as can be seen in such a phrase as this: 'Cette mort . . . laisse vivre Dieu en nous . . . ce néant . . . donne lieu en nous de son être' (BREMOND, op. cit., t. III (Paris 1923), p. 375, and this can be seen perhaps more clearly in OLIER but in fact the emphasis on annihilation in various tones of voice, so to say, dominated the tradition.

[27] Condren was enigmatic in himself but also in his writings. It is not yet known exactly what his genuine writings were; all were edited and published after his death. For our purposes here it is not a matter of the first importance. His ideas were prevalent, characteristic of a whole school. His ideas can be seen in CHARLES DE CONDREN, *The Eternal Sacrifice*, Eng. trans., London 1906.

[28] So many of these famous 17th-century characters seem to have suffered from various kinds of neuroses. Details can be seen in BREMOND, op. cit., t. III.

interpreted not as a statement about the priestly quality of the people but as one about the ministerial priesthood. For him (and perhaps he was misled by the terminology of 1 Pet. 5:1-4) the letter was speaking of the fullness of the priesthood as seen in the episcopate. With this he associated priests (*presbuteroi?*) who, through their shared life of grace with their bishops, presented an image of the union of Christ with his Father.[29] This was the Church and it may be regarded as an improvement on the views of some at the council of Constance who would have it that the mystical body was made up of the pope, its head, and the cardinals, its members. But ecclesiologically speaking, Olier's views are hardly happy.[30]

The Importance of the Clerks Regular

One of the most striking features of the post-tridentine period is that the presbyter, the priest in the conventional meaning of the term, entered into his own. Over the whole period there were in different countries great bishops, but at the level of ordinary and missionary life, it was the priest who played the most prominent part. The status of the parish priest became ever more important and the power of the old corporate bodies declined. New ones took their place although they were usually not part of the diocesan structure. These were the numerous companies of clerks regular from which the renewal of the pastoral clergy can largely be said to have taken its origin. Before the renewal of the Church got under way small groups of priests gathered together to perform in a fitting manner the ordinary duties of the parish clergy, above all preaching. The Company of Jesus was no more than this, at least at first, and they were followed by others, the Oratory in Italy and the French Oratory of Bérulle in France from which came the communities of St John Eudes and of Jean

[29] See TÜCHLE, BOUMAN, J. LE BRUN, *Réforme et Contre-Réforme* (Paris 1968), p. 282.

[30] From an analysis by L. Cognet of OLIER'S *Traité des saints ordres*, it is possible to see that his vision of the ministry was wholly inward-looking and the annihilation theology of Condren is carried to an extreme: the priest is to be hidden in Christ 'dans un éloignement intérieur et dans une distance infinie du monde . . . *dans une impossibilité morale d'aimer rien de la creature*'! It is not surprising that, as Cognet remarks, 'les aspects apostoliques (du sacerdoce) s'estompent'. See *La Spiritualité Moderne*, t. I (third part of *Histoire de la Spiritualité Chrétienne*, ed. L. Bouyer, J. Leclercq, F. Vandenbroucke and L. Cognet) Paris 1966, p. 405.

Jacques Olier, the 'Messieurs de S. Sulpice'. The purpose of these institutes was precisely to help the priest to sanctify himself so that he could become a worthy minister of Christ, but their effect was to enhance the office of priesthood; as population increased and the great diocesan territories began to fill up, the priest and especially the parish priest, came to assume an ever greater place in the minds of the people. The bishop inevitably became more remote and the fact that until well into the 19th century bishops were usually chosen from the nobility or the gentry meant that there was a social remoteness as well. This became painfully clear at the time of the French Revolution and it says much for the renewal of the French clergy that thousands of them, without any support from their bishops, resisted the pressures of the revolutionary state either by going underground or by exile. But all this, coupled with the unsatisfactory theology of the episcopate of the time, meant that the theological status of the bishop became ever more ambiguous. It was not until the trend of theological reflection was decisively reversed, as it was at Vatican II, that the episcopate could be seen in its true light as the primary participation in the priesthood of Christ. It was not until then that the bishop would be seen as primarily a pastor, the chief shepherd of the flock entrusted to his care, and not as an administrator nor merely as a liturgical functionary to confer confirmation and ordination.

It would be interesting, but not possible here, to examine the notions on ministry held by the Jansenists. Before they became (or were driven into becoming) a sect they were much influenced by the ideas of Bérulle and Condren through St Cyran and it was not until Jansenism became mixed up with Gallicanism that in a man like Quesnel one begins to get 'presbyterian' or even 'democratic' theories of the Church.

Catholic Presbyterianism

The origins and course of Gallicanism are extremely complicated, its history reaching from the early 16th century until the French Revolution and beyond. From one point of view it can be seen as an effort at what we call decentralisation, though as it was under the control of a monarchy that became absolute with Louis XIV and the connection between altar and throne became uncomfortably close, it cannot be regarded as a happy development. As it took expression in the 17th and 18th centuries, it was the result of an unsatisfactory theology of the ministry, at one level being a continuation of the tensions that had remained unresolved at the council of Trent. At another it was a sociological protest at the continuing remoteness of the bishops from the 'lower' clergy. A recent writer observes that Edmond Richer, who was the chief protagonist in all this matter, *le champion de l'ecclésiologie gallicane*, wrote explicitly against the invasion of the Roman and Bellarminian theories of the Church into France.[31] From him stemmed all that followed for two centuries: 'It is impossible to find words to express the influence of this little treatise (*De ecclesiastica et politica potestate libellus*) of thirty pages which dominated the Church of France up to the Civil Constitution of the clergy and beyond.'[32]

For Richer the Church was a sort of democracy though really an aristocracy for he had every intention of keeping the control of affairs in the hands of the lower clergy. Christ, the founder of the Church and its true head, entrusted authority to the collectivity of the faithful. These are the unique source of all authority and it is they who commit the power of priesthood (*ordo*) to all the pastors, to the *Ecclesia sacerdotalis*. But the power of *jurisdiction* belongs sovereignly to the bishops, each in his own diocese. General councils are, by divine authority, the supreme authority in the Church and they delegate to the pope the executive power to govern the Church – his power then is not of divine origin – though always under the control of the councils which shall meet regularly.[33] With Richerism was associated what the French writers called *parochisme* which may be described as the divine institution of parish priests (though not apparently of curates).[34]

[31] See L. WILLAERT S.J., *La Restauration Catholique*, 1563–1648, t. 18 of *Histoire de l'Eglise* (Fliche et Martin), Paris 1960, pp. 388–9.

[32] WILLAERT, op. cit., p. 388.

[33] WILLAERT, op. cit., p. 388.

[34] The most famous book on this subject was *De antiquo iure presbyterorum in regimine ecclesiastico* (1676) by JACQUES BOILEAU, the brother of the poet. The Church should be governed by bishops and priests together, the latter to have deliberative vote in synods and councils. It is interesting to learn that some canons of Chartres

There is no need to delay any longer over these ecclesiological *bizarreries* but it will be noted that all this jumbled up theology is the remote result of the failure of the council of Trent to produce a coherent theology of the Church and the ministry. It should be noted also however that there was a political Gallicanism, largely a matter of state. The monarchs of the time were determined to keep a strong control over the Church and especially the bishops. There was an episcopal Gallicanism which strove for freedom to manage its own ecclesiastical affairs and resisted the 'ultramontane' tendencies of the post-tridentine Church. Thirdly, there was a kind of presbyterianism which sociologically was a resistance movement against the high and mighty episcopate, and theologically was the result of an old but bad theology of the ministry which had failed to establish the nature of the episcopate as a divinely given structure of the Church.

Febronianism

There was another strain of episcopalism, first cousin to Gallicanism, in Germany, of which the most notorious representative was J. Nikolaus von Hontheim, better known as Febronius, though other theologians and canonists held views very similar to his.[35] There is in fact nothing new here and the theological penetration is not as impressive as the lucid, easy Latin they wrote. Their views can be summed up like this:

(i) Bishops who are the successors of the apostles have by the nature of their office a universal pastoral charge over the Church.

(ii) They receive not only their orders directly from Christ but also their jurisdiction.

(iii) Their pastoral activities are confined to certain regions –

---

sent to their bishop a declaration in which they said that in the early ages of the Church there was no difference between bishops and priests, citing Acts 20! The distinction was one of custom only. (For the Boileau reference see E. PRÉCLIN and E. JARRY, *Les Luttes politiques et doctrinales aux XVIIe et XVIIIe siècles*, first part, p. 210 and for the detail about the canons of Chartres, ibid., p. 164, n. 4.)

---

[35] See J. BEUMER S.J., 'Die Kollegiale Gewalt der Bischöfe für die Gesamtkirche nach der Theologie des 18. Jahrhunderts,' *Gregorianum*, Vol. XLV, 2, 1964, pp. 281–7.

dioceses – simply for good order. In other words, the limitation of their jurisdiction is of ecclesiastical institution.

(iv) But the bishop cannot be a bishop with jurisdiction unless he is in communion with the pope.[36]

It is clear that these writers, whatever their animus against the papacy, had a high doctrine of the episcopate and it is not merely a benign interpretation of their views to say that they were groping towards a collegiality that was to be expressed by Vatican II. If we are inclined to blame them for their inadequate theology, we might remember that Vatican II itself has not produced a totally satisfactory teaching on the matter.

The First Vatican Council

Although we instinctively think of the first Vatican council as wholly occupied with papal infallibility, this was not so. First, it was very much occupied with the *primacy* of the pope and second-ly, we forget that the constitution *Pastor Aeternus*, defining papal infallibility, was part – or became part – of a whole schema called *De Ecclesia*. In fact if the council fiercely debated infallibility, the bishops were almost equally concerned about their own status in the Church. Nor was this a pre-occupation merely of the anti-infallibilist (or anti-opportunist) minority. Wholly moderate men like Ullathorne of Birmingham[37] showed a constant concern about the matter. It is one of the tragedies of Vatican I that the whole *schema De Ecclesia* never achieved the status of a conciliar decision. As a recent writer has said:

'(We can now realise) how much we lost through the sudden interruption of the council. . . . We can see that many inconveniences both in respect of the faith of the people and in

[36] It may be wondered what was the difference between the doctrine of Feb-ronius and French Gallicanism. It would appear that there are two differences: (a) Febronius paid little attention to the Erastian element in it (though his followers were to suffer from the sacristy mentality of the Emperor Joseph); (b) he wanted to make a sort of ecclesiastical constitution out of the privileges acquired (or arrogated) by the French Church and to justify his view that authority resided in the body of the Church, an authority however which was to be exercised by its pastors (See *Les Luttes politiques et doctrinales* . . . 2nd part, p. 773).

[37] See CUTHBERT BUTLER, *The Vatican Council*, 1869–1870 (2nd ed., London 1962), pp. 119–20.

respect of relationships with the separated Christians have
resulted from the truncated presentation of the Catholic Church
which the *Pastor Aeternus* gives and which is limited to an
exposition of the headship of the Church. It is not less certain
that Catholic theology suffered grave damage from this situation and we can indeed speak of the temporary disappearance
of certain subjects (from theological discussion). We cannot but
deplore a tendency among certain theologians to consider the
pope, in practice if not in theory, as the sole holder of the
teaching office (*magisterium*) of the Church. Have not we had to
wait until recent years for the conception of the Church as the
mystical body of Christ to be appreciated? And it is still more
recently that research on the theology of the episcopate has
taken place. There can be no doubt that a second constitution
De Ecclesia . . . would not only have eliminated these obscurities
but still more, would have enriched theology by providing it
with material for reflection on the structure of the Church.'[38]

The first reactions to the first draft schema *De Ecclesia* came
from three bishops whom some would perhaps describe as
'Gallicans' though the truth is that their minds had evidently been
formed on an earlier tradition than that of Trent or 17th century
Gallicanism. They were Ketteler, Bishop of Mainz, Ginoulhiac of
Grenoble and Devoucoux of Evreux, the last described as a
moderate Gallican who yet was content to work with two untra-
montane vicars-general! On the publication of the draft, they prepared and put in statements pointing out that the draft has said
nothing about bishops – a fact which scandalised them and many
others – and offering to supply the want. It is impossible even to
summarise these reports here. One can merely say that they saw
the episcopate as an essential structure of the Church, as necessary
as the papacy, that bishops enjoy an ordinary jurisdiction not
mediated by the pope and though the word is not used, that the
bishops form a college with a pastoral charge, in union of course
with the pope, the head of the college, over the whole Church.
These men were moderates, in no way hostile to the papacy, but
with a strong grasp of what had been traditional doctrine in the

[38] JEAN-PIERRE TORRELL O.P., *La Théologie de l'Episcopat* (Paris 1961), pp. 277–8.

Church. Their reports constitute an almost classical argument *ex traditione* which seems to have been unknown to or forgotten by some of the fathers of Vatican II.

While the famous draft of *Pastor Aeternus* was making its painful way through the sessions of the council, the Deputation for Faith, to which had been attached the great Kleutgen, was preparing the rest of the *schema* on the constitution of the Church and on bishops in particular. This statement took up all the traditional doctrine about the episcopate, establishing with greater theological precision than that of the three bishops, that the bishop is superior to the presbyter not only by orders but also by jurisdiction, that they have a share with the pope in the universal pastoral work of the Church, that their office can be described as teaching, ruling and sanctifying and that – surprisingly – the subject of infallibility is twofold, namely the papacy and the episcopate. All the debate about this at Vatican II and since was anticipated by the fathers of Vatican I.

It is because this draft never got to the stage of decision that Torrell can say that it was a calamity for the Church in the next seventy or eighty years.

Conclusion

It is difficult to say what conclusions are to be drawn from this brief study of these notions about the ministry. No doubt a more detailed investigation of the whole theological tradition from Trent to 1870 would produce a richer theology than appears here. One is inclined to agree with A. Michel that the theology of orders in this period was static, still carrying the burden of the medieval aberrations. Practice for the most part was a great deal better than the theory but it is not surprising that in our own time both the theory and practice of the ministry has come in for severe criticism and that many if not most priests have great difficulty in establishing their sacerdotal identity. All the traditional and sociological moulds in which the priesthood has been expressed are now seen to be obsolete and the task for the future must be an ever more searching examination of what the priesthood is so that it can receive an expression that is consonant with its fundamental nature and apt to serve the needs of our time.

INTRODUCTION

The Anglican communion has been able to contain a wide range of theological opinion and liturgical practice within its framework. This has sometimes given the impression that there is no such thing as a consistent or systematic Anglican theology.

Nevertheless, the Anglican position can best be explored in the line of scholars, from Hooker to the present day, who have been sensitive to the many currents of thought active in their own times, and who have expressed them in a form which very many of their contemporaries would accept. This approach is reflected in this paper.

BIOGRAPHICAL NOTE

THE REV. R. P. MCDERMOTT *is an Anglican priest and a lecturer in the Faculty of Theology in the University of Durham.*

9 An Anglican's Reflections on Priesthood

R. P. McDERMOTT

THERE IS A PASSAGE IN GEORGE TYRRELL'S AUTOBIO-graphy where he describes his first visit to Grangegorman Parish Church, the old-fashioned Irish high Anglican parish church, where he was to become a regular worshipper:

> The first visit to Grangegorman attracted and interested me. It was not merely the choral service, which was a relief as contrasting with the unutterable prosiness of St George's; nor that the devotion and reverence, which I marked, made any particular appeal to my godless nature; but rather that I felt instrinctively what I long afterwards understood clearly, namely: that the difference between an altar and a communion table was infinite; that it meant a totally different religion, another order of things altogether, of which I had no experience.[1]

The passage illustrates obviously enough the divisions and conflicts within Anglicanism, and it raises a question whether indeed the divisions of the 16th century produced two conflicting and irreconcilable types of religion. Probably few today would

[1] GEORGE TYRRELL, *Autobiography*, p. 98.

care to assert that the difference between an altar and a communion table is infinite, but the question of what is signified by an altar, the corporate priesthood of the Church and within this the priesthood of the ministry in the Church, is of the greatest importance and raises fundamental theological issues.

Christian bishops and presbyters have for centuries been called priests. The usage is even in some ecumenical circles regarded as at best little better than a tolerable archaism, at the worst a seriously or even totally misleading description of the Christian ministry. In the 16th century the other Reformed Churches abandoned this title for the ministry, and among them it has disappeared both from official documents and from popular usage. In the Ordinal which the Church of England adopted at the Reformation the word priest was retained. Sacrificial language was entirely removed and the ministry described as a ministry of the word and sacraments with a special emphasis on its pastoral character, an emphasis which has been very marked in Anglicanism ever since.[2] In the noble exhortation which the ordaining bishop addresses to the candidates for the priesthood, he says:

> ... we exhort you, in the name of our Lord Jesus Christ, that you have in remembrance, into how high a dignity, and to how weighty an office and charge ye are called: that is to say, to be messengers, watchmen, and stewards of the Lord; to teach, and to premonish, to feed and provide for the Lord's family; to seek for Christ's sheep that are dispersed abroad, and for his children who are in the midst of this naughty world, that they may be saved through Christ for ever.

Then after an interrogation, the *Veni Creator*, and a prayer, the bishop ordains them with these words:

> Receive the holy Ghost for the office and work of a Priest in the Church of God, now committed unto thee by the imposition of our hands. Whose sins thou dost forgive they are forgiven;

---

[2] This pastoral emphasis is characteristic of the classical Anglican works on the clerical life, G. HERBERT'S *Country Parson*, BISHOP TAYLOR'S *Rules and Advices*, BISHOP WILSON'S *Sacra Privata*, BISHOP HENSON'S *Ad Clerum*.

and whose sins thou dost retain, they are retained. And be thou
a faithful dispenser of the Word of God, and of his holy Sacraments; In the name of the Father, and of the Son, and of the
Holy Ghost. Amen.

But although the Church of England retained the word priest, and
asserted in the Preface to the Ordinal 'that from the Apostles'
time there have been these Orders of Ministers in Christ's Church;
Bishops, Priests, and Deacons' and that these were to be 'continued and reverently used and esteemed in the Church of
England', many Anglicans, and among them theologians of the
highest rank like Hooker in the 16th century and Lightfoot in the
19th were uneasy with the word. It is really with Hooker that
anything that can be called a distinctive Anglican attitude in
theology emerges. He says, in taking note of Puritan opposition
to the retention of the word priest:

> the clergy are either presbyters or deacons. I rather term the
> one sort Presbyters than Priests, because in a matter of so small
> moment I would not willingly offend their ears to whom the
> name of Priesthood is odious though without cause . . . whether
> we call it a Priesthood, a Presbytership, or a Ministry it skilleth
> not: although in truth the word *Presbyter* doth seem more fit,
> and in propriety of speech more agreeable than Priest with the
> drift of the whole Gospel of Jesus Christ.

Hooker's main point really is that the Christian minister and the
Jewish priest do not exercise the same office and therefore cannot
univocally be called priests:

> Seeing then that sacrifice is now no part of the Church ministry,
> how should the name of Priesthood be therunto rightly applied?
> Surely even as St Paul applieth the name of Flesh unto that very
> substance of fishes which hath a proportionable correspondence
> to flesh although it be in nature another thing. Wherupon when
> philosophers will speak warily, they make a difference between
> flesh in one sort of living creatures and that other substance in
> the rest which hath but a kind of analogy to flesh: the Apostle
> contrariwise having matter of greater importance wherof to

speak nameth indifferently both flesh. The Fathers of the Church of Christ with like security of speech call usually the ministry of the Gospel *Priesthood* in regard of that which the Gospel hath *proportionable* to ancient sacrifices, namely the Communion of the blessed Body and Blood of Christ.[3]

With the fuller development of the doctrine of the eucharistic sacrifice that begins with Hooker's contemporaries and friends Lancelot Andrews and Richard Field, the hesitation about the use of the term priest disappears in the main stream of Anglican theology. As far as the doctrine of the ministerial priesthood is concerned this theology culminates in the 19th century in the work of F. D. Maurice and R. C. Moberley.[4] Thus to quote Maurice, whom many would claim to be *the* typical Anglican theologian:

Now as I have so carefully connected the idea of sacrifice with the Eucharist, it follows from this statement, that if I suppose it to be administered by human hands at all, I must suppose those hands to be in some sense of the word sacerdotal. Nay, it would seem to follow by almost necessary inference, that if I suppose the Jewish sacrifice to have passed into something higher, I must suppose the Jewish priesthood to have passed into something higher. And this is in fact my belief. I do think that a Melchisedec priesthood has succeeded to an Aaronical priesthood even as the power of an endless life has succeded to the law of a carnal commandment. I do think that he who presents the perfect sacrifice before God, and himself and his people as redeemed by that sacrifice, has a higher function than he had who presented the daily offering, or made the yearly atonement before God.[5]

[3] HOOKER, *Ecclesiastical Polity*, Book V, ch. lxxviii, 2.

[4] F. D. MAURICE, *The Kingdom of Christ*, and R. C. MOBERLEY, *Ministerial Priesthood.* Typically Anglican treatment of priesthood and sacrifice will be found in *Doctrine in the Church of England* (The Report of the Archbishops' Commission, 1938), and in such writers as H. B. SWETE, *The Ascended Christ*; OLIVER QUICK, *The Christian Sacraments*, and *The Gospel of the New World*; ALAN RICHARDSON, *The Theology of the New Testament*; J. G. DAVIES, *The Spirit, The Church and the Sacraments.*

[5] MAURICE, op. cit. Part II, ch. IV, Section IV: 'The Romish System', 4.

The hesitation about the word priest has had several roots. First, there is the conviction that since the one 'full perfect and sufficient sacrifice, oblation and satisfaction' is the sacrifice of Calvary, any other sacrifice would detract from its uniqueness and sufficiency, and therefore the minister cannot exercise a sacrificial function and be a priest. This would be valid only against a doctrine which made the eucharist a sacrifice supplementing Calvary. Again, there is the tendency to forget that sacrifice is not merely expiatory – the sin offering, but is also latreutic and a means of fellowship – the burnt offering and the peace offering. With Andrews the important point is made that the one true sacrifice is Christ's sacrifice, and that both the Jewish rites which prefigure it and the Christian eucharist can be described as sacrifices only by their relation to it, so that the eucharist is in its own way as much a sacrifice as the rites of the temple – a line of thought which receives a more adequate development in Maurice. More generally, I think, the hesitations about the use of the word have sprung from the fear of sacerdotalism, in the supposed sense of religious officials believed to be endowed with individual powers of manipulating the divine. It is in some such sense that many, probably the great majority of Anglicans would have understood a well known phrase of Cardinal Vaughan's at the time of the controversy over Anglican orders in the pontificate of Leo XIII. When the Cardinal spoke of 'the power to produce the actual living Christ Jesus' he used language which seemed dangerous and offensive even to a high Anglican like Moberley. For Maurice the heart of what he called in the language of his time 'the Romish system', by which he meant what he believed to be the distortion of Catholicism in Trent and the Counter-Reformation, was the error of regarding the priesthood as *vicarial* rather than *representative*:

In the word *vicarial* the Romanist means to embody his notion that the priest is doing the work of one who is absent, and who, only at certain times and under certain conditions, presents himself to men. By the word representative, I mean to express the truth that the minister sets forth Christ to men as present in His Church at all times, as exercising those functions Himself upon which He entered when He ascended on high.[6]

In his great work *Ministerial Priesthood*, the first edition of which appeared in 1897, R. C. Moberley remarks:

> ... the Christian ministry is not a substituted intermediary – still less an atoning mediator – between God and lay people; but it is rather the representative and organ of the whole body, in the exercise of prerogatives and powers which belong to the body as a whole.[7]

It could perhaps be argued that the foundation of the view which sees the ministry as the organ and agent of the corporate priesthood of the people of God had been laid in Hooker's teaching on the primary subject of both the power of order and the power of jurisdiction. The power of order, he writes:

> is received at the hands of the whole visible catholic Church. . . . They whom the whole Church hath from the beginning used as her agents in conferring this power are not either one or more of the laity. . . . The whole Church visible being the true original subject of all power, it hath not ordinarily allowed any other than bishops to ordain.[8]

And of the power of jurisdiction he writes:

> The greatest agents of the bishop of Rome's inordinate sovereignty strive against no one point with such earnestness as this, that jurisdiction (and in the name of jurisdiction they also comprehend the power of dominion spiritual) should be thought originally to be the right of the whole Church; and that no person hath or can have the same, otherwise than derived from the body of the Church.[9]

The Christian ministry, which is possessed in its fullness by the bishop, exercises a threefold function, pastoral, kerygmatic, and liturgical. The Christian minister is pastor, preacher and teacher,

[6] MAURICE, ibid., Section V; The Romish System, 1.

[7] MOBERLEY, op. cit. (the new edition, edited with a valuable introduction by Professor Antony Hanson), p. 241.

[8] *Ecclesiastical Polity*, Book VII, ch. xiv, 11.

[9] Ibid., Book VIII, ch. vi, 2.

and priest. But should the liturgical and priestly aspect of his work be singled out to give the distinctive appellation of his office? I wish to argue that the priestly function has a priority both for the ministry and the Church, because in the three offices of Christ the priestly office has a priority over the prophetic and the regal. And where this priority of the priestly function is not recognised, whether in Christ, or in the Church, or in its ministry, or where a misleading account of its nature is given, a distortion of the Gospel is inevitable. If this be so, it is proper to consider priesthood the distinctive appellation of the ministry provided that the notion of priesthood is taken as incorporating the kerygmatic and pastoral functions.

Jesus came into Galilee proclaiming the Gospel of the kingdom of God, the Good News, fulfilling the hopes of the people of God, that the ultimate manifestation of the sovereign majesty of the true and living God was coming upon men. As prophet he proclaimed the Gospel with unique authority, as Son of Man and servant-Messiah he exercised the divine dominion proleptically in his humble and obscure life and death and then in his glorification at the right hand of the Father; as priest he hallowed the name of God the Father in his life and death, and in his heavenly glorification he remains for ever the Great high Priest, the minister of the true sanctuary, presenting himself before God and making intercession for us. In his totally obedient and selfgiving love, culminating in the self-surrender of the Cross, he completely and adequately acknowledged the glory of God and hallowed the divine name, he manifested the divine judgement upon human sin, he broke the barrier of alienation between mankind and God, and made it possible for men to glorify God in that communion and fellowship with God for which man exists. Jesus is the man for God, and because of this he is the man for others. Gerhard Ebeling has written in his essay on 'the Protestant Idea of the Priesthood':

Moreover the significance of this sacrificial surrender is not that it is a substitute for our surrender, but it is intended to set that surrender in motion. This is the true vicarious activity, the absolute being for others accomplished in Christ. Vicarious activity in this sense means keeping a place. Jesus Christ has kept the place where the reconciliation between God and man can take place. So he is the keeper of a place for God among men, and of a place for men before God. This is the whole object of his being for others, to awaken faith. For faith means being before God as those who are loved by God, and therefore being among men as witnesses of faith, witnesses of the love of God. This is Christ's vicarious activity, his keeping a place, namely, that he is for others in such a way that true being for others originates with him. True being for others, however, is being for God and for one's fellow-man on the basis of the fact that God is for us.[10]

The priesthood of Christ is his being for God, his complete acknowledgement of the divine glory (oblation), which requires complete self-giving (immolation), a self giving which under the conditions of sin means suffering and death.

On its own level and derivatively, the Church which is Christ's body participates in his *triplex munus*. As participating in the prophetic office, it proclaims in the power of his Spirit and in the varying cultural circumstances of human history, the one eschatological Gospel; as sharing in his kingship it has to live after the pattern of the servant-Messiah and Good Shepherd in its own life as a brotherhood of freedom and in service to men; as the priestly body, through the atoning sacrifice of Christ its eternal High Priest, it has access to God and fellowship with him, and in him can offer that worship in spirit and in truth which the Father seeketh (John 4:23) through Him and in Him offering the sacrifice of praise and the burnt offering of its self-oblation. As Jesus is the man for God, so the Church's primary function is to glorify God – its priestly function – and this requires the proclamation of the Gospel, and the fellowship of brotherhood and service to men. And this Christian service is not only a matter of charity in personal relationships but the fulfilment of social and political obligations, just as the prophetic office of the Church requires it to witness to justice and brotherhood among men. As Moberley wrote:

[10] GERHARD EBELING, *The Word of God and Tradition*, p. 202.

The priestliness may be spoken of as essentially towards God: only then this offering to God involves and contains a *manward* devotion also. Or *qua* priesthood it may be thought of as immediately to and for man; only then this manward devotion means the presentation of humanity *as an offering to God*. The offering to God is an offering of humanity. The service for others is *ipso facto* to Godward. It is this intense 'to Godwardness' which makes the Church in the world – whether surrounded by external contradiction or no – a perpetual aspiration, and offering to the Father; and therefore also, by inherent necessity, a perpetual reflection of what He is, as revealed to the world in the Person of Jesus Christ. It is this intense 'for-otherness', this marvellous spirit which – Calvary apart – finds its highest expression historically in the 'Blot me I pray Thee out of the book which Thou hast written' of Moses, or the 'I could wish that I myself were anathema from Christ' of St Paul . . . it is this which is the expression in ordinary terms of human life of the true inwardness of the priesthood of the Church. This is sacrifice taking practical form in the protectiveness of pastoral love: and there is no true pastoral love without sacrifice. It is no unique fact only, but an eternal principle which is recorded in the words: The Good shepherd giveth his life for the sheep.

I do not suppose that as an Englishman of his particular background Moberley would have agreed, but there are Irishmen who would see in the death of James Connelly, who received the last sacraments before his execution as a social revolutionary, an exemplification of this eternal principle. Moberley's argument goes on:

All this is the inherent privilege of the members of the body of Christ. What, then, is the priesthood of Christ's ordained ministers? The priesthood of the ministry follows as corollary from the priesthood of the Church. What the one is, the other is. If the priesthood of the Church consists *ceremonially* in her capacity for self identification, through Eucharistic worship with the eternal presentation of Christ's atoning sacrifice, and *spiritually* in her identification of inner life with the spirit of sacrifice which is the spirit of love uttering itself in devoted ministry to others, so it is by necessary consequence with the priesthood of the ministry. For the priesthood of the ministry is nothing distinct in kind from the priesthood of the Church. The ordained priests are priestly only because it is the Church's prerogative to be priestly; and because they are, by ordination, specialised and empowered to exercise ministerially and organically the prerogatives which are the prerogatives of the body as a whole.[11]

The whole Church is a corporate priesthood in which every member by his baptism participates, 'a holy priesthood, to offer spiritual sacrifices acceptable to God through Jesus Christ' (1 Pet. 2:5, cf. Rev. 5:10). With all its faults and limitations modern Anglicanism has had a fine tradition of social thought from Maurice to William Temple. And the attitude of that tradition was well expressed in William Temple's observation that it is not the case that conduct is important and worship helps it, but that worship is important and conduct tests it. The priestly function of the Church, its worship, is prior to all else, but its reality as worship of the true and living God, rather than as an emotional escape from reality, is tested by the sacrificial life of its brotherhood. Man is indeed by nature a priest. As Archbishop Leighton wrote:

All created things indeed declare and speak His Glory; the Heavens sound it forth, and the Earth and Sea resound and echo it back. But His reasonable creatures hath He peculiarly framed both to take notice of His Glory in all the rest, and to return it from and for all the rest in a more express and lively way.

And in this lower world it is Man alone that is made capable of observing the Glory of God, and of offering Him praises. He expresses it well who calls man 'the World's High Priest.'[12]

[11] MOBERLEY, op. cit., p. 256.
[12] Leighton was Archbishop of Glasgow in the reign of Charles II. His commentary on I Peter and other works of piety influenced many of the Evangelicals and S. T. Coleridge. The quotation is from his comment on I Pet. 5:11.

Leighton is referring here to George Herbert's poem 'Providence':

> Man is the world's High Priest: he doth present
> The sacrifice for all: while they below
> Unto the service mutter an assent,
> Such as springs use that fall, and winds that blow.

But such a natural priesthood, the capacity and the duty to eternal glory is only a part of the truth. It is not merely that by redemption man has been forgiven and enabled to acknowledge the majesty of deity – though in this respect some anthropocentric Christianity falls below the nobler paganism. It is in Christ that 'all things were created . . . all things were created through him and for him' (Col. 1:5), and man is created not simply in the relation of creature and creator to acknowledge the glory of God, but by incorporation into Christ and adoption to sonship, to share in the worship and love of the Son for the Father, to participate in the spirit of glory and of God (1 Pet. 4:12), and in this age to be the shrine of the Divine indwelling (1 Cor. 3:16). To quote Leighton again, commenting on 1 Pet. 2:4f. ('To whom coming as unto a living stone . . . ye also, as lively stones, are built up a spiritual house, a holy priesthood'):

> As they are living stones built on him into a spiritual temple, so they are priests of that same temple made by him (Rev. 1:6). As he was, after a transcendent manner, temple, priest, and sacrifice, so in their kind, are Christians all these three through him: and by his Spirit that is in them, their offerings through him are made acceptable.

Accepted and reconciled to God through Christ's sacrifice as a sin offering (2 Cor. 5:21), the Church offers itself to God in and through the self-oblation of Christ its High Priest, offering its whole life to God in the threefold sacrifice of soul and body (Rom. 12:1f.), of praise (Heb. 13:13), and of brotherly love and service (Heb. 13:16). Of this life of priesthood in Christ, the eucharist is the sacramental enactment. A sacrifice is liturgically a symbolic act of worship, in the full range of the meaning of worship. The Church offers bread and wine, which symbolically represent both its own sacrifice of praise and self offering in acknowledgement of the Creator, and also the sacrifice of Calvary, of which they are the memorial. The gifts thus offered, by the Church's eucharistic prayer, and accepted by God, become the sacrament of the body and blood of Christ, the efficacious sign of his presence who is the glorified Lord, the great High Priest, and the enthroned Lamb of God. He is present to the faith and in the midst of the eucharistic assembly, a manifestation of his presence which is invisible but as real as the visible manifestation of the risen Lord in the midst of the disciples on the first Easter Sunday evening in the Upper Room, or in the breaking of bread at Emmaus. By communion the worshippers are united to Christ, participate in the benefits of his sacrifice, and in and with him offer themselves as a living sacrifice to God.

Of the five aspects which Brilioth distinguished in the eucharist there is a current tendency to stress its character as a fellowship meal, a tendency which is not without its difficulties and dangers. A fellowship, a *koinonia*, is constituted not by mutual interest in one another but by a common sharing, a joint participation in some common object. We are united in one fellowship with one another because we are partakers in the one Christ. We are one fellowship in the eucharistic meal because we are partakers in the one food, the body and blood of Christ. A hymn by an 18th century Non-Conformist, Philip Doddridge, is in common use in Anglican churches:

Hail, sacred feast which Jesus makes,
Rich banquet of his Flesh and Blood!
Thrice happy he who here partakes
That sacred stream, that heavenly food.

The theologically instructed are often unaware how difficult and even repellent this Johannine language is for many modern people. And yet if the fellowship meal is not a participation in precisely this supernatural food, it is not the eucharist, and is likely to become a humanistic *agape*. Indeed the whole symbolism of the sacred meal is much more difficult for contemporary minds than the idea of sacrifice as symbolic offering. For the notion of a gift which symbolises and enacts the will of a group or an individual is perfectly familiar to us, e.g. in the laying of a wreath on a memorial, the presentation of a testimonial, an engagement ring, a birthday present. I am not denying the value of the idea of a fellowship meal in the eucharist. It has been well expressed by Hort, one of the greatest of 19th century Anglicans:

> Before all things it is the feast of a brotherhood united in a Divine Head, setting forth as the fundamental law of their existence the law of sacrifice towards each other and towards Him, which has been made a reality by His supreme Sacrifice. This is entirely obscured in the Roman and Anglican rites alike.[13]

Roman Catholic theologians, for example Fr Bouyer in his *The Spirit and the Forms of Protestantism*, have enquired why it was that fundamental principles of the Reformation which must be regarded as Catholic and true, e.g. justification by faith, *soli Deo gloria*, the priesthood of the laity, the supremacy of scripture, in fact issued in what a Roman Catholic must consider heresy and schism. Some twenty years ago a group of high Anglican theologians considering the results of the Reformation, in the report to the Archbishop of Canterbury published under the title *Catholicity* saw the explanation in the fragmentation of Christian truth which had been brought about first by the separation of east and west and then by the further schisms of the 16th century. This explanation resembles and presumably descends from F. D. Maurice. In the first part of his *Kingdom of Christ* he examines the different fragments of western christendom, sees each with insights into the fullness of the Gospel, which have been distorted by isolation from the rest and being then made the basis of a theological system. Such a distortion of the Gospel results when the doctrine of justification by faith is separated from a real assertion of the priesthood of the Church.

Considered apart from the controversies of the past, there is no contradiction between justification by faith and the eucharistic sacrifice; indeed to assert the sacrificial character of the eucharist and the priestly character of the Church is to assert precisely those truths which the formula justification by faith properly expresses.

[13] *Life and Letters of A. J. F. Hort*, Vol. II, p. 343.

For it is to assert that the redemptive work of Christ is the only basis of our approach to God, and it is to *proclaim the Lord's death till He come*, the Lord's death which at once manifests God's saving love and the divine exposure of and judgement on human evil; and it is to confess that we are sinners, that as Hooker put it, the best things we do have somewhat in them which needs pardon. But isolated from the wholeness of Christian truth the doctrine of justification by faith can come to mean that the essence of Christianity is trust in a forgiving God; the Gospel becomes identified with the message of forgiveness, and the function of the Church is seen almost entirely as the proclamation of the word of forgiveness. But Christianity is more than trust in a forgiving God, it is life in Christ. Paradoxically the intention to give God alone the glory turns into a man-centred religion which all too easily admits of an existentialist reduction of a 'dekerygmatisation'. For a man can seek God because he wants forgiveness or a liberated conscience or an authentic life or whatever it may be, but this is like – on the human level, seeking a man's friendship as a cure for one's own loneliness or marrying to find a solution of one's psychological problems. Unless the friend or the marriage partner is valued for his own sake there will be no true friendship or love.

By some curious principle of *enantiodromia* this isolated apprehension of justification by faith, where it does not issue in an individualistic pietism, tends to turn into some form of moralism, more or less sentimental, more or less profound in varying circumstances. From the question 'How shall I find a gracious God' there is a swing to the question 'How shall I find a gracious neighbour' or whatever formulation of reduced Christianity may be current. Thus in some forms of moralism Christianity is regarded as a life of self-sacrifice *simpliciter* and this can result in a fussy activism, a living for others which can be insensitive and egoistic. Where, as in its better forms, the Christian is seen after the example of Christ as the man for others, this too often seems to ignore the fact that to love another is not merely a matter of sensitiveness and openness to him, important as these are. The quality of our love depends upon our total vision on life; love for another is a genuine concern for his fulfilment as a human being, and our conception of that fulfilment depends on what I have called our total vision of life.

For the Christian human fulfilment is fellowship with God. This does not mean forcing religion upon another as in some crude forms of evangelism and ecclesiastical propaganda. Indeed we may recognise that this particular man or this group of men, because of their cultural conditioning, must be regarded humanly speaking as incapable of conscious relation to God in this life. To these divine grace will come anonymously, and the Christian will seek in honesty and humility to promote with them and for them the true values which they do or can recognise. He will honour the goodness they show in any true effort for justice and love, and he will remember the last fifteen verses of the twenty-fifth chapter of St Matthew. Whether he knows it or not, every man is for God, and will stand before the throne of Christ his redeemer and judge. The Church exists to glorify God by its worship, its preaching of the Gospel, and the quality of its concern for brotherhood and justice. Corporately it is a royal priesthood called to proclaim the wonderful acts of God the creator and redeemer (1 Pet. 2:9).

Where the priesthood of the Church is forgotten the distortions of the Gospel are inevitable. But the priestly character of the ministry is the sacrament, the efficacious sign, of the priesthood of the Church. To quote Hort once again:

... the uniqueness of the great sacrifice seems to me not to consist in its being a substitute which makes all other sacrifices useless and unmeaning, but in its giving them the power and meaning which of themselves they could not have. Christ is not merely our Priest but our High Priest, or priest of priests; and this title seems to me to give reality to Christian, as it did to Jewish priesthood; both to the universal priesthood of the Church and to the representative priesthood of the apostolic ministry, without which the idea of any priesthood vanishes into any empty metaphor.[14]

The evidence of history seems to support Hort's judgement. In those Churches where the priesthood of the ministry is denied the

[14] Ibid., p. 158.

priesthood of all believers becomes at the best an individualist religion. At its worst it has come in some Protestant circles, as Bishop Stephen Neill remarked,

> to make of the minister nothing more than the employee of a group of Christians, to be retained only on the condition of strict conformity to the general opinion and of saying nothing that could disturb the complacency of the hearers.[15]

If this seems a harsh judgement, it may be supported from a recent essay on the pastor and social conflict by J. R. Bodo, Professor of Practical Theology at San Francisco Theological Seminary. He remarks that in the presence of social conflict the pastor may feel that he is called to speak a word from the Lord, but that the congregation's expectations may be different, and he quotes 'a prominent citizen of Georgia' who stated recently:

> If their advocacy from the pulpits (in which they are, in the last analysis, the paid guest speakers) becomes sufficiently obnoxious to cause a substantial decline in attendance and gross receipts ... the clergyman mustn't be too surprised when the church fathers arrange for his transfer to more favourable climes.[16]

The most superstitious sacerdotalism of Mediterranean folk religion is not as terrible a corruption of Christianity as this view of the Minister of the word of God which regards him as 'the paid guest speaker', like a hired performer at a Rotary luncheon. Such gross corruption is of course not characteristic of the major forms of Protestantism. In these the idea of the priesthood of the Church tends to become either a piece of academic theology or an empty metaphor, and the functions of the Church come to be regarded as primarily evangelism, the proclamation of the word, and service. The idea of a royal priesthood is without real content.

Where, on the other hand, the priesthood of the ministry becomes wrongly distinguished from the corporate priesthood of the Church the results are clericalism, a mixture of institutionalism and individualism, instead of the organic community of brother-

---

[15] S. NEILL, *The Church and Christian Union*, p. 237.
[16] J. R. BODO in *Religion and Social Conflict*, R. Lee and M. K. Mart (eds.), p. 158.

hood in Christ, and a false conception of the priestly character as an individual endowment, a false conception which approximates to the sacerdotalism of manipulating the divine. Protestant criticism has fastened on the development of the concepts of holy order as a sacrament conferring a *character indelibilis* as the source of these distortions. Undoubtedly the whole theology of the powers of order and jurisdiction needs a thorough reconsideration. But the concept of holy order as a sacrament stands for certain very important truths; firstly, for the sacramental character of the ministry as an effectual sign of the priestly character of the Church; secondly, for the truth that this minister is not merely the holder of an office in a particular Church or institution, but an agent, instrument, and sign of the universal Christian fellowship, the body of Christ, so that his presiding at a eucharistic assembly is a sign that this eucharist is not merely an act of fellowship of a local congregation but the actualisation here and now of the universal Church; thirdly, for the truth that the ministry as part of the sacramental structure of the Church is a symbol and instrument of its succession and continuity, its unity and identity through time.

Most of the difficulties that have arisen from the indelibility of order can be dealt with, I think, on certain conditions. First, it should be recognised that schism is normally not so much separation from the Church as a breach of fellowship and violation of brotherhood within it. This is the view of nearly all Anglicans, and the second Vatican council, by its recognition of the ecclesial reality of communities not in union with the Holy See appeared to be moving towards it. Secondly, the character is indelible since ordination consecrates a man for life to the service of Christ in the ministry of the Church, but the effects of this consecration may be totally suspended, so that we are not committed to recognising the validity of the ordinations performed by a disreputable or half crazy *episcopus vagans.*[17] Furthermore, the ministry of a Church which lacks or even denies apostolic succession may be recognisable as valid from its fruits. If such a community has baptism, the scriptures, the preaching of the Gospel,

---

[17] The Anglican Bishops in the Lambeth Conferences have refused to accept ordinations by *episcopi vagantes.*

and the Lord's Supper, its ministry is discharging apostolic functions, and in the conversion of sinners, the feeding of a part of Christ's flock, and contributing to the building up of the body of Christ, its ministry has the signs of an apostle. Can we say that in the ordinations which confer this ministry Christ plays no part? Somewhat as it is held that in a grave emergency a priest without jurisdiction can validly absolve, the Church supplying jurisdiction, so should we not hold that where an ordination conferred without the normative ministry and rite is thus validated by its fruits, the Church, the whole body of Christ, supplies holy order? Thus where there is a re-union between two separated parts of Christendom, one of which lacks the apostolic succession, if the episcopate is accepted for the union, if the priesthood of the Church and ministry is affirmed, and any denial of these abandoned, then surely the ministry lacking the succession should be accepted as it stands and incorporated into the normal succession by such acceptance and the consecration of some of the ministers to the episcopate, with an adequate conscience clause for genuine conscientious scruples. Some Anglicans have felt doubtful and unable to vote for the scheme of reunion with Methodism, partly because they could not find any theological description of the proposed service for reunification of the ministries which would justify their taking part in it, partly because they were not satisfied that the denial of any special priesthood of the ministry was abandoned completely, and partly because they were not certain that the way forward in reunion is the amalgamation of existing denominational structures into a larger denomination.

We may distinguish between the theological structure of the ministry and its empirical organisation, and between its theological character and its sociological status. Its theological structure is its articulation into the three major orders, of which the bishop possesses the ministry in its fullness. By its organisation I mean the way in which its functioning is arranged. Thus our normal system is 'the bishop with restraint', that is, a territorial diocese ruled by a bishop, and divided into territorial parishes each in the charge of an incumbent. Now the principle of territorial jurisdiction has great value in providing everywhere a pastor of the church responsible and available in a given area. And where the territorial principle is completely abandoned, as in some forms of American Protestantism, the results can be very bad. But although the territorial principle is valuable, it is not part of the theological structure of the Church in the form we know it. In theory each diocese is a local church of which the bishop is the chief pastor, priest and teacher. But in fact, in the way we all behave, we tend to regard the diocese as little more than a territorial subdivision of a larger unit. We need to think first of the universal Church, the whole fellowship of which Christ is head and king, and in which he has set the apostolic ministry, and then to ask ourselves what a local church is and should be. The Church Catholic is a universal fellowship, and in this age there is a tension between universality and fellowship, so that for purposes of fellowship and community the members of the universal Church must be gathered in particular fellowships, particular and local churches.

What is the desirable size of a particular church, whether properly local or in some way a 'gathered church'? And should every true local church have a bishop at its head? One might imagine as a future development a Christian community of some five hundred members, committed Christians in an entirely secularised community, with a bishop as their chief pastor and a presbytery of perhaps a dozen priests functioning with the bishop as a corporate body, and perhaps the bishop the only full-time minister, and all the rest earning their living in some ordinary occupation. This brings me to my second distinction, between the sociological status and theological character of the ministry. For centuries, both before and after the Reformation, the bishops of the English dioceses ranked with the nobility and lived in the style of the nobility, and for a shorter period after the Reformation – mainly in the 19th and early 20th centuries – the Anglican clergy were regarded as belonging to the upper middle class or the gentry. They had become one of those learned professions considered suitable for these classes. (There are pessimists who say that, given the unique English capacity for combining continuity and change, in less than a century the average Anglican bishop will look like a minor meritocratic tycoon, that some of them are already beginning to look like this. But the merciful calamities of history will probably refute this pessimism.) We should distinguish between a priest and a clergyman. A priest is one ordained to the sacred ministry, an agent and representative of the priestly body of Christ, a clergyman is a priest who earns his living by being a priest, priesthood is his profession as a professional man, his full time work and source of income. The Church will always need full time priests, but if a man can be a priest and earn his living as a schoolmaster or a university teacher there is no theological reason why a priest should not earn his living by any other honest employment. For there is no distinction between the spirituality of a priest, and the spirituality of a Christian layman. Each is baptised into the death and resurrection of Christ and has to live this out in a daily life in the fellowship of the eucharistic community. The priesthood is not a monastic vocation nor is a monk necessarily a priest, and the married clergy of the Uniate Eastern Churches prove that there is no binding theological significance in the celibacy of the Latin rite. Celibacy and the monastic life are states to which particular individuals are called by God but there is no incompatibility between the priesthood and married life or ordinary secular work.

In essence, then, there is no distinction between the spirituality of the priest and any ordinary member of the *laos*. But the priest, whether full-time or part-time, is a witness to the lordship of Jesus Christ, a steward of his mysteries, and a messenger of his Gospel. His faults and failures can be a scandal to his brothers and to unbelievers. If he is to strengthen his brethren he must be genuinely a man of prayer, and because he is a representative the Church can properly demand of him the recitation of the Daily Office. In the circumstances of our time it could be said that every Christian according to his opportunities should take seriously prayer, poetry, and politics – prayer as contemplation and living contact with God; poetry, or at any rate the keeping sensitive of the imagination in the vulgarity of a decaying culture; politics, for a responsible attitude in the revolutionary transformation of the coming years. And in these respects the priest has an even greater responsibility than his brethren, since he has to stand at the altar and in the pulpit. When I think of the good priests I have known, I recollect that everyone of them had in very different ways integrity, simplicity, humility, and an entirely unconscious dignity, but the best of them would have said with a profounder understanding what any of us their commonplace inferiors must say, that it is only possible to be a priest 'not having a righteousness of my own, based on law, but that which is through faith in Christ, the righteousness from God that depends on faith'. This was said magnificently by one of the greatest of Anglican priests and finest of English poets, George Herbert in his poem *Aaron*.

> Holinesse on the head,
> Light and perfections on the breast,
> Harmonious bells below, raising the dead
> To lead them unto life and rest:
> Thus are true Aarons drest.
>
> Profaneness in my head,
> Defects and darknesse in my breast,
> A noise of passions ringing me for dead
> Unto a place where is no rest:
> Poore priest thus am I drest.
>
> Only another head
> I have, another heart and breast,
> Another music, making live not dead,
> Without whom I could have no rest:
> In him I am well drest.
>
> Christ is my onely head.
> My alone onely heart and breast,
> My onely musick, striking me ev'n dead:
> That to the old man I may rest,
> And be in him new drest.
>
> So holy in my head,
> Perfect and light in my deare breast,
> My doctrine tun'd by Christ (who is not dead
> But lives in me while I do rest)
> Come people: Aaron's drest.

PART THREE

INTRODUCTION

The first of the two papers from professional sociologists stands on the fundamental assertion that the relationship between religion and society is neither independence, nor dependence of one on the other, but inter-dependence in mutual influence. As a consequence of this it is of the first importance for the priesthood as a social institution that contemporary society is based on an occupational structure; because the occupational position of the priest is not clearly evident, uncertainty and strain are inevitable. The society in which we now live recognises a member in terms of what he does in society, and allots his place in terms of what he has achieved. Any examination of the priesthood must recognise that the whole historical approach is called in question by these fundamental considerations: the social function of the priest in the remote past is no longer relevant to his position and role in the present.

As a social group within the Church and within society the full-time ministry has changed: there has been a steep decline in numbers and in social status, and increasing uncertainty amongst its members about its role in society. The 'secularisation' of contemporary society is not necessarily the explanation for the change, for it is related more specifically to the general rise in education, the increasing responsibilities assumed by the laity, and the emergence of other clearly defined professions which have taken over functions which were once fulfilled by the clergy.

If it is difficult to think of the priesthood as an occupation, in the sense of a specialist activity for the performance of a particular kind of job, it is also difficult to see it as a profession if this involves all three characteristics of a clear area of technical skill, a body of systematic knowledge, and a professional ethic based on the idea of service to clients. Only the third of these factors applies clearly to the priesthood.

Such radical considerations are essential before there can be any reliable conclusions about the possible lines of development open to the Christian ministry in the present sociological context, let alone before conclusions about recruitment and training can be drawn.

BIOGRAPHICAL NOTE

ROBERT TOWLER *is a lecturer in sociology in the Department of Social Studies at the University of Leeds. He graduated in Psychology-Sociology from Leeds in 1964 and subsequently did doctoral research on the changes of attitudes and values of men in training for the ministry of the Church of England. This paper and other material from his thesis will form part of the basis of a book forthcoming with Anthony P. M. Coxon on the Sociology of Ordination Training in the Anglican Church.*

10 *The Role of the Clergy*

ROBERT TOWLER

IT HAS BEEN SAID THAT WHEN, IN THE 4TH CENTURY, Christianity ceased to be persecuted by the state and was adopted as the official religion of the Roman empire, this dramatic change, though it affected both Church and state, made a greater difference to the Church than it did to the empire. I mention this by way of introduction because the sociologist of religion is interested in studying just such a situation. He is concerned with religion as a social institution, and with its relationship to society. In a social system, as in any other kind of system, the relationship between the component parts, or between one part and the whole, is a two-way relationship. There is neither independence, nor dependence, but inter-dependence. Thus religious institutions are to be seen as influencing society and also as themselves being influenced by it, and any satisfactory theory which the sociologist of religion may put forward must account for this mutual influence. It may often seem that the sociologist tries to reduce the religious component in society to a mere function of the other components; but this is not really so. In fact he is only trying to state some hypothetical relationship in specific terms which can be tested. The student of church history may suggest that the Roman empire's acceptance of Christianity profoundly affected the Christian religion; the sociologist of religion will try to explain subsequent developments in terms of this social change. It is along these lines that I shall try to offer some observations about the Christian ministry and the state in which it finds itself today.

One of the distinctive characteristics of all religions, and of the various groups within any particular religion, is the position occupied by their functionaries or leaders. Thus, in studying Judaism, one of the most significant areas to be examined is the several functions which were served by prophets, priests, seers and so on. We shall find exactly the same is true if we examine the particular functions within the Christian ministry from the apostolic period onwards. In the post-Reformation period the types of ministry have been as diverse and almost as complex as have the corresponding doctrines, from the traditional Catholic pyramid on the one hand to the complete absence of any designated leaders in some sects on the other hand. This variation between different types of ministry is something to which we are all accustomed. At the present time, however, a reassessment of the nature and functions of the ministry is taking place in all Christian denominations, and as a result is a situation which is as fluid as the present questionings have made the content of the Christian faith itself.

The sociological explanation most often proposed for this reassessment is that the ministry is now set in a secular society. Contemporary culture is not based on religious beliefs, and so the clergy are essentially out of tune with the age. As a group they are regarded as being fundamentally irrelevant in the present day. Thus Dr Bryan Wilson has spoken of the 'alienation of the clergy' and has drawn a comparison between them and

'. . . the charcoal-burners or alchemists in an age in which the processes in which they were engaged had been rendered obsolete, technically or intellectually.'[1]

This explanation may well be part of the truth. However, it is a very general explanation which does not account for many of the particular changes. For that reason I want to look at the ministry itself, and at its history and development as a social group within the Church and within society. It may be possible to explain many

[1] B. R. WILSON, *Religion in Secular Society* (London 1966), p. 76.

of the changes presently taking place without recourse to the general process of the secularisation of society. Furthermore, if this alternative explanation is satisfactory, it will imply that the changes which face the ministry were inevitable, and would have occurred anyway. This is not to deny the importance of secularisation of society, but merely to question whether it is necessary to invoke it in order to understand the dilemma in which the Christian ministry finds itself today.

The first task is to state clearly what these changes are, and then to go on to look for causes. The changes are three-fold. First there is the shortage of priests, secondly the decline in the social status of the ministry, and thirdly there is uncertainty about the role of the priest. As far as numbers are concerned, the ministry faces a crisis. This is a rather dramatic word to use, but it is strictly appropriate since the problem of recruitment to the ministry in all Churches has assumed dramatic proportions. A crisis is a turning-point: it is a moment of danger and suspense. Although it is this critical decline in numbers which demands attention, it is of the utmost importance that we realise that this decline is only a symptom. The shortage of priests is not itself the problem, but the sign of an underlying problem. So although we must pay attention to the shrinkage of the ministry and grasp the full extent of it, we must do so only in order to get the measure of the problem which it indicates. The underlying problem is two-fold. On the one hand there is the sharp decline in the status of the ministry, that is to say the prestige which is accorded to the clergy by society; on the other hand there is the uncertainty of the clergy as to what is precisely their role within the Church and within society. Each of these factors will be considered in turn.

First the drop in numbers. Here I must restrict myself to the Church of England, though its predicament is by no means unique. There is an overall shrinkage in the ministry of the Church of England. This is not confined to the shortage of recruits, but has itself to be considered under four separate headings. In the first place the numerical strength of the ministry has declined in actual numbers by 20 per cent since the turn of the century. This fact, however, by itself, does not give the full extent of the shrinkage, for during the same period there has been a very considerable rise in population. So the second point is that relative to the population of England as a whole, the Anglican ministry has declined by more than 40 per cent.[2] But these figures merely indicate the shrinkage in terms of the number of men involved. The third point is that the shrinkage is still further aggravated by the increasing proportion of recruits to the ministry who are over thirty years of age: the so-called 'late vocations'. These men increase the actual numbers in the ministry but they enter it with markedly fewer years of work ahead of them. So if the strength of the ministry is estimated in terms of potential years of work, it is seen to have shrunk still further. Finally there is the increasing number of men who quit the ministry who have to be taken into account. Since the majority of these are young priests, men who are still young enough to find alternative work and an alternative source of income, this fourth aspect of the shrinkage of the ministry makes the age profile of the clergy as a whole even more biased; so this is yet another aspect of the total shrinkage and it is necessary to remember how complete it is. If the process is to be reversed – and there are no signs of such a reversal in the Church of England – each one of these four trends would have to be reversed.

The second aspect of change to be taken into account is the decline in prestige which the clergy, considered as a group, have suffered. Whereas they were once among the most respected members of the community, their present position is now very much less clear – and it is the ambiguity of their present position which has to be emphasised. Studies which have examined the relative status accorded to the clergy by people in general, as compared with other occupational groups, have shown that the clergy still come out high on these rankings.[3] This evidence, so far as it goes, suggests that the clergy have retained their high degree of prestige, but one is compelled to question its validity. For there is no doubt at all that in European society the clergy have lost the social standing which in former ages they were accorded. This discrepancy in the evidence is central to the prob-

[2] This is based on the Census data for 1901–1951; it should be noted that there was no 1941 Census.

[3] For details of two such studies see WILSON, op. cit., pp. 82–3.

lem. On the one hand there is the popular respect in which they are held, the attention which their views command, the social positions which they are called upon to fill; on the other hand there is the fact that so many of the functions which the clergy once fulfilled are now discharged by professional people in the welfare services. This contradiction between what appears to be high evaluation on the one hand, and the low value attached to their services on the other hand lies at the heart of the crisis, and will be returned to below.

The third factor to be considered is the uncertainty on the part of the clergy as to what precisely is their role. In England as elsewhere this problem is evidenced most clearly by the number of priests who leave the parochial ministry. Often they go to teaching posts or to work in the welfare services. It is when he attempts to define his role and the activities which he thinks ought to fill his day that the individual priest is most aware of the crisis. Though this is the aspect of the crisis which is most readily apparent to him it does not necessarily mean that it is the most important one, but simply that this is the point at which it hurts the individual priest most. The priest's role is obviously a complex one which contains many separate aspects. The most common distinction is that drawn between the priest as prophet, priest and king. The sociological utility of this distinction is limited for it is basically a theological one, derived from the theological roles attributed to Jesus Christ. If the roles of prophet, priest and king are to be useful they have to be translated into a more readily understandable form, such as teacher, liturgical minister and leader, whereupon they lose three parts of their original theological connotation. Anthony Spencer has pointed to the special importance of the prophetical role of the priest and has interpreted it in a fairly concrete way:

'Social and cultural change in Britain calls for creative innovators among the clergy, for prophetic men who are deeply rooted in society and see the need to re-express fundamental Christian values and to restate norms.'[4]

[4] A. E. C. W. SPENCER, in his presidential address to the Ninth International Conference on the Sociology of Religion, reprinted in *Herder Correspondence*, Vol. 4, 1967, pp. 361–4.

Even this statement, however, is not precise enough to allow the sociologist to distinguish which actions pertain to the prophetic role, for it refers more to the quality of a man's actions than to a set of acts which can be specified. The individual priest – or bishop – may fulfil a prophetic role in the Church or in society, but this is dependent on the charismatic authority of the man himself rather than on the authority which inheres in his office.

The sociologist must limit himself to distinguishing between those aspects of the priest's role which may be described and observed empirically. Furthermore it is necessary to restrict the analysis to those aspects of the role which are common to all priests because they are inherent in the office itself, rather than functions of the individual, otherwise it will cease to be an analysis of the priesthood. Professor Samuel Blizzard, in his useful analysis, distinguishes six components which go to make up the total priestly role.[5] He aims to cover all the various types of Christian ministry, and this means that some of the components which he enumerates receive greater emphasis in the ministry of one denomination than they do in that of another. The six components of the priest's role which he distinguishes are:

  (i) Teacher of the Christian faith
 (ii) Organiser of Church societies and affairs
(iii) Preacher of the Word of God
 (iv) Administrator of parish business
  (v) Pastor of his people
 (vi) Priest in his liturgical functions as administrator of sacraments and leader of public worship.

At one time all these activities were recognised components of the priest's role, and he alone was responsible for their performance. Each of them now, however, is being subjected to a process of erosion. Thus the role of the priest as a teacher dates from the time when he was distinguished from those to whom he minis-

[5] s. w. blizzard, 'The Minister's Dilemma', *Christian Century*, 23 April 1956, pp. 508–9; it should be noted that the present discussion is concerned with *role ambiguity* which must not be confused with *role conflict* which is the subject of much of Blizzard's discussion, cf. s. w. blizzard, 'Role Conflicts of the Urban Minister', *The City Church*, Vol. 7, No. 4, 1956, pp. 13–15.

tered by his theological learning and the level of his general education; but today the relative decline in the educational level of the clergy is too well known to need comment. The latest statistics for the Church of England show that only 35 per cent of those offering themselves for ordination are university graduates.[6] Even in the field of theology the clergy no longer have a monopoly of learning for, as Dr Trevor Long has pointed out, the proportion of those who read for theological degrees and who do not intend to be ordained is increasing.[7] Thus at the University of Leeds, of those who passed through the Department of Theology between 1961 and 1965, 57 per cent were planning to teach as religious specialists whereas only 23 per cent were ordinands.[8] So we see that while on the one hand the educational level of the clergy is declining, on the other hand there is an increasing number of lay people, both men and women, who have obtained theological degrees. Many of the latter are teachers, and this means that in the future more and more parishes will have among the laity people who are well equipped to teach the Christian faith, far better equipped than their clergy in fact, who have had less theological education, and no training at all in teaching methods.

The second component of the priest's role that Dr Blizzard distinguishes is that of organising the church activities, but it is well known that the clergy are handing over a substantial amount of this to the laity. Church societies, guilds, youth clubs and so on are increasingly becoming not only organisations *for* the laity, but *of* the laity, and this removes from the priest a considerable amount of work which was formerly regarded as being his responsibility. As Dr Joan Brothers has pointed out in a survey of Catholicism in Liverpool:

'... perhaps the most significant rejection discovered in the course of the survey lies in the rebellion expressed by some at

[6] The report, 'First Report on the Reorganisation of the Theological Colleges', of The Advisory Council for the Church's Ministry to the National Assembly of the Church of England, C.A., 1708, 1968, p. 14.

[7] T. O. LONG, 'Religion, Society and the Teacher', *The Modern Churchman*, Vol. X, 1967, pp. 142–51.

[8] Ibid., p. 144.

the extent to which the parish priest controls all parochial affairs.'[9]

So far as the priest's role as preacher is concerned, in the Church of England this responsibility has not been his exclusively since the institution of the office of Lay Reader.[10] So in recent years the third component of the priest's role has been opened to participation by the laity. Similarly so far as Dr Blizzard's fourth component is concerned, the priest's role as administrator has been diminished by the growing practice of laymen accepting responsibility for parochial finances and for a number of similar jobs.

The fifth component which Dr Blizzard distinguishes is that of the priest as pastor. Traditionally it has been regarded as an important part of the duty of the clergy to care for the members of the local church as their pastor. Today, however, it is no longer the priest's sole responsibility for his flock which is stressed, so much as the mutual responsibility for all the members of the church for one another. In the Church of England this is reflected in a variety of different ways such as the institution of street wardens, and in particular campaigns such as that conducted ecumenically under the slogan 'People Next Door'. So at the same time as the clergy have been freed from their obligations in the organisational and administrative fields in order to be able to spend more time exercising the pastoral component of their role, the obligation of the laity to discharge this last function is also being stressed. The result is that in all these ways the distinctiveness of the priest's role is becoming more and more eroded. The only component which necessarily remains distinctive, at least in the Catholic Church and in other Churches with the same sacramental tradition, is the liturgical one. But even in this sixth component of the priest's role the whole aim of the liturgical movement is directed towards encouraging the participation of the laity, leaving the priest as the president of the eucharist rather than as the sole celebrant of it.

[9] J. BROTHERS, 'Social Change and the Role of the Priest', *Social Compass*, Vol. X, 1963, p. 484.

[10] The office of Lay Reader in its modern form was introduced in the Church of England in 1860.

This may be an inadequate way in which to analyse the various components of the total priestly role, but the differences in detail matter relatively little. The essential point is that in each component of his role, the priest is less sure of what precisely is his job. He is less sure of what is expected of him, and it is the expectations which others have of a social actor which, sociologically, determine the actor's role. His formally defined position in a social system tells us little of what is expected of him in practice. An actor's behaviour, as the incumbent of a social position, is determined by the expectations which the incumbents of counter positions have of him. His role is defined by what is expected of him.[11]

Three areas have been outlined in which the present changes in the ministry are to be seen most clearly. The ministry is a group in society which is shrinking in size, declining in the status accorded to it by society, and displaying uncertainties as to its role. Obviously these are not three separate problems. They are three aspects of a single problem: three points at which a whole process of change becomes recognisable.

As has already been said, the drop in numbers, though it is often treated as the most important and therefore the one which receives the most attention, is in fact only a symptom. Indeed it is only to be expected that it should result from the other two problems. A group which suffers from declining status and a progressively less clear self-definition must expect a crisis in its recruitment. So I propose to leave the question of numbers on one side. It is epiphenomenal, and should be treated as such.

That leaves two problems. The question we have to try and answer is how to account, in sociological terms, for the appearance of these problems. Part of the answer, so obvious that it is often overlooked, is the general rise in the level of education among the population as a whole. Hitherto, because of its nature as a social group, the ministry, at any rate in England, has had a more or less continuous tradition of learning. This has not been universally so, of course, but it has been true, broadly speaking, of the

[11] This usage follows N. GROSS, W. S. MASON and A. W. MCEACHERN, *Explorations in Role Analysis* (New York 1958); see chs. 1–5 for a summary of older usages and a justification of the one presently employed.

established Churches in most countries. This characteristic of the clergy as an educated group was one of the sources of the respect accorded to them and of their comparatively high social status. When, however, higher education became available to everyone, the clergy no longer enjoyed this privileged position in society. This means that within the Church there was no longer the same educational gap between the clergy and the laity, and the laity are no longer in the same relationship of dependence as they previously were. In the case of the Roman Catholic community of Liverpool this change has been quite recent. In fact it is only since the 1944 Education Act that its impact has been felt. Dr Joan Brothers has discussed the effects of it in an article on 'Social change and role of the Priest' and she concludes that

'... educational change has altered the social status of some of the young parishioners, and in doing so has disturbed the balance between priest and parishioner. As a result, tension has developed, not because of individual disharmony or disagreement, but as a consequence of the changing social system which sometimes leads to confusion in loyalties over religious institutions and responsibilities. ... Lack of familiarity makes it difficult for each to understand what the other expects of him. No longer are both as clearly aware as they used to be of the rights and obligations which they are required to respect and discharge towards one another.'[12]

As Dr Brothers points out in the same article this shift in the relative educational levels of clergy and laity has led to a desire on the part of the laity to assume responsibilities in matters which had been previously regarded as the concern of the priest. This sharing with the laity of what had previously been defined as components of the specifically priestly role has inevitably resulted in a role uncertainty on the part of priests themselves.

So far the ministry has been described simply as 'a social group' – it has not been described as a profession, or even as an occupation. However, it is very common practice to speak of it in these terms. If one is looking for a contemporary model of priesthood, it is the model of a profession which is most often employed. It is

[12] Brothers, op. cit., pp. 487–8.

employed outside the context of theological debate but that is all to the good, since it is only the small group of trained theologians who think of the ministry in such terms. A recent document on the ministry of the Church of England provides an excellent example of the way in which the model of a profession is used, and, incidentally, illustrates the present concern over the priest's role. Speaking of what it calls the distinctive role of the clergy, it says:

> 'The clergy of the Church of England still take their place within the tradition of the learned professions of men whose responsibility is to serve people. There are responsibilities which are peculiar to the clergy and yet have to be spelt out more fully, but these as well as their more general responsibilities, can be discharged in a fashion which can be compared with the best practice of doctors and social workers.'[13]

If, as the document claims, the ministry is a profession it must be possible to define its professional duties and responsibilities. Yet this is precisely what it is difficult to do.

The erosion of the priest's role and the uncertainty in defining it which have been observed at the parish level are paralleled by a corresponding uncertainty and erosion of the role of the clergy in society as a whole. This becomes obvious when it is seen in an historical perspective. Many of the functions which the clergy fulfilled in the early middle ages have been gradually taken over by the various professions which have emerged from the ministry. So there is uncertainty among the clergy as to their role both within the Church and within society. At the parish level the priest is forced to ask what is his precise function; what does he do that only he can do? Some, like Dr Wilson, answer that the priest does not have a specific role. Thus, he says,

> 'The role of the priest is diffuse rather than specific. Of all social roles the priest's calls for the widest use of his *untrained* capacities, and calls into play, more than in any profession, his personality dispositions. . . . It is because of this diffuseness of

---

[13] The Report, 'The Church and the Social Services', of the Board for Social Responsibility to the National Assembly of the Church of England, C.A. 1703, 1968, p. 16.

the priest's role that there is an irreducible qualitative element which is not capable of precise formulation.'[14]

If this is so, clearly the priesthood cannot be regarded as a profession at all in any meaningful use of that expression. The same uncertainty exists in the wider context too. We are forced to ask what is the precise role of the clergy in society?

Dr Wilson's doubts about whether the ministry is a profession have been noted. Similar reservations have been expressed from a quite different standpoint by another well-known English sociologist, Dr David Martin.[15] In the face of these opinions Professor Gordon Dunstan still maintains that the ministry is a profession and that it has its own unique contribution to make alongside the other professions. He argues that this is so on the grounds that it conforms to certain criteria of professionality put forward by Professor Robert Merton.[16] These criteria by which an occupation is judged to count as a profession are three-fold. It must, in the first place, be an occupation characterised by a technical skill and trained capacity which is, in the second place, based on a body of systematic knowledge; and thirdly it must be an occupation imbued with a professional ethic based on the idea of service to its clients. Taking this last criterion first, there is no doubt that the ministry is imbued with an ethic of help and service to people. This is something which it does indeed share with the professions, and because of it the ministry is often found trying to co-operate with the professions in pursuing their common aim. It is just possible to interpret theology as the systematic knowledge which is characteristic of the ministry, though many people would doubt this both on theoretical and also on pragmatic grounds. Professional knowledge is relevant, however, only insofar as it is the theoretical foundation upon which the professional skills and techniques are based. It is precisely this characteristic skill and practical service which the ministry as a profession is supposed to offer which eludes definition. Unless theology can be shown to be

[14] B. R. WILSON, 'The Paul Report Examined', *Theology*, Vol. LXVIII, 1965, pp. 89–103.

[15] D. A. MARTIN, *A Sociology of English Religion* (London 1967), pp. 119–22.

[16] G. R. DUNSTAN, 'The Sacred Ministry as a Learned Profession', *Theology*, Vol. LXX, 1967, pp. 433–42.

the basis of a definite professional activity it is no more systematic professional learning than is a knowledge of classics or philosophy. The professions must be seen as occupations which demand highly specialised skills, and skills which are grounded in systematic theory. On neither of these criteria does the ministry show itself to be a profession.

However, the main point at which I take issue with Professor Dunstan and with all those who maintain that the ministry is a profession is a much more fundamental one. This point is the assumption that the ministry is an occupational group. In my view the ministry, so far from being that type of occupation which we describe as a profession, is not an occupation at all. This will become clear if we take a brief look at the history of the development of the professions. The essential sociological nature of the ministry as a social group may also emerge a little more clearly.

In the early 18th century Addison spoke of the 'three learned professions of divinity, law and physic'.[17] This is one of the earliest examples of the use of the word 'profession' to describe particular occupations or callings. The learned professions were those vocations which, in contrast to the contemporary crafts and trades, required learning as well as skill for their exercise. Addison mentioned three, but at an earlier stage in history both law and physic were practised by men within the ranks of the clergy. This is not surprising, since, in the early middle ages, when society was stratified into estates, the first, second and third estates were the social groups in which were located respectively leadership, learning and labour. So it is natural that, as Carr-Saunders and Wilson said in their book on the professions:

'The earliest phases of certain vocations, which have grown into professions, were passed within the Church. Education was so closely bound up with ecclesiastical functions that the priest and the teacher were distinguished with difficulty. Lawyers, physicians and civil servants were members of the ecclesiastical order who had assumed special functions.'[18]

Thus it is clear that to be a cleric in that period of history was not

[17] Quoted in the Oxford English Dictionary under 'Profession'.
[18] A. M. CARR-SAUNDERS and P. A. WILSON, *The Professions* (Oxford 1933), p. 290.

to have an occupation. It was to occupy a social position of an entirely different kind. In the medieval period a person's social position was defined primarily in terms of what he *was*. The prevailing mood of the social system was static. Society itself changed little from generation to generation. There was very little social mobility, either within or between generations. When a person did change his status it was, as it were, by fiat. He might be created a knight, or he might be ordained a priest. Generally speaking, however, positions within medieval society were ascribed rather than achieved; the society itself was ascription-orientated. Twentieth century society is in the sharpest possible contrast to this. We live in an achievement-orientated society, where a person occupies the social position which he has achieved, and which is defined in terms of what he *does*. So it is almost meaningless to ask what the medieval clergy *did*. They fulfilled a most important function in society, but it was a function not restricted to ministry within the Church. It extended to the effective ministry of society as a whole, and comprised many occupations and various callings. The present crisis of the ministry must be viewed against the background of this sociological role of the clergy in medieval society which was formative in its subsequent development, for it puts the relationship of the ministry to the professions into perspective.

Another erroneous account of the present difficulties of the ministry in terms of the professional model is to regard the former as an under-developed profession. This view also is corrected by considering the ministry in its historical perspective. We have seen that the ministry was the matrix of the learned professions. Freed from the restrictions imposed by their clerical origins, physic and law were able to develop as separate professional associations with increasing specialisation. The body of theory underpinning these skills was also able to develop, though slowly at first, after it had been released from the theological presuppositions by which it had hitherto been bound. In other words, it was precisely their separation from the clergy which made the evolution of the older professions possible. To explain the dilemma of the contemporary ministry as the result of professional under-development, as Dr Osmund Schreuder for instance has done, is therefore absurd.[19] The similarities which the ministry bears to medicine and law are obviously due to the clerical origin of those professions, especially their inheritance of the common ethic of service to people; the *differences* are due to their separation. But the evolution of the professions is a continuing process. Medicine and law are themselves in process of change. The once familiar general practitioner of medicine is on the way out. Rapid scientific advance, among other things, requires that medical treatment should become increasingly based on hospitals and other institutions where developments in modern skills and techniques are readily available. The complexity of modern medicine leaves less and less room for the contemporary doctor to fulfil his old role of friend and counsellor of the family. Indeed the paradigm of the modern professional is no longer the physician as it was twenty years ago; it is rather the industrial chemist in the employment of a large corporation who represents the new norm. When this pattern of development within the professions is recognised, it makes the idea of the clergyman becoming fully and contemporarily professional look as ludicrous as it really is.

I have argued that the sociological development of the ministry from the middle ages to the present day show it to be neither a profession, nor even an occupation. The characteristics which it assumed at that crucial period of history have indeed confused the picture. As Carr-Saunders and Wilson observed,

'Divinity found a place in the list only because it was at one time either the only profession or the basis on which other professions were built. It took its place with physic and the law, as it were, by ancient right. Man had not observed that, *since it had divested itself of duties relating to the ordinary business of life*, its position on the list was anomalous.'[20]

When these authors say that the ministry 'divested itself of duties relating to the ordinary business of life' we should observe the important implication that the ministry was not always concerned with the ordinary business of life. There was a time in the early

[19] O. SCHROEDER, 'Le caractére professionnel du sacerdoce', *Social Compass*, Vol. XII, 1965, pp. 5–19.

[20] CARR-SAUNDERS and WILSON, op. cit., p. 294 (emphasis added).

Christian centuries when the functions and responsibilities of the ministry were confined to the Christian Church. The priest's role was defined in terms of his relationship to the members of the Church, and it was only in this context that his role had significance and meaning, just as, for example, the master and officers of a Masonic lodge have no significance or meaning outside Freemasonry.[21] When Christianity became the sole religion of the state, the members of its ministry came to have significance for the whole of society, which had become coterminous with the Christian Church. So what has in the past been known as the clerical profession is a particular institutional form of the Christian ministry which arose in a particular type of society and which was relevant to that particular society. It is, of course, a sociological common-place that institutional forms have a remarkable habit of persisting long after they have ceased to be appropriate. The probability that the traditional ministry faces imminent collapse provides internal evidence that it is an institutional form which is no longer viable. External evidence is furnished by the examination of the sociological function which the clerical profession has fulfilled in times past, thus confirming the conclusion that this particular institutional form is now outmoded. As society becomes increasingly de-Christianised the significance of the clergy is once more confined within the boundaries of the Church. Such wider significance as remains is residual. It is a hang-over from the period of Christian imperialism.

The foregoing analysis of the sociological nature of the ministry did not originate as an *a priori* theory. It was prompted by the need to make some sense of empirical research. In studying the changes in attitudes and values of a group of Anglican ordination candidates in five English theological colleges I had assumed that they were preparing to enter a profession. I have argued that the ministry is fundamentally different from the medical profession, but I have come to this conclusion only after having set out with precisely the opposite assumption. The comparison is very tempting. Much of the training for the medical profession consists of training individuals to be a particular type of person with appro-

---

[21] I am indebted to Mr Giles Ecclestone for suggesting this comparison which, though frivolous, is quite useful.

priate attitudes and values. Medical students must be trained, not only to perform the technical skills of their trade and to understand its theory, but also to *be* physicians as well. They must learn to think of themselves, of their patients and of their colleagues in particular ways; they must learn appropriate forms of social interaction; and they must adjust their whole pattern of behaviour so as to be consonant with the professional role. This professional socialisation has been studied sociologically, and my research has been an attempt to study the equivalent process for the Anglican clergy.[22] Difficulties, however, arose immediately. It is quite clear that ordination candidates are training for the ministry, and yet an examination of that training shows that they are not being prepared to do anything outside a broadly liturgical context. Emphasis in most theological colleges is concentrated in two areas: in learning a certain amount of fairly elementary theology, and in learning to live a particular style of clerical life. Other aspects of training are accorded so little time and attention that one is forced to conclude that they are thought to be peripheral. When confronted with the question of what ordinands are being trained to *do*, one cannot escape the answer that they are not being trained to do anything, but only to *be* clergymen. One is forced to recognise that the training is not much related to what the clergyman is going to occupy his time and energies doing. Rather, it is a preparation for a theologically defined role which might involve almost any sort of practical activity. It is well expressed in the use of the term *formatio* to describe priestly training. All jobs have more to them than the simple performance of an activity, and in the case of some highly specialised jobs which involve much social interaction the manner in which the duty is performed assumes an importance almost equalling that of the duty itself. The manner clearly needs to be learned. Basically, however, the job is defined by the specialised activity in which it consists. This is what the man does. It is this skill that the training cultivates. With the priesthood this is not so. The precise activities are left openended, and it is the manner of their performance which is trained for. It is the formation of a particular kind of person, rather than

---

[22] For an example of work on this aspect of the sociology of medical education, see H. S. BECKER, *et al.*, *Boys in White* (Chicago 1961).

the training for a particular job. Clearly, this is not training for an occupation.

Contemporary society is based on its occupational structure. A social group of clergymen who have no occupational positions is thus in a highly anomalous position. The evidence, both internal and external, which I have outlined indicates that this anomalous position of the Christian ministry is no longer viable. The material for the analysis has been drawn primarily from the Church of England but it has a much wider application. One might suppose that the Roman Catholic Church in England is an exception since it is a minority group, but there is little to support the supposition. Although its present position may not yet be grave, it displays all the same symptoms. Thus Charles Davis, in the careful comments he made when he left the Catholic Church, said explicitly that he believed the institutional structure of the Catholic ministry hindered rather than helped the discharge of that ministry. The state of the Roman Catholic Church in France more closely resembles that of the Church of England, and if anything, the problem has been more clearly perceived there. This awareness may have been stimulated by the recent tradition of anti-clericalism, but it is fundamentally the same as that found in England. The problem was articulated by the group of fifty priests who wrote, in a letter to their bishops, that:

'Ce que nous avons vécu et ce que nous vivons, aux côtés de chrétiens et de non-chrétiens, nous révèle avec plus d'évidence que notre statut de clercs nous conduit à des impasses.'[23]

Prompted by the reactions of other priests, of working class origin, who felt the letter was marred by an attitude of self-centredness, the original signatories further elucidated their position by writing that,

'... notre analyse nous mène à penser que le statut clérical impose aux prêtres avec le style de vie et le mode de relation aux hommes qu'il implique est l'un des obstacles majeurs à cette révélation de Jesus-Christ. En conséquence, le rejet du

[23] Quoted in *La Croix*, 22 November 1968.

statut clérical nous apparait comme un préalable nécessaire pour définir à nouveau la Mission.'[24]

Examples could be cited to show that this analysis applies in varying degrees to all major Churches.

If the ministry in its present form is outmoded and is in real danger of collapse, one is obliged to ask what new sociological forms it might be possible for the ministry to assume. Broadly speaking, I think there are two lines of development open to it. These lines are completely different from each other, and both would have far-reaching implications for the Churches. The first of these developments would be for the full-time ministry as we know it to be allowed to die the death which now seems to be probable. The tendency for the laity to assume many of the responsibilities once restricted to the clergy could then proceed without hindrance. Priests could earn their livelihood in normal occupations; and in the Catholic Church, as in other Churches, this would certainly involve their being free to marry. It is obvious that these changes in the form of the ministry would require a corresponding reorganisation of the parochial structure. Organisation in units the size of parishes would be impracticable. A smaller unit would be needed, which might be something like that recently described by Father Jean-Paul Audet:

> 'What I would like to see is the creation of an "assembly" (*ekklesia*) mid-way between the family and the kind of large "congregation" we know today. Such an intermediate "assembly" would then be considered as our true "base community" – flexible, mobile, diversified and at grips with the realities of human life.'[25]

This would entail a new type of church structure, served by a ministry of an entirely new form. Far from simply making the best of a bad job, or making a virtue out of a necessity, it could be a creative innovation. Such a transformation, however, which would accurately be described as an *aggiornamento*, could not

[24] Ibid.

[25] J.-P. AUDET, *Structures of Christian Priesthood*, Trans. Rosemary Sheed (London 1967), p. 169; this book has subsequently been published in the original French as *Mariage et Célibat dans le Service Pastoral de l'Eglise* (Paris 1968).

happen spontaneously, but would require positive action to make it possible. It would involve the dispersal of the Church and would result in a much more flexible structure. There would, of course, still be need for a basic bureaucracy, consisting of full-time officials, but the institution it would serve would be organised in an entirely new way.

The other possible way in which the ministry might develop is diametrically opposed to this, and would involve the kind of changes which have been observed taking place in the United States. Since contemporary society is based on occupational groups, the ministry might seek to adapt itself in such a way as to constitute an occupation itself. If this happened, the local church could become a community centre with a religious basis, providing its members with amenities and welfare services to supplement those provided by the state. Within this context of a rational organisation, with definable ends in addition to its strictly religious ones, the role of the priest would be that of an organiser, administrator and professional counsellor as well as that of a priest in the liturgical sense. It would be his responsibility to share out many of the tasks this would involve, and he would become the full-time head of a religious organisation. Such a form of ministry could indeed be regarded as an occupation, and all the appropriate judgements as to its effectivity, vitality, efficiency and so on could be applied to it since the priest would be competing for members with all the other voluntary associations which exist to pursue secular interests and activities. It would thrive to the extent to which it provided effective leadership for an organisation which was able to do this successfully. Starting from the present state of the ministry of the Church of England, such a development would require every bit as much effort as the other innovation described. The training of the clergy would need to include substantial instruction in counselling techniques, sociology and welfare work, business promotion, management and so on. Salaries would have to be raised to a realistic level as in America. In the Church of England this would mean increasing them by a factor of three or four. There is no reason why, given adequate capital investment, such a development could not be a viable alternative, even in England. Indeed, the first signs of such a movement are already visible, although it has not sought or received official sanction. This is seen in the formation of CORAT, Christian Organisations Research and Advisory Trust, under the chairmanship of the Earl of March and with the Anglican Bishop of London, the Roman Catholic Bishop Butler and the sociologist Dr David Martin among the members of its Advisory Council. CORAT 'brings the techniques of modern management consultancy to bear on the special problems of Christian organisations'. It is a beginning, but the changes will have to be far-reaching and swift if they are to alleviate the present difficulties of the ministry.

I have tried to describe the two alternatives as I see them. They may sound fanciful but given the present crisis in which the ministry finds itself, they are no more than extrapolations from tendencies already in operation. If neither line of development is pursued with sufficient vigour, then I think that stagnation and a further shrinkage in the ministry is bound to follow. There is, however, a third possibility which combines both the lines of development I have described. In the course of my research I found two quite distinct orientations among Anglican ordinands.[26] The distinction was not, of course, clear-cut in every case, nor did every individual fall neatly into one category or the other. But what emerged was, on the one hand, a type of ordinand with a highly religious orientation, an indifference to secular interests, and strongly committed to the institutional church. On the other hand there emerged another type of ordinand who was characterised by a comparatively low level of interest in institutional religion and religious beliefs, but highly committed to secular interests and activities. These two orientations correspond, it seems, to the two possible lines along which the ministry can develop. Each of them shares a common characteristic which will be no surprise to those familiar with Emile Durkheim's basic theory of religion: the tendency to make the society in which they live, and the religious group to which they are committed,

---

[26] These types of vocation emerged from a factor analysis of the results from a battery of tests comprising thirteen variables in all; for details see ROBERT TOWLER, 'Puritan and Antipuritan' in D. A. MARTIN (ed.) *A Sociological Yearbook of Religion in Britain*: 2 (London 1969).

coterminous.[27] The one creates for itself a totally religious environment by retreating into a clearly defined religious organisation; the other achieves the same result by defining the whole of society as the Church, and looks for religious inspiration within the sphere which is usually designated as secular.

Thus the third possibility is that the full-time ministry should gradually disappear and be replaced by a ministry of worker-priests in a radically restructured Church. But at the same time full-time religious functionaries such as the members of Religious Orders, so-called secular institutes, and teams of evangelists would play an important role within the Church and provide adequate outlets for those whose religious orientation demands such expression. This third possibility might take place most naturally within those Churches which have preserved the Catholic tradition, but it may be significant that the Protestant Church in continental Europe are at present seeking to re-introduce the Religious Life in a variety of forms. It may be that this is, for Christians, the most hopeful way forward.[28]

[27] The tendency of a religious group to become coterminous with society, which Durkheim interpreted as a society's veneration of its own collective identity is reflected powerfully in the words of Dostoievsky's Grand Inquisitor: 'But man seeks to worship what is beyond dispute, so that all men would agree at once to worship it. For these pitiful creatures are concerned not only with what one or the other can worship, but to find something that all would believe in and worship; what is essential is that all may be together in it. This craving for *community* of worship is the chief misery of each man individually and of all humanity from the beginning of time. . . . And so it will be to the end of the world, even when gods disappear from the earth they will fall down before idols just the same.'

[28] It may be noted that Ernst Troeltsch came to a very similar conclusion fifty years ago within the terms of his church-sect typology when he suggested developments 'to help us to overcome our miserable ecclesiastical situation, which is daily becoming worse'. (Trans. OLIVE WYON, *The Social Teaching of the Christian Churches* (London 1931), p. 1006.

The second sociological paper takes advantage of the symposium form — in which the speakers can move on from positions reached in earlier papers — by developing considerations which emerged in the first sociological paper, within the general question of what the sociologist can be expected to achieve. The fact of change is again taken as fundamental, and this has important consequences for the kind of model which is selected and used for an investigation of the position of the priest in contemporary society. Static models evolved in a static society are no longer effective, and this precludes the use of a functionalist model, a model drawn from a state of equilibrium, or even a systems model. Secularisation, which was only mentioned in the previous paper, receives a more extensive treatment, defined as 'the rejection or by-passing of ecclesiastical institutions by individuals or society at large, together with the religious values represented by the Church. Secularisation means simply that the Church — at least in the form in which it has emerged — is not wanted.'

The main problem for a sociologist examining the present position of priesthood is the society of useable information; his aim is to understand and interpret existing patterns of social structure, rather than attempt to evaluate plans or speculation about social structure which does not yet exist. There have already been changes in theological perspective in the contemporary Church but these changes have not yet altered the Church's structure to an extent which a sociologist would find significant. If the changes are occurring there is still very little known about them, in terms of answers to such questions as the parish's evaluation of the work of its priest or minister, the quality of the relationship between priest and people, and the ways (if at all) in which a priest or minister is wanted in his parish. Answers are needed which can be empirically verified or rejected.

Obtaining reliable answers to these questions is only one of the fundamental needs. There is need for recognition that the problem is not confined to one particular church or is great; it is a universal one despite local variations and factors such as culture which are characteristic of only one situation. The causes are wider and deeper than is suggested by particular problems or concerns. It is necessary to go back to the beginning and rethink the issues involved.

It is an unsatisfactory situation for the sociologist. The church leaders who ask him the questions and commission his research are disappointed with the result, for they seem no more than a sophisticated description, often written in repulsive jargon, of a situation already known, and they provide no clear solutions to the problems posed. For reasons already mentioned the sociologist himself is dissatisfied with his results, for he is frustrated by the awareness that he has not penetrated very far below the surface, and by the scarcity of reliable material.

Under these circumstances it is inevitable and valuable that this paper is open-ended and inconclusive. It could not have been anything else.

INTRODUCTION

The second sociological paper takes advantage of the symposium form – in which the speakers can move on from positions reached in earlier papers – by developing considerations which emerged in the first sociological paper, within the general question of what the sociologist can be expected to achieve. The fact of change is again taken as fundamental, and this has important consequences for the kind of model which is selected and used for an investigation of the position of the priest in contemporary society. Static models evolved in a static society are no longer effective, and this precludes the use of a functionalist model, a model drawn from a state of equilibrium, or even a systems model. Secularisation, which was only mentioned in the previous paper, receives a more extensive treatment, defined as 'the rejection or by-passing of ecclesiastical institutions by individuals or society at large, together with the religious values represented by the Church. Secularisation means simply that the Church – at least in the form in which it has emerged – is not wanted'.

The main problem for a sociologist examining the present position of priesthood is the scarcity of useable information; his aim is to understand and interpret existing patterns of social structure, rather than attempt to evaluate plans or speculation about social structure which does not yet exist. There have already been changes in theological perspective in the contemporary Church but these changes have not yet affected the Church's structure to an extent which a sociologist would find significant. If the changes are occurring there is still very little known about them, in terms of answers to such questions as the parish's evaluation of the work of its priest or minister, the quality of the relationship between priest and people, and the ways (if at all) in which a priest or minister is wanted in his parish. Answers are needed which can be empirically verified or rejected.

Obtaining reliable answers to the right questions is only one of the fundamental needs. There is need for recognition that the problem is not confined to one particular church or area; it is a universal one despite local variations and factors such as celibacy which are characteristic of only one situation. The causes are wider and deeper than is suggested by particular problems or customs. It is necessary to go back to the beginning and rethink the issues involved.

It is an unsatisfactory situation for the sociologist. The church leaders who ask him the questions and commission his research are disappointed with the results, for they seem no more than 'a sophisticated description, often written in repulsive jargon, of a situation already known', and they provide no clear solutions to the problems posed. For reasons already mentioned the sociologist himself is dissatisfied with his results, for he is frustrated by the awareness that he has not penetrated very far below the surface, and by the scarcity of reliable material.

Under these circumstances it is inevitable and valuable that this paper is open-ended and inconclusive. It could not have been anything else.

II A Search for New Approaches to the Sociological Study of the Priesthood

WILLIAM PICKERING

IT IS PROBABLY A TRUISM TO SAY THAT EVERY INTELLECTUAL and scientific advance has been made by the enunciation of a problem. The problem may be postulated by a group of people who view it in the light of their own wants or needs, or it may present itself only to the mind of the academic. Some problems are solved and so cease to be problems, but those that are old are frequently shelved because they become so thoroughly worked over that little more can be said or done about them. It then becomes more fruitful to turn to other problems which show some prospect of solution. Again, discoveries or the emergence of new social situations give rise to fresh problems, thus allowing the

BIOGRAPHICAL NOTE

WILLIAM PICKERING *has been Lecturer in Social Studies in the University of Newcastle upon Tyne since 1966, after eight years as Associate Professor of Sociology at St John's College, University of Manitoba. He edited* Anglican-Methodist Relations: Some Institutional Factors, *and was co-author of* Taken for Granted: A Survey of the Parish Clergy of the Anglican Church of Canada. *He has been an Anglican priest since 1951.*

older issues, at least for a time, to be forgotten. The development of sociology is no exception to this movement. New problems are tackled as old ones are set aside. Quite often shifts in sociology have occurred through the awareness of a particular social problem or evil, or through the advent of political changes. Further, it is not unknown for changes in theoretical issues to have been initiated by problems of expediency. Alongside this there exists another factor. What the sociologist studies theoretically, and more frequently what he undertakes of a practical kind, is determined to a large extent by research grants. These are usually given for specific projects and are related to what might be generally held to be important social issues.

It is a common charge that the sociologist has a poor record of solving the problems with which he is presented or which he sets himself. He does not move on to new ones as a result of having solved the old ones. Where he has been successful has been in tackling issues that are little more than superficial. But leaving this argument aside – and it is open to considerable debate – it can be stated without fear of denial that the sociologist makes the claim that at least he sheds light on a given problem and may point to possible ways of solution, without at the same time necessarily producing answers of the kind comparable to those of the natural scientist. However, often the charges levelled against the sociologist by the outsider are unrealistic. The sociologist is often asked to tackle problems that are not within his powers to solve for he may not possess the tools necessary to find the answers. Frequently the question he is asked is not a valid question within the terms of his science: he thus becomes the butt of criticism when he fails to prove himself to be the *deus ex machina* the outsider may think he is. These points become well illustrated in examining studies made in the sociology of the priesthood.

The priesthood or professional ministry of the Church has of recent years been the subject of a fair amount of enquiry, sociological as well as theological. The reason is obvious. Issues have presented themselves which have emerged out of a new religious and social situation, and which add up to something bordering on a crisis. Observers in the Churches and beyond them all appear to be agreed on the phenomenon itself, namely, that the contemporary priesthood or ministry is characterised by uncertainty, turmoil and depletion. Fifty or a hundred years ago such qualities were either not so pronounced or were completely absent. The so-called hard facts, which have given immediate rise to the problem, can be spelt out in more detail, and although they have been well rehearsed and commented on elsewhere, they might briefly be mentioned here in the light of what is to be said later.[1] They are:

1. A relative or absolute decline in the numbers of priests or ministers.
2. An increase in the average age of those in training and a decline in the level of academic achievement.
3. The fact that many leave the parish ministry for teaching and other specialised work in the Church.
4. That men leave the priesthood altogether though they may work as laymen.
5. That others again leave both the priesthood and the Church.
6. That there exist dissatisfactions and confusions about the required duties of priests, especially among younger men.
7. A relative loss of social status.

Most of these characteristics apply to all the major denominations and occur irrespective of country. Certain characteristics of course may not be applicable in all cases and they may be more marked in one country than another. For example, the Episcopal Church of the United States has reported an increase in the numbers ordained between 1960 and 1967.[2] In England, the Anglican and Free Churches are particularly pressed by falling numbers, an increase in the age structure of the clergy, and a decline in academic standards. However, without pressing the matter further it is reasonable to hold that the characteristics that have been mentioned are well nigh universal in the Christian world.

The contemporary state of the priesthood has its own fascination for the academic who, as a disinterested outsider, may feel

---

[1] See previous paper by R. Towler.

[2] *Canadian Churchman*, November 1968, Toronto. Statistics for the same church in certain categories of membership also showed increases; in other categories there were decreases.

drawn to study the situation. But those within the institution itself have a concern which is of a different order. They are alarmed or dismayed by what is happening and ultimately wish to see the current trend halted, or at least some kind of readjustment effected. The result has been that church leaders, perhaps too late in the day, have encouraged professionals to tackle the problem of analysis, in some cases offering research grants. In addition, individual scholars within the Church have felt compelled to tackle the issue on their own initiative.

Assuming that the starting point of the sociological studies is directly or indirectly the fact that the contemporary priesthood is failing to function according to its long accepted goals and ideals, how have sociologists approached their task and how far have they been successful? These are large questions, which if they are to be answered carefully, need detailed documentation inappropriate to a paper such as this. All that can be done for the purposes on hand is to indicate directions and trends. There has been a considerable amount of statistical work on the clergy viewed as a professional or occupational group. As well as the production of basic demographic material, which has been particularly in evidence in the Roman Catholic Church, extensive studies have been carried out in most churches on recruitment and training. But in line with the contemporary trend in the sociology of the professions, questions have been raised about such matters as adequate pay, job-satisfaction, uncertainty of function, and so on. Surveys have taken into account the ways in which the clergy view their parishes or congregations and attention has been given to such questions as: Do the clergy feel lonely or isolated? Are their energies overtaxed? Do they experience conflict in their work? Do they find congregations meet their expectations? These and similar issues have been closely analysed and refined, and no doubt adequate answers have been obtained. Certainly in the United States, and to a lesser degree in England, much emphasis has been placed on the problems of organisation and administration – problems which to say the least are strongly disliked by the clergy at large. Research along the lines just mentioned has been carried out in nearly every major denomination and in almost every country, though obviously some studies have been more thorough than others, and certain denominations or countries have emphasised one aspect more than another. The extent and number of the studies indicates at least the universality of the acceptance of the problem and the realisation of its seriousness for the Churches.

Yet the results of the surveys that have been carried out, useful though they have been in underlining the problem, do not seem to answer the basic question. To talk about role-conflict, job-satisfaction, poor salary, or celibacy does not penetrate to the heart of the matter. Dissatisfaction with the results is frequently expressed and it stems from two sources. The first comes from those who frequently pay the piper – the church leaders themselves who commission the research. The tunes that are played do not please. Leaders give half-hearted applause because as they say: 'We have heard it all before; the tune is an old one.' In their eyes all the sociologist does is to produce a sophisticated description, often written in repulsive jargon, of a situation already known. Instead of revealing the hidden, or what is operating beneath the surface in the way for example that Marx did for class analysis, all the sociologist succeeds in doing is to substantiate gossip. The second source of dissatisfaction stems from research workers themselves, and amongst them I include myself, who have become increasingly aware of the fact that they have not plumbed the depths. They have dealt with only peripheral matters and their sense of frustration matches that of the clergy themselves. It may well be that those who have been undertaking the research may have been asking the wrong questions, not of the clergy, but of themselves. Objective though the sociologist may claim to be, he may be blinded by the facts, or only accept those that are in some measure reassuring. He may not be bold enough to see the consequences of his findings. Is it that he does not apply a ruthless logic to his conclusions?

The problem has to be approached afresh. To do this it is necessary to go back to the beginning and to try to re-think the issues. Questions of a more fundamental nature may have to be raised: at least, the questions will have to be checked and if possible refined. However, in order to proceed with this task certain assumptions have to be made at the very beginning and three such assumptions are put forward which I hold to be implicit in any re-thinking of the problem.

The first is the acceptance of the facts about the contemporary priesthood which give rise to the problem and offer the means of defining it. These must form the starting point – a point on which observers inside as well as outside the Church can agree. Further, the problem to be analysed represents a social fact that is to be found in all the larger Churches within the Christian world, though in some Churches it may be of different proportions than in others. Objections might be raised that the situation is not as universal as it appears in the first instance. For example, an important sociological factor exists in the Roman Catholic Church which is absent in all the other Churches. I refer to celibacy. No one can deny that a celibate priesthood may limit recruitment, and at this time, with certain social and religious pressures, may be the cause of many priests leaving the ministry in order to marry. Withdrawal may also be an act of protest against what is seen to be an unfair system. It has been estimated that in the United States alone in the two years, 1966 and 1967, 711 priests ceased to hold office, of whom about 500 were diocesan priests.[3] Yet although celibacy is a burning issue in the Church and will probably be so for some time to come, it is wrong to assume that it is the only problem of the priesthood, or that if marriage were allowed all would be well. Studies carried out in Canada have shown that loneliness, for example, is as prevalent among married clergy of the Anglican Church as it is among the unmarried.[4] It is better to view the problem of celibacy on its own and to see the dissensions to which it gives rise as an effect rather than a cause. Again, objections might be raised on the grounds that the Roman Catholic Church, unlike other Churches, is undergoing considerable reforms and it has moved a great distance theologically and ecclesiastically in an incredibly short time. The changes have given rise to bewilderment among clergy and laity alike. In many respects the Church is accepting

---

[3] *Toronto Star*, April 3, 1968.

[4] W. S. F. PICKERING and J. L. BLANCHARD, *Taken for Granted: A Survey of the Parish Clergy of the Anglican Church of Canada*, 1967, Toronto: The General Synod of the Anglican Church of Canada, p. 22.

ideas and practices which have marked resemblances to what heretofore have been characteristics of the Protestant Churches. But a certain amount of turmoil can also be found in these Churches with a growth of radicalism in the form of secular theology. The Roman Catholic hierarchy faces severe problems in trying to contain the flood of changes that are taking place; some of which stem from the 16th century Reformation ideas and others from modern theological and liturgical research. But despite all this, despite the fact that the crisis is a crisis of authority and control, what is going on in the Roman Catholic Church is sociologically similar to that which is occurring in non-Roman Churches, and this is particularly the case of the doubt, uncertainty, and frustration which is found to exist among the clergy. It is possible to argue that the problem of the priesthood or ministry is basically different in each of the major Churches and therefore separate explanations have to be sought in every Church. But the case for separation or differentiation is not justified in the light of the evidence we possess. Behind denominational differences there lurks a common problem, that of a malfunctioning and depleted professional ministry. Social forces are at work which affect not one Church but all the Churches. It is a matter of common sense to assume that the problem is universal. If this is taken for granted, then the explanation of what is happening must also be applicable *mutatis mutandis* to all Churches. To examine one Church and select features which are in some measure unique to that Church is to miss the wood for the trees.

The second assumption is a search for right questions. This means a selection of questions, the answers to which help to explain the problem under consideration. But the questions must be those which can be answered sociologically, that is, they must invite answers which can be empirically verified or rejected. Worthwhile research turns on the formulation of relevant questions. This point cannot be too strongly emphasised because not only is it crucial to good research, it is frequently an issue of misunderstanding between the professional sociologist and the church leader. The leader has been known to ask questions that are impossible to answer with the somewhat crude tools the sociologist has at his command. When the sociologist tries to comply with such demands he usually ends up by losing face with the authorities and he becomes accused of doing bad sociology by his fellow professionals. Further, leaders up to now have requested information which can be immediately used to right what they see as a bad or worsening situation. They want sociologists to produce formulae which will bring about a given end. This kind of thinking is not only a grave misunderstanding of what sociology is about, it also assumes a great deal, for example, the possibility of achieving the given end adopted by the leaders. But this consideration is of secondary importance. What is more important is the positing of questions which are sociologically valid and which are of such a kind as to make a contribution to explanation and understanding. This is in fact the most difficult part in the building up of sociology itself.

In order to dispel any misunderstanding a point is raised which is nothing more than a rider and which emerges out of what has already been said. The task of the sociologist is that of establishing an explanation and understanding of social phenomena of the past and present. Although his eventual aim may be to predict in the manner of many natural scientists, he has not yet reached the stage where this is a likelihood. For this reason if no other, he cannot forecast the future. He debases his profession if he substitutes guessing for prediction. Nor is it his job to dogmatise over solutions to social problems. Contrary to a lot of misinformed opinion, sociology is not a reformist study.

The third assumption is that any relevant examination of the priesthood must be seen in terms of change. The 'hard data' on which the problem rests all indicate that what is happening is something new or something which is part of a continual process of change which has been taking place for some period. No matter how the problem is approached the assumption must be the same, namely, the phenomena under review display elements of change. The model that the sociologist is forced to use can only be, therefore, one of change and this would apply whether he looks at the situation as a whole and selects a 'grand model' of change, or whether he selects elements within the whole and estimates how far they have changed. Thus, a functionalist model, an equilibrium model, or even a systems model, can have but limited application and such models are better avoided. Role-analysis has at least this merit that it can be adapted to the notion of change. Roles at different periods of time can be compared and changes noted. The division of the overall problem into elements which are not analysed in a way as to show change is a lost labour. To demonstrate the existence of inadequate salaries, or role-conflict, or the fact that the priest is or is not a member of the professions, is not enough: what is necessary, supposing for the moment that such lines of analysis are selected, is to show whether such conditions existed in the past, whether such conditions were formally held to be important or significant, and whether the changes are significant for the present situation. It is all too readily assumed that the implications of a given factor are obvious, and because they are not spelt out, the research appears unconvincing and often superficial. For example, poor salaries or celibacy hinder recruitment to the priesthood only under certain social and religious conditions. Role-conflict is a threat only to people of certain psychological dispositions. A depleted ministry means poor recruitment only on certain assumptions. And one may well ask: Why should not the uncertain and weak state of the Churches act as a challenge to young men to enter the priesthood rather than a deterrent? What is called for in analysis is the establishment of changes that have occurred and at the same time a demonstration that the changes are relevant to an explanation of the problem under consideration. In brief, any explanation of changes associated with the social dimension of the priesthood has to take into account the milieu or changes in the milieu in which the priesthood exists.

For the rest of the paper I shall consider this third assumption in more detail but before I do so it might be helpful to try to analyse the basic work the priest undertakes – a necessary task in any attempt to go back to first principles.

The sociologist is not in a position to determine how far traditional concepts of the priesthood or ministry have been faithful to New Testament ideas or those of the early Church. He can but accept the model that has been established with the passing of centuries. The two basic terms for consideration are priest in the Catholic Church and minister in the Protestant Churches.[5]

The very nature of the priesthood is to create, sustain or mediate relationships. The priest is the chief functionary of liturgical worship or cultic practice and as such stands before God and in the name of the people who claim allegiance to God. He is the operator of sacraments by which it is believed the people enter into a particular relationship with God. The authority of the priest is his ordination by the Church in the name of God but at the same time the priest acts as leader of a group of people who wish to be or who are in some measure related to God. People are encouraged to see the priest as their representative, chosen or sent. It is he who is able to control or sustain their relationship to God. The priest does not act in a vacuum: as a functionary he is tied to the people by acting on their behalf, for both he and they claim loyalty to God and to one another. In some sense it can also be claimed that God speaks through his priest to the people so that the priest both acts and speaks in the name of God in carrying out basic tasks and in maintaining doctrine. His position can be represented thus:

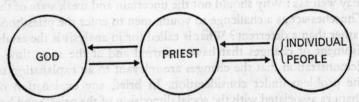

The Protestant minister sees his work in a different way. The Reformers openly rejected the idea of a priestly functionary who comes between the individual or the community and God. The individual enters into a direct relationship with God albeit through Christ, and he does not require the work of a human mediator. Crudely put, every man is his own priest. Salvation is not to be obtained by partaking in priest-controlled sacraments.

---

[5] The role of bishop is of the utmost importance in the structure of the Catholic Church but within the terms of reference of the paper the notion of bishop is excluded.

Nonetheless the traditional Protestant Churches created an order of ministers who are ordained and who are held to be leaders of congregations. They are the chief though not exclusive functionaries in liturgical worship. They represent their congregations and even direct them. In their work of preaching and performing pastoral duties, ministers see themselves as leading their congregations to God. It can also be said of ministers that God speaks through them to his people and this is taken to be part of the task of preaching. Clearly Protestant ministers do not claim to act as mediators in the Catholic sense but they can be seen as 'midwives' in bringing people to God and in helping them to be better Christians. In this respect they are mediators, but they, like the Catholic priests, stand with their people – are tied in with their people – in establishing relationships between God and His elect. Thus the position of ministers can be seen to be like this:

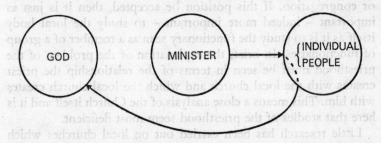

The sociologist is not immediately concerned with the relationship that the priest, or minister, or people claims to have with God. But he does see that both the priest and the minister have defined relationships with the local church and it is on these relationships that he initially focuses his attention.[6] Indeed, the difference between the Catholic priest and the Protestant minister is not significantly different for the larger problem which is the

[6] It is not necessary for the purposes on hand to delineate precisely the group with which the priest or minister is associated – the worshipping body, the congregation, or the parish in the technical sense of the word. The argument is that the functionary has to be viewed in relation to a reference group, which perhaps he himself has to define. If the group is taken to include non-believers or the lapsed, it would most likely have at its centre a worshipping body with which the priest is closely tied.

subject of this paper.[7] They are both religious leaders who stand within a group of people whom they represent and for whom they bear a responsibility. Their aim, Catholic or Protestant, is to endeavour to see that their people sustain their relationships with God. It is here that the very *raison d'être* of the priest or minister is to be found. For the purposes of studying the contemporary situation and of examining changes that may have occurred over the centuries, it is sociologically valid to see in the first instance the work of the Catholic priest and Protestant minister not only of the same order, but in terms of relationships maintained with local worshipping bodies.

The priesthood cannot be understood in itself as if it consisted of an isolated group of functionaries performing purely technical operations, as for example, machinists in a factory. Rather, it has to be seen against the immediate background of the local church or congregation. If this position be accepted, then it is just as important – indeed more important – to study the local body itself as it is to study the functionary seen as a member of a group of functionaries. In brief, the explanation of the problem of the priesthood must be seen in terms of the relationship the priest creates with the local church and which the local church creates with him. This means a close analysis of the Church itself and it is here that studies of the priesthood seem most deficient.

Little research has been carried out on local churches which directly elucidates the problems associated with the priesthood or ministry. Sociologists are hard pressed to find material from secondary sources that will immediately help them deal with the issues of the contemporary priesthood. In fact there have been very few studies which have had as their subject matter the formal or informal relationships between the priest and the parishioners nor any which show how parishioners evaluate their relationships with the priest.[8]

---

[7] Cf. TH. M. STEEMAN, 'The Priest as Socio-Religious Leader', n *Actes de la Conférence Internationale, Clergy in Church and Society*, 1967, Rome: Conférence Internationale de Sociologie Religieuse.

[8] Of the books which have in some way dealt with the subject, the following might be mentioned: C. K. WARD, *Priests and People*, Liverpool 1961; F. BOULARD, 'How Christians regard the Priest Today', in *The Sacrament of Orders*, London 1962, pp. 297–313; J. H. FICHTER, *Dynamics of a City Parish*, Chicago 1951. The results are

It might be suggested at this point that we proceed no further. If, as it has been maintained that the relationship established between priest and people be examined in the light of the people who constitute the local church and no such studies exist, extended exploration along these lines is, for the time being at least, an impossibility. However, it seems worthwhile to consider briefly approaches that could be made in the examination of the local scene and at the same time employ findings of a wider kind, as well as the results of small limited surveys which deal with the local church and the place of the priest within it. As soon as the parish door is opened, all kinds of possibilities are presented. However, three questions are singled out which are useful avenues of approach. They cannot now be answered adequately but they might be empirically examined in the future and lead to a fresh understanding of the emergence of a depleted and unsure priesthood. They are:

1. How does the parish evaluate the work of the priest or minister?
2. What is the quality of the relations between priest and people?
3. Is the priest wanted in the parish?

Surveys which deal with the attitude of parishioners towards the clergy are not only few in number, they are by their very nature unreliable. Respondents frequently do not understand the nature of the questions put to them, nor are they accustomed to think along the lines set out by them. C. K. Ward found in answer to the question 'Which do you consider the three most important of the various duties of a priest in a parish?' that some parishioners either disregarded liturgical duties or assumed they were not included.[9] Although half the respondents mentioned such functions, just under two-thirds referred to visiting homes of parishioners as the most important of the priest's duties; and Ward

keenly awaited of a large survey being undertaken in the area of Lille. See J. VERSCHEURE, 'Les évolutions d'une recherche psycho-sociologique sur le prêtre dans la region nord de la France', in *Actes de la Conférence Internationale, Clergy in Church and Society*, 1967, Rome: Conférence Internationale de Sociologie Religieuse.

[9] C. K. WARD, *Priests and People*, Liverpool 1961, p. 56.

concluded: 'there would appear no doubt that those interviewed expected the priest to be in close contact with parishioners and considered such contact extremely important.'[10] From a survey that was carried out in a large Anglican parish in Winnipeg, the response to a similar question produced results close to those found in the Roman Catholic parish in Liverpool in which Fr Ward conducted his research. Only 15 per cent referred to liturgical functions but half the congregation gave pastoral work, which included visiting, counselling, working with young people, as one of the most important duties of the parish minister.[11] The members of the same congregation also listed personal qualities they wanted their minister to have and these indicated a wish that he should be a good pastor. Despite the meagreness of the information and the likelihood of unreliability, a common attitude in all probability exists in parishes in the west that the most popular duties that can be carried out by the priest are those associated with pastoral work. Surely with the passing of years there is a marked change in this matter? Parishioners now want to enter into close contact with the clergy. The social distance which formerly separated the priest or minister from his people is diminishing in the face of a relatively more democratic form of society. His office may still be respected but people want to have a priest whose personal qualities they can admire and accept and who at the same time can be treated as a friend on near or equal terms. Once again, relative differences will be found between denomination and denomination, country and country, class and class, but the tendency is doubtless universal. In this connection it is interesting to note that more attention is being given in theological colleges to pastoral training or to specialised training in clinical theology, and the clergy themselves are often reported as saying that they feel most satisfied in their work in the performance of pastoral duties.[12] A cleavage thus becomes apparent. On the one hand the priest's major work is traditionally that of a cultic functionary; on the other, his own parishioners – let alone people outside the Church – appreciate him mostly in terms of pastoral and personal relationships and do not welcome him

[10] Ibid., p. 57.   [11] Quoted in PICKERING and BLANCHARD, op. cit., pp. 224–5.
[12] E.g., PICKERING and BLANCHARD, op. cit., p. 56.

adopting the role of social worker or political agitator, except in extreme conditions in the parish. If this is in fact a real conflict and can be empirically shown to be extensive then its importance can hardly be overestimated, for it shows at least the existence of a conflict of ideals between priest and people or a conflict between old essential duties and new ones. It may also indicate the existence of a conflict in the mind of the priest himself who finds that he spends more time counselling people than in performing priestly duties. But it is not certain that the conflict does exist. While parishioners apparently place high values on pastoral concerns, they may not fully appreciate, or verbally express opinions on the role of the priest as a cultic functionary or even as a preacher. The surveys, so far, tell us little more than the kinds of qualities congregations want of their ministers. Those congregations which have been questioned may not have faced the possibility of being involved in a church where there is no permanent functionary, or they may not have learnt from experience what happens when the parish system or congregation is no longer supported by a professional leader. It has to be admitted that one of the difficulties in pursuing this question is the impossibility of obtaining comparable data for previous decades. How can the attitudes of parishioners towards the clergy be determined now that former parishioners are dead? All that can be done is to make deductions from historical material and this has limited value compared with the data that can be collected about the present situation. Nevertheless, studies along these lines need to be undertaken on the attitudes and concepts parishioners have of their priest.

We turn to the second question about the qualities of the relations between the priest and people. In times past the lines of communication between the priest and his flock were mainly unidirectional. The priest was often an educated person – relatively speaking perhaps the only educated person in the parish – and parishioners came to be instructed by him or had instruction thrust upon them. They learnt the facts of their faith which was summed up in the creeds or based on the Bible. Instruction was of a catechetical kind. The information they received was seldom challenged or thought out by the parishioners. The priest saw his teaching accomplished when his flock had absorbed the facts of orthodoxy. Some changes to this generalised pattern occurred at various points in history, for example, during the Reformation and again in the 19th century with the growth of secular thought and of new methods of teaching. The prevailing attitude in western society today is that people should not learn facts by rote but that the facts should be accommodated through experience and reason, and further, that in certain categories of data people should be encouraged to apply a freedom of interpretation. As a result of his theological education, the priest today may hold these new ideas himself, but his parishioners despite their own education may not view religious belief and education in the same light. As in former years they want to be told facts and they become bewildered if a priest adopts a method that calls for their own decision and interpretation. He may well desire to teach in a dialectical method but this does not 'work' in many parishes because of the wide difference in background between the priest and the people. The priest would like to be involved in greater theological discussion, but in most parishes at least the response is meagre.

There is another aspect of the new relationship of the priest to his people. Just as it is no longer unidirectional in terms of teaching, so it is no longer unidirectional in terms of administration and influence. He not only influences parishioners; they also influence him.

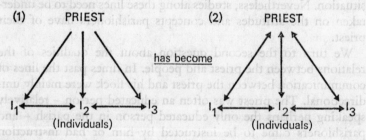

The priest is now involved in a network of mutually dependent relationships and these occur at both the level of official organisation as well as at an informal or even unconscious level where the thought and practice of the laity may make considerable impact on him. This change has been brought about partly by the reduction of social distance between priest and people, and also because, as in the Protestant Churches and now more recently in the Roman Catholic Church, the involvement of lay people in the affairs of the Church has inevitably brought about a closer relationship between priest or minister and his people. As a result of what has recently happened in the Roman Catholic Church, the priest may find that he is inadequately trained to deal with the new types of leadership that are demanded and which are more democratic in form than was formerly the case.

The types of relations established in a social group are in part determined by the nature of the group itself. Where the group is formal relations between officials or members may well be of the same order. If the group is loosely structured relations may be informal. In classifying a contemporary congregation or local church, a sociologist describes it as an organised voluntary association. It consists of a group of people who, of their own volition, enter into membership, or who as children are made members, and who again may withdraw their membership if they so wish. The law of Britain and most western European countries does not force people to be members of a Church nor prevents them from so doing. Indeed, the law may protect people over and against the Church. Basic physical and social needs of individuals are fulfilled without the requirement of church membership. Religious persecution is absent. In these ways the Church is a voluntary society alongside other voluntary societies which are such a marked feature of social life in the modern western world. They attract people in terms of a common interest, particularly leisure-time pursuits, and I have drawn attention elsewhere to the parallels that exist between a leisure-time association and certain elements of some contemporary Churches.[13] To be sure, the Churches claim to deal with issues which have eternal significance but their form of association is close to that of a Friendly Society or an Old Age Pensioners' Club. By contrast, the Church in the middle ages can hardly be said to have been a voluntary society, nor indeed were the Churches which were formed by the Reformation in the

[13] W. S. F. PICKERING, 'Religion – a Leisure-time Pursuit?' in D. Martin (ed.), *A Sociological Yearbook of Religion in Britain*, London 1968.

16th century. Up until the 18th or 19th centuries a national Church was viewed as a society which was or had to be embraced by everyone. Membership was enforced by law and penalties were exerted on those who would not comply. There is now complete freedom to become involved in church life or to withdraw from it. This has meant both locally and nationally that the Church has lost considerable status in society and with it considerable power. The clergy as a consequence may be of the opinion that they are now asked to be leaders of groups which are in a sense voluntary and relatively unimportant. The links that are created between clergy and people are thus no longer 'professional' links, for they have ceased to be links associated with power.

And so to the third question. To what extent are the clergy wanted by local congregations? Contrary to the expectations of Marx and Durkheim, organised religion has shown remarkable powers of tenacity and persistence, though contemporary prophets might proclaim the end is at last at hand. The outward structures remain; many parishes still flourish; there are signs of fresh impetus in such a movement as *aggiornamento* (bringing up to date). There is thus the continued need for priests in terms of the demands of parishes. That ordained men feel they are no longer wanted is in part a loss of nerve. Most men who enter the priesthood have a sense of service both to the Church as an organisation as well as to the people who make up the Church. The priest is likely to respond where he sees a need. To date, whether or not he feels he is needed has depended on his own estimation of the parish situation and perhaps that of his superiors. He has not based his sense of need on what the parishioners themselves say. Apart from personal likes and dislikes, can it be said that a priest is wanted by his flock? Very few attempts have been made to answer this question and there are critics who will hold that the gathering of information of this kind is of little worth owing to its unreliability. I think it can be assumed that most local churches do want a full-time functionary in so far as they need someone who will perform liturgical functions and who will act as their leader or representative in various matters. Once again variations may well exist between denominations. In some churches, such as those of the Roman Catholic Church, parishioners realise that as matters stand their church would cease to function without a priest. But even where lay people are empowered to perform liturgically, and as in fact they do in the Methodist Church, a minister is usually given high status, and local churches closely associated with a minister are held to be 'superior' to those which only receive visits from a full-time functionary. Although there is in all probability a general wish on the part of a parish for the services of a professional priest or minister, parishioners tend not to convey to their appointed functionary the fact that he is wanted. They take it for granted that they will have a leader: often they take him for granted. They assume that he can deal satisfactorily with their situation and with the fact that the parish is in a milieu beset by secularisation. The clergy complained in the Canadian survey that the parishioners did not go out of their way to discover the problems the parish minister had to face and to help him deal with them.[14] That parishioners want to have their own priest or minister doubtless stems from an elementary realisation that as a group of worshippers or active believers they need a leader, and in Catholic groups an ordained functionary. They do not have to be sociologists to know that some form of leadership is essential for the persistence of most types of groups. Those trained in leadership are the obvious people to be in charge of the congregation or parish. As a national Church is at present constituted, for example the Church of England with its 15,000 parishes, a sudden switch to a part-time ministry with perhaps the ordination of many lay people, would bring about sheer socio-religious havoc. In terms of what members would like in the matter of leadership, there is little shadow of doubt that it is a full-time functionary where obviously the size of the local church makes some sense of the demand. That men are not responding to such a need – that many are withdrawing from parish work – points to two facts. (a) That potential leaders are considering their own needs and satisfactions rather than those of the Church, that is, there may well now be a decline in pastoral concern as classically understood. (b) That parish work in itself does not satisfy a sufficient number of potential leaders. To perform the cult and to

[14] PICKERING and BLANCHARD, op. cit., pp. 14ff.

lead the group does not attract the would-be full-time functionary to the extent it did.

Although the priest may not be in the demand he once was for leading worship on Sundays and for conducting weekday services, in so far as attendances may be declining, he still finds himself wanted in other ways. Until recently at least, reports of surveys showed that where the worshipping body declines, there still persists a demand for *les rites de passage*. People may show but limited inclination for regular worship, but they seldom hesitate to approach the priest or minister for marriage, for the baptism of their offspring; for the burial of their relatives; and even first communion or confirmation for their children, where such is the practice of the Church. In this sense there is demand for the priest who alone can perform the rites. No priest, no rite; and where a layman can act as a functionary, people feel it is better to have the services of the priest. *Les rites de passage*, it can be argued, are the last ditch of the confessing Christian. They are related to important points in a person's life and if religion means anything at all, it has significance at moments like these. The demand arises from the people themselves. However, there exists a dilemma at this point because many priests do not cherish functioning at rites when the persons involved are not regular worshippers. The task is to be welcomed for the faithful but not for those whom Fichter calls the 'dormant' Catholics[15] or, we should add, the 'nothing-arians'. The priest maintains the rites are held out of context and here he passes theological judgment. There are signs that the number of outsiders who are applying for *les rites de passage* is now declining. It may well be that the reason for such a change is a more honest and logical approach to religion on the part of those outside the Churches. But also the clergy themselves may be undermining the demand in that they are making it increasingly difficult for the outsider to participate in *les rites de passage*, and they are bringing this about by tightening up regulations and by laying down new conditions for participation.

Careful documentation is hardly required to show that by and large the number of active parishioners who constitute the worshipping body has declined with the passing of years. The amount

[15] Ibid., p. 35.

of contraction may vary with denomination or region. Frequently, though not always, it is the established Church or the Church supported by the nation which has contracted the most. Churches in cities have suffered more, relatively speaking, than churches in rural areas. In terms of worship on Sundays the priest may find that overall demands have diminished and that his usefulness as a consequence is less obvious. He may of course be conscious of the fact that he still dealing with a large congregation but in previous generations it would have been larger than it is at the present time. In terms of active worshippers the parish has shrunk from P_1 to P_2 (see Diagram below) and the functionary will inevitably realise that he is working in a contracted situation.

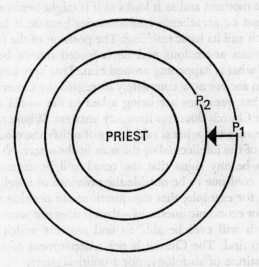

The change from P_1 to P_2 is generally explained as the result of secularisation and no analysis of the priest-parish relationship in contemporary society can be understood apart from a consideration of those forces loosely grouped under the name of secularisation. Secularisation is here defined as the rejection or by-passing of ecclesiastical institutions by individuals or society at large, together with the religious values represented by the Church. Secularisation means simply that the Church – at least in the form in which it has emerged – is not wanted. Its services are not

required to the extent they once were: its ideology is considered
to be irrelevant to modern demands. In the context of society at
large rather than within the worshipping body, the priest feels he
is not wanted. The world is changing and what the priest has to
offer is openly disregarded. The logic is that in time he will go
out of business and therefore out of existence. The priest can be
likened to a lamp-lighter. Lamp-lighters were in demand in the
19th century when gas lamps were used extensively to light the
streets. Few such lamps still exist in London, and perhaps lamp-
lighters will be no more for the very simple reason that there will
be no more lamps to light. If there are no local churches for the
priest to lead he will inevitably cease to exist. Secular society, as
it is at the moment and as it looks as if it might become, does not
need priests or preachers or missionaries because it has rejected
the Church and its basic teaching. The position of the functionary
thus becomes anomalous and he is forced out of business by
reason of what is happening around him. That very large sections
of modern society now completely disregard the Church is due to
the fact that questions are being asked in the world at large to
which the Church does not have any answers. Where the Church
does have answers, what is said does not satisfy the modern mind,
be it that of the intellectual or the man-in-the-street. Nor do there
appear to be any signs that the trend will be reversed. If the
questions continue to be outside the province of religion and the
Church – for example, that the questions are nothing more than
technical or economic questions – then it does not seem likely that
the Church will ever be able to find answers which society is
striving to find. The Church is not a department of economics,
nor an institute of sociology, nor a political party.

Seen over a broad spectrum, the changes that have taken place
within the Churches over the past century can best be analysed in
terms of ecology. By that is meant that the Church has tried to
adjust itself internally to meat external threats to its own existence.
The external threat has been secularisation, which has in some
form penetrated into the Church itself. At the Reformation
changes occurred largely, though not entirely, by reason of a
shift in religious thinking. From the 19th century onwards the
changes that have taken place have been those which have

emerged from the fact that the Church found itself in an environment that was becoming indifferent to religion in any shape or form. The Church responded then and continues to respond by internal change but the questions arise, 'Have the changes been effective?' and, 'Are there any limits to the changes before the identity of the institution is lost?'

In what has just been said, an extraordinarily brief attempt has been made to answer the question of why the clergy at this present time suffer from a loss of nerve and to account for the dichotomy between an expressed need on the part of congregations for a full-time functionary and the poor response on the part of potential respondents.

PART FOUR

INTRODUCTION

In this paper Dom Sebastian Moore suggests that the Christian faith looks back to an historical person, but it finds there a person who proclaimed as fact the Kingdom to which we all aspire, and who was himself plunged into darkness and death just as we in our aspirations are contradicted by the facts of this world.

'Celebration' is a key concept in the view presented here, for celebration comes from the heart of man set free, and is shared enjoyment of that freedom. The eucharist expresses the quality of celebration which we have learned from him who set us free and shares in our celebration. This solemn, Christ-centred ritual, expresses the insistent truth that man is one and lives fully only in one world, and that he is prepared to be crucified rather than compromise this freedom. Christ does not stand outside and legislate for a cult he has initiated; he acknowledges himself to be one of our brethren, enters into the spirit of our celebration and empowers it with the life he has earned in dying.

Man is a concrete reality beyond ethnic and cultural limits, and his celebration cannot be expressed through a eucharist which is frozen in the thought forms and theology of any particular period or culture.

BIOGRAPHICAL NOTE

SEBASTIAN MOORE *is a monk of Downside Abbey who read English at Cambridge and a D.D. at St Anselmo in Rome. He has taught theology at Downside, edited* The Downside Review *and been parish priest in the centre of Liverpool. He is the author of* God is a New Language *and* No Exit *and* The Experience of Prayer.

12 The Secular Implications of Liturgy

SEBASTIAN MOORE

WHAT A TITLE! IF EVER THERE WAS AN INVITATION TO BE dreary, this is it. For me however, this title is an invitation to be contemplative. I have to look at Jesus instituting the eucharist. I have to look at him as only I can: which means that I must, in looking, be knowing myself, recognising anew the life that stirs in me and has so many sources – all that I have read and made real sense of, all that I have learned of life and love and friendship, the experience of prayer, all that here and now makes me tick. And I have to look at Jesus making the eucharist as only a modern man can look: which means that I must wonder whether he did institute the eucharist. As a modern man I am by nature critical. I have lost the ease and innocence with which an earlier age moved between the worlds of fact and of imagination hardly perceiving the difference between the two. And when I come to Jesus I am made most acutely conscious of this difference between fact and myth, or between life and liturgical celebration. For Jesus seems somehow to unite in his own person the diverse worlds in which man lives, and it is only because he does this that he is for the believer the creative centre of the world. But I want to know how he does this, and what it would mean to do this, and what it would have meant for him to do this and for his disciples to understand him as doing this.

I am incredibly puzzled here. I must take stock of the fact that past Christian ages did not have this puzzle. For them the worlds of man had not come apart, and so there was no problem as to how Jesus could have made them all one. It was no odder for Jesus to move from the ritual supper table to the cross than it was for them to move from the accolade to the bloody combat. They would not have had that feeling of oddness that I have at the thought of a man celebrating his own death with ritual and solemnly enjoining this celebration on his followers. And I must note that even today the men we call theologians show a disturbing unawareness of this kind of oddity. For them 'the supper' and 'the cross' are pieces to fit together in a theological jigsaw. How precisely do they fit together? Theory follows theory. The deeper question as to how they *can* fit together and in doing so have any human verisimilitude does not enter the game. Hence the glazed look which shows in the eyes of scientist and philosopher when two theologians at a conference start going for each other. What are they *doing*, these theology men? They seem to have a discipline of their own whose only distinguishing feature is that it ignores the disciplines that must control the study of the very things with which they profess to deal.

Now such a workout as I am here proposing to myself is essential to the task I have undertaken. I mean that an alert and contemplative awareness of what stands at the origin of our Christian worship is essential if we are to find the latter's 'secular implications'. It is itself the first and critical step in that enquiry. An enquiry which takes our liturgy as given, which starts off from an understanding of the liturgy that employs a preferred theological theory as to how it works, and then seeks to relate *this* liturgy to the world and the world to it, is doomed to become the latest example of religious gimmickry. The bread of life which it offers to an increasingly puzzled world will have been processed by that out-of-this-world thinking that usually goes for theology.

Nevertheless I think and write as a believer. For me, in an experience which I believe to be of God the very truth, Jesus *is* the meeting and oneing of the worlds. Indeed it is only because he is that that the question as to *how on earth* he can be this has such urgency for me.

So let me try to pose the problem as exactly as I can. Biblical scholarship took a big leap forward in awareness when somebody said 'Jesus preached the Kingdom, but Paul preached Christ'. Awareness is awareness of differences, and it was an increased awareness that first registered as odd the difference between a man with a message and that man *as* the message. That Jesus is himself the message comes easily to the theologians as the burden both of his teaching and of Paul's, but only because of a deadly facility for making equations which the study of theology seems to engender. In reality there is a bewildering shift of perspective when the preacher becomes a sort of mystic object contacted through ritual. A fresh awareness of this shift sent the scholars in search of a convincing bridge-passage: and for those who could not wear the simpliste account which saw sacramental Christianity as the creation of Paul (a position very hard to hold in face of what is now known), the bridge-passage was the Resurrection experience. If the men who but a few years ago had followed the teacher to Jerusalem and death were now able to baptise 'into him' and share mystically in his body and blood, this was because of a transformation of consciousness in which the crucified leader became the risen Kurios.

Now of this placing of the Resurrection experience at the centre, many things can be said. It has involved for instance, a shift in believing apologetics from the whodunnit theology of the empty tomb to the validity of the experience itself. With this shift I am not here concerned. The point for me, a believer trying to understand, is that the emergence of the crucified leader as Lord is a process in which the whole experience created by the Galilean teacher goes into the melting-pot and is there new-minted as the faith of the Resurrection. Let me spell this out. You had the impact of his personality, the awakening of the messianic hope, the essentially puzzling nature of its personification in the teacher himself, culminating in the fiasco of the cross: and what the cross said was: 'that's the only Messiah you're going to get, that's all the real world has to offer to the soul which aspires to an earthly reign of God'.

The point is that all this experience is real, terribly real. The hope for a Messiah, meaning a man who will come from God and 'take over' our wretched attempts to found a true polity – this is unreal. But in the Gospel, this hope is made to converge on a figure whose proclamation as 'Messiah' is nothing if not realistic: 'Jesus the Nazarene, King of the Jews'. The 'fulfilment' of the hope is ironic, bitter, this-worldly. The ingredients – starry-eyed Messiah-gazing, the whole idea of a people of God entering into its own and confounding the Romans – are unreal, but the whole event is real, what happens 'in the event' (understanding this phrase idiomatically) is what ought to happen. Now for me, this is precisely where the Christian faith becomes convincing. I mean that the passing of the irony of the crucified Messiah into the faith of the Church is manifestly a liberation of consciousness from its worldly limits: a liberation that is not an escape into mysticism but on the contrary feels its way into the light *through* the exiguous passage, through this world's crucifixion of our dreams, insisting on this crucifixion as the very gateway into glory. A woman said to me the other day 'the reason why I can't get round the Gospels is that the mission of Jesus failed and the evangelists are at pains to emphasise this'. Such trueness to *life* in a document concerned with *religion* is, well, it's simply uninventable. This to me is revelation, revelation into which I with all my worldly expectations must die, revelation which *is* revelation *because* it demands my dying as the price of its appearing, revelation which comes of him who said 'no man can see me and live'. The early Church did not bypass the cross. It did not pass from this bitter disappointment into another dream, the ecstasy of the hellenistic mysteries. It gloried in the cross and found there the very coining of *its* mysteries.

This is the process whereby Jesus becomes the meeting and oneing of the worlds and is believable as such: a process in which both Jesus and his followers get lost in this world, this world that is ruled, according to the scriptures, by the powers of darkness, and that is dominated, according to a more modern idiom, by 'the stubbornly promoted end of all life on this planet'. It is only in this way that Jesus is believable. And I don't mean this in any loose sense, as we say that a man is believable when he shows the ordinary signs of honesty. I mean that it is only such a Jesus that can be the ground of that act which, fully alive to this world and going beyond it, deserves the name of faith. We cannot believe in a Messiah who, in his physical life, is larger than life, a Messiah who comes and 'takes over', who in his worldly existence and consciousness is beyond the difference between life and ritual, a Messiah who says to struggling and world-despairing man 'just do this, go through this rigmarole that I am teaching you, and you will be in touch with the simple truth that your experience fractures'. And the problem at last is just this: that it seems to be just such a larger-than-life Messiah that rises before my eyes when I read the story of the institution at the last supper enjoyed with his followers. Here the dualism of Jesus–Christ, of Jesus the preacher and Christ the preached, of Galilean preacher and mystic being contacted through ritual, seems to be simply resolved. Here the proclaimer of God's reign and the sacrament man are as it were *pictorially* the same person. Here we seem to be given a rest from the tempestuous unknowing journey through disillusion into light, while the man responsible for it all stands outside it and teaches us to say Mass. Here, to be a little naughty, is the most Roman Catholic moment in the whole Gospel.

It is not any perverse disinclination for simplicity that makes me say that this will not do. The whole strength of Christian faith, its capacity to endure and grow until the end of time, consists in this: that it looks back to an historical person only to see him proclaiming as fact the Kingdom to which we shall always aspire, and plunged into darkness and death just as we in our aspiration are contradicted by the facts of this world. Thus even the historical consideration of Jesus brings us with a bump into the present. And for its present power, Christian faith looks to the Spirit, to that victory over death that can take as many forms emotionally and imaginatively as there are and will be societies and cultures of men. Any way of thinking which attributes to Jesus in his historical condition that power on which the believer is now to draw is fatal to the efficacy and catholicity of Christian faith. The dualism between the Jesus of history and the Christ of faith, really sensed and rightly understood, is essential to the vitality, the flexibility, the *dunamis* of Christian faith. For in this dualism, in the *feel* of this difference, we see the price that has to be paid and was paid in blood for a real passage from darkness to light. This dualism assimilates the proclaimer of God's reign to this world, it enables us to see him in his actual crunch-situation without prerogatives borrowed from the Resurrection, so that we of this world, recognising our struggle in him, can enjoy his victory in us. The ecclesiastical hands raised in horror at any suggestion of a disjunction between Jesus and the Christ are the hands of those who cannot take life but want a legislator, human so that we can quote him, divine so that we can be sure he's right, who will tell us what to do. The denial of the disjunction is ecclesiastical, its discovery is secular and is part of the whole disinterested thrust of worldly science. But the actual disjunction itself is the most secular thing of all. For it is the cross. And it has ever been the Christian tradition, starting with Phil. 2:11 and the magisterial opening of Romans, that whatever is to be said meta-physically about the person of Jesus in the flesh, his emergence as decisive power in people's lives is only through the cross and the glory to which the cross has led.

There is another way of getting the point I am making about the Last Supper. The new covenant is everlasting because it is human, because its language is one that will endure as long as men are born, work, love, suffer and die. It is a law implanted in the heart, as Jeremiah says. Its handing over to us is not the institution of a priesthood, not the creation of a ritual order, not an investiture. Because it is for man for always, its foundation is the life and death of a man, and the New Testament applies all the old religious words, such as priesthood, investiture, sacrifice, to the bleeding body on the gibbet, applies them with an irony of which we of a subsequent age are more conscious than could have been the original writers, and of which the intervening Christian ages seem not to have been conscious at all. Now if *this* is how Christ is going to carry in himself the burden of God's new order, he cannot do this after the old manner, of ritual, of ordination, of what our journalists call organised religion.

Or put it this way. We hear the gospel account of the institution. In what context do we hear it? Almost certainly in a Christian religious sacramental context. We automatically read back into the story the eucharist as we have it, priests and all. We frame the story with a tradition which, for all its radical emancipation from religion in its sectarian sense, has most of the marks of a particular religious tradition. Clearly *this* is not the context in which the thing actually happened. If we are more enlightened, we hear the story in the Jewish ritual context. But this context cannot contain the whole story. It cannot contain the special reference to himself that Jesus is said to have given to the Jewish ritual meal: I mean the crucial words: 'my body, my blood.' This reference can have had *no* context, no ritual context. The only context was the death that awaited him and that dogs every man who awaits eagerly the reign of God. Clear your mind of the only available ritual contexts, the Jewish and the Christian, and you will experience, perhaps for the first time, the extraordinary strangeness of those words: 'my body' (hunk of bread), 'my blood' (cup of wine). And when we remember that the evangelists themselves were describing current liturgical practice, the original event, its flavour, becomes even more manifestly unavailable to us.

Whatever Jesus was doing, he was not founding a new religion with himself at the centre. The *new covenant* to which he refers has mysterious overtones that take us right outside the restricted world of religion: overtones of a humanity at last released from all provincialism, of the sons of God waiting to be revealed. And it is in this way, and with these overtones ringing in our ears, that we must hear the words 'in my blood'.

In my blood. In our lives as men and women. In the only real coin so far as man's real relationship with God is concerned.

The institution takes place much more under the shadow of the cross than we customarily think. And the reference that Jesus in the institution makes to himself should I think be thought of not in terms of a serene and clear knowledge that he was the Christ but in terms of the *sense* he seems to have had that his death was the inevitable conclusion of his proclamation and, *very* mysteriously, its fulfilment. I would dare to attribute to him, in this conviction of his that his death was the end of the world, a seeming madness that begins to look more and more like the only sanity as we develop in the sense of our own lives, when we cease to look upon this life of ours as an interim during which we keep ourselves occupied as best we can, and dare to challenge the universe in the name of God and as the sons of God that we are. When Loisy said that Jesus thought his death would be the end of the world, he was only seeking to understand in real psychological terms sayings of Jesus that had been understood hitherto on the hypothesis of a psychology in Jesus that was omniscient and could as it were legislate for this world until the end of time. According to this psychology, the end to which Jesus referred in his eschatological discourses was *the* end of the world which he foresaw would occur when the Church he was founding had completed its mission. Now we have abandoned this simpliste account of the mind of Jesus, and at the same time a more mature understanding of psychology allows for a 'madness' that is really saner, that is, more attuned to the heights and depths of man in the world, than what commonly goes for sanity. Thus the acceptance of Loisy's hypothesis *now* does not involve the crude notion of a simply deluded Jesus which was all that the psychology of Loisy's time allowed for. And don't forget that according to Mark's Gospel Jesus's relatives thought him 'out of his mind'.

Be that as it may, what I am positing is a reference, in the words of Jesus at the supper, to his own imminent death, seen in a manner not entirely out of our reach when we think with the whole of ourselves of our own death: a reference of this kind, and not a reference to future aeons of church life passed in compliance with a liturgy he was bequeathing. Further, the reference to his own death, being the end of the old order, of sacrifice, of ritual, of religion, carries as its implication that henceforth it is man himself that is the theme of the celebration, carries with it the command to his followers to have this meal in his memory knowing that it is *their* lives, in his Spirit and as his body, that they are celebrating.

This interpretation of the institution fits in well with an important insight first made plain, to me at least, by Gregory Dix in his great pioneer work *The Shape of the Liturgy*. Jesus was not saying 'here's a new thing you've got to do, my special memorial service' but 'in future, when you do this, when you eat this celebratory meal, or any other meal for that matter, remember me'. In other words, the thing to be *done* is already being done.

All that is new is the motive, the motif. And when the thing done, the celebration of our common life and death in food and drink, is done in his memory, then it expresses incomparably more fully, and with a wholly new and authoritative certainty that it is meaningful, our whole life and struggle and suffering as an acceptable worship, since it is from Jesus dying into the pleroma of Christ, which we are, that we have this empowering of the sheerly *human* as *worship*. '*Gloria Dei vivens homo*', as Irenaeus said.

What has happened in Christian history is that the reference to himself on the part of Christ has eclipsed the celebratory meal which it originally empowered in its basic human significance, with the result that the reference to Jesus loses its original sense. This was due presumably to the fact that the convert pagans had no such meal in which to receive the words of Christ as a new orientation. The result of this eclipsing was to give us the reading of 'do this in commemoration of me' that has dominated the Christian centuries and created the notion of Jesus as a liturgical innovator, which, being necessarily a provincial notion, is fatal to a full Catholic Christian understanding. This inversion has been well illustrated by a friend of mine in the following manner. Suppose a friend said to us 'I'm very fond of London. So please, whenever you go up to London send me a picture postcard' and we interpret this by travelling daily up to London *in order* to send him a picture postcard. The wrong order.

Once we realise that the meaning and intention of Jesus's words is to give to our celebration of man and his life and death that significance which it has in a humanity liberated for God and from religion, we have in principle liberated the eucharist from its clerical ritual straitjacket and realised it as our celebration of our life to God. Gone then is the dualism which demanded that two things, our life in this world and a solemn Christ-centred ritual, be somehow united. No longer does the initiator stand outside and legislate for a cult that he was initiating. Glad to acknowledge himself as one of our brethren, as Hebrews puts it, he enters into the spirit of our celebration and empowers it with the life that he has earned in dying.

Such a liberated eucharist, such a celebration of man, is surely closer to the intention of Christ than the theologically frozen eucharist that we take from more recent days. Closer to that intention which is not 'the mind of the legislator' but an intention shaped by the pressure of the whole this-world-situation upon him whom a design far more dark and mysterious than we emotionally recognise placed at the centre of the vortex. It is the intention that was hammered out in the bloody sweat of Gethsemane. It is the insistence that, everything to the contrary notwithstanding, man is one and lives fully only in one world (or, in traditional language, that man is called into the kingdom of God) and the insatiable need to live that one world in freedom and be crucified by the compromisers, the decent inhabitants of many worlds and no world, the men of unfreedom.

A eucharist that is, simply and singly and beyond the complications created by our endemic obtuseness, *our* celebration, is the eucharist as it comes out of the broken heart of Jesus. Is it not strange that a radically reappraised eucharist has this 'trad' quality about it? I find more and more that it's a question of cutting one's way through layers of pretentious hierophantic rubbish (that's what 'the liturgical movement' now looks like) to the heart of things which is the heart of Christ.

Who shall dare to say in what tone of voice, and with what 'intention', the words 'my body' were first uttered? We have not the humanity, the humour, the sense of tragic yet redeemable irony, the simplicity or the poetry, the feeling for man and his history, to know. But one thing we do know. The eucharist is a celebration, and you cannot celebrate two things at once, you cannot have two sources of joy. Of its essence, celebration comes from the heart of man set free and is the shared enjoyment of that freedom. This in the end is the celebration we have learned from him who set us free, even though for all the Christian centuries we have learned it after the manner of a schoolroom task, from a divine schoolteacher rather than from man alive. It is only now, when the whole crisis of man is upon us, that we begin to appreciate those words in the upper room as a powerful hint thrown out from the centre of the human vortex, a hint which the Christian ages have taken – too seriously? No, with the wrong kind of seriousness, a seriousness which, when we consider the amount of influence the celebration has had on the world's growth looks more like frivolity. If there is joy among the angels for one sinner that repents, there is surely laughter among them at the prodigious literalism of Christians which so inerrantly misses the point.

The world. What of the world today? When we consider the world in relation to the celebration of man, we encounter a paradox. For on the one hand we seem to have a world that has no place for celebration. Cult is dying on us. On the other hand, the world now is for the first time in a position where the celebration of man could be meaningful. For the liturgies we have so far had are each of them tied to a particular culture. In the past, man has been a concrete reality only as this or that race or culture. But today, man is becoming a concrete reality beyond these old ethnic limits. The human as such is becoming increasingly our object of concern. The future of man himself is for us a theme of anguish as in the past it was the future of this or that race or culture that alone occupied men's thoughts. Now if man himself is our concern: if he is becoming the centre of our consciousness and concern, must he not become a theme of celebration? Do we not want, on pain of allowing our anguish for men to degenerate into a sort of hectic hopelessness, to celebrate man, our life as man, our hope, our problematic mortality?

Where shall we find such a celebration? We cannot produce one just because we want one. The mechanics of celebration are delicate, as are the mechanics of making love. They resist production-to-order. Indeed the similarity is striking. For the making of love too is ruled by a queer mixture of the immemorially old and the spontaneously now. I can imagine nothing quite so horrible or heartless as a celebration of man produced by UNESCO or even Amnesty International. A valid celebration of man, albeit a new phenomenon on this earth, will have to be totally without the thought-up, the fictitious, the consciously appropriate. It will have to be something that has in essence been done before. It will have its roots deep in man's past, for man's extension in time is as much part of his catholicity as his extension over the globe at one time.

Are there not in fact strong indications that a liberated freedom-celebrating eucharist, which is precisely the celebration of man, and a newly emergent need for just such a celebration, could coincide?

The possibility of this coincidence is strictly dependent on an imaginative leap forward in our eucharistic thinking. The dualism at the heart of current eucharistic theory makes it impossible, the dualism, I mean, between a liturgy allegedly taught by Jesus and a world which a liturgy so externally considered *cannot* be part of. In reality our eucharistic liturgy came out of Jesus in his very subjection to that world, and by this very fact could not have the serene legislative quality that small men have attributed to it.

It is time to sum up. The purpose of our eucharistic liturgy is to celebrate our life, our work, our joy in being, our impossibility in loving, our hope, our victory over the death that ought to sour all these things: to celebrate all these things, that is, *as* victorious over death, or better, as embracing of death. We celebrate all these things as alive in God. We celebrate a freedom that wells up in ourselves and is sure of its ultimate reality and consummation. We celebrate man and all his history, all his struggle towards single truth and beatifying truthfulness. All which is to say that we celebrate the life, death and resurrection of Jesus, that massive transmutation of the human in which we glory. If there is any dualism here, if 'our life set free in God' and 'Christ's death and resurrection' refer to two different things, then is the resurrection of Christ not all-pervasive: and if the resurrection is not all-pervading, then it is not at all. The resurrection is that kind of thing.

But there has been just this dualism in the Christian ages and in their autumnal baroque aftermath. And this is because – or perhaps is itself the reason why – there has stood at the origin of Christian worship a Jesus who commissioned and empowered it, a walking wonder-man, a man who could legislate for the human, a supreme legislator – and a supreme legislator could only touch our lives from the outside, and could only impose his celebration on us from the outside of a life with which it will never be compounded. As thus imposed, the celebration is a most extraordinary thing, *seeming* to touch us from within but somehow not doing so, creating problems rather than enlarging our human mystery. This supreme legislator, this man who by a fiat of his will (and not the desperate fiat of Gethsemane) could initiate and empower the Christian eucharist, is an undead man rather than a dead and risen man. There is no reason why he should die. He could institute and empower the eucharist without dying – except for the fact that the reference of the eucharist is to his death, a fact which no theologian has been able successfully to compound with the institution itself. This incoherence between the crucified Messiah and the undead magic-man of the institution has dogged all our eucharistic theology, which has been able only to think up problematic theory after problematic theory – and the number of these theories when I was a student was just approaching the half-century.

The Christian tradition has been strangled by the image of a man who was able to achieve in anticipation the lordship which was only his in the Resurrection and, there, is ours too: to achieve it, that is, in the static hieratic terms of order and priesthood of which the actual way of its achievement is the surpassing. And has not the Christian tradition been dogged, sometimes comically, by the contradiction at its heart between a priestly establishment and the denial of all priesthood. When Francis of Assisi took off all his clothes in the presence of the bishop and went out into the snow crying 'our Father who art in Heaven', I suppose everyone sort of knew that what he was doing was what the bishop really stood for.

Christianity is too big and too deep, too much what we simply are, too much the very self of men, too *us*, too bloody obvious, for anyone to have *started*.

And yet of all the so-called world-religions, Christianity is the most associated with one man, is associated with one man in a way that the religions are not.

The resolution of this paradox, the rise of Christianity in a man who *is* man, is called the Resurrection.

Christianity lives in its roots at this level, where a man originates it yet does not found it, or institute it, or stand at its beginning in any way that we can conceive of a movement taking its origin. But Christian tradition, Christianity trying to remember, conceiving and talking, is never wholly faithful to this manner of its beginning. It makes of the beginning-man a Founder. It talks of him instituting its celebration. It assimilates his role and work to those various influences of man on man that are the stuff of cultures and that are swept away when their enclosing cultures die. And thus the man whose *life and death* is its beginning becomes the man by whose *inspiration*, or by whose *organising genius*, or by whose *God-given mandate*, it conceives itself to have started. At this level the liberal ineptitude which speaks of an original inspirer, and the ecclesiastical ineptitude which speaks of the institutor of a familiar and time-bound order of ritual, are but facets of one ineptitude, the ineptitude endemic to articulate Christianity. And liberalism and priestcraft are both of them cultures and will perish. Christianity comes from that man in a deeply mysterious manner which is conveyed more truly by the Johannine reference to the blood and water flowing from the side of Christ than by any of our models for the creation of societies.

It is only the Spirit, it is only Christianity's essential life, that can send us aright to Christianity's man and reveal him as *the* man, as us, and that can draw from our flesh the praise and the celebration that is his only evidence.

APPENDIX

Note 1

The thinking in this paper depends, not perhaps overtly enough for clarity, on certain theological assumptions that have now become part and parcel of the author's mind. Let me give these assumptions in telegraphic form, in a sort of litany of Christian re-appraisal.

To say that Christ is a priest, without appreciating the irony of this statement, is to be hardly a Christian but rather an imitation Christian. To say that Christ is king, without appreciating the irony of this statement, is to be barely a Christian. To say that we have a sacrifice, without appreciating the irony of this statement, is to be barely a Christian. To say that Christ is God, without appreciating what an embarrassing notion of God this implies, is to be hardly a Christian. To say that God is our Father, without appreciating the irony of such a statement, is to be barely a Christian.

It is because of the irony of these statements that Christ is lost in the world; it is through the power of the Spirit transfiguring their irony, that the world is raised up in Christ.

To say that Christ is a priest is to say that priests are out. To say that Christ is a king is to say that kings are out. To say that he is our sacrifice is to say that sacrifices are out. To say that Christ is God is to say that gods are out.

And now to God the Father, God the Son, and God the breath of life. . . .

Note 2

On theological method. More important than what a theologian says are the cultural assumptions on which he feels able to say it. If those cultural assumptions are not adverted to, and if the culture that once supported them has now been shed by a world grown more aware, then he is in fact saying nothing at all. I look back along years of theologising, chiefly on the eucharist, trying to compound two entities called respectively the Last Supper and the Cross. The cultural assumption was that they *could* be compounded, that there was a single order to which they both belonged. And this was a huge cultural assumption, that unification of the world which medieval man took for granted – one world that could accommodate both a ceremonial and a living and dying Jesus without registering the extreme difference of treatment that these two concepts, really thought about, require. I see now that every time I tried to fit together what I called the Last Supper and the Cross I was thinking within this cultural assumption, in which I cannot and do not *really* think about *things*. I was not aware of the fact, but really I was talking about nothing at all. A theology once culturally based, and doggedly persistent while the base has collapsed, becomes a kind of no-culture or anti-culture – which accounts for the glazed look in the eyes of scientist and philosopher to which I referred earlier.

INTRODUCTION

Central to the problems of the Church's ministry is the question of what constitutes the original data of the Church, and above all the evaluation of the constitutive value and the definitive character of the ministries which exist in her. This depends in its turn on the answer given to the question, What is the Reign which Jesus proclaimed, and how does the Church understand herself in relation to it?

The Church's mission consists not only in being, by its community life, a circle of interpersonal relationships, but in opening up for the world today the prospect for the future shown forth in Christ crucified. She is God's final action, for salvation is already proclaimed and lived in her, but she is not yet the harvest.

So the Church's life is a continuity, but it is not one founded on an unalterable Law or on a formal structure similar to the constitution of a secular state; nor is it a timeless eternity whose institutions are preserved from the vicissitudes of history. Consequently, function in the Church is exercised in the perspective of waiting, and not from the point of view of an organisation permanently settled in history. The Servant, who bears the sufferings of the many, is the model, rather than any hierarchical principle based on power or personal qualities.

Community is one key to the paradox, for it is only at the heart of the community that the deepest level of being of the Church can be discovered, the life which remains hidden in Jesus Christ. All the charisms are given in community, for the Spirit is given in different ways, but the charisms work together for the good of the community.

It is from this point of view that the functions of the president of the community are understood: to preside at the eucharist, which makes the Church; and to bind and loose in the service of the community's internal discipline. These functions are exercised within the eschatological event of the death and resurrection of Jesus Christ, which is commemorated in the liturgical celebration, through faith in his presence. (*Canon Houssiau's article has been translated from the French by Christopher Lash.*)

BIOGRAPHICAL NOTE

CANON ALBERT HOUSSIAU *is Professor of Sacramental Theology and President of the College of the Holy Spirit in the Catholic University of Louvain.*

13 The Church and her Ministry from the Viewpoint of Eschatology

ALBERT HOUSSIAU

'THE KINGDOM OF GOD HAS DRAWN NEAR.' THIS MESSAGE of Jesus enables the Church to understand her situation and guides her in her action. The idea one has of the Church, her mission and her organisation is effectively conditioned by the way in which one evaluates and interprets this fundamental theme of the New Testament. What reality is present in the Church? What is her mission in the world? In what way is she, like the *eschaton*, definitive, while remaining, like history, subject to change?[1]

For liberal Protestantism the kingdom preached by Jesus was no more than the peaceable and powerful force of God in men's hearts; a kingdom on earth, but wholly interior. The Gospel is reduced to preaching the fatherhood of God and the brotherhood of man. The concern of the kingdom is for souls not things. But this kingdom lives at peace in the world of authorities, work and culture, since its religion acts as a foundation for the moral

[1] On the history of the theme of the Kingdom, see W. NIGG, *Das ewige Reich. Geschichte einer Hoffnung* (Zürich 1954) réed. (Siebenstern, 105-6), Munich-Hamburg, 1967.

culture of nations; in short it is a bourgeois religion. The liberal Christian experiences no feeling of being torn in two directions in this world, since, as was said at the time, 'the eschatology office is normally shut nowadays'. On this view the Church becomes nothing more than a community of men who are united in brotherhood, its word contains no paradox, and any element of organisation is simply an outer shell which stifles liberty.[2]

It was Johannes Weiss and Albert Schweitzer who delivered the fatal blow to the biblical pretensions of this bourgeois Christianity. They held that Jesus preached nothing but the imminent and dramatic arrival of a wholly different world. He was no more concerned with laying down moral principles for a world that was about to disappear than he was with organising a Church. 'Jesus preached the kingdom; but it was the Church which arrived.' (A. Loisy). But how can one hear this uncompromising message except by freeing it from every outward form of representation. For Schweitzer it remains the challenge of will to will; the enthusiasm and the heroism of this view of the world are what matter. For whereas Jesus expected the intervention of God, we have to create the kingdom by our moral effort. But we must envisage the kingdom in the radical spirit of Jesus himself, so that, moved by the same driving force, we may be able to do everything possible to bring it about. There is no longer any place here for dogma, for sacraments, or for an historical institution. United with Jesus we must communicate to the world in his infinite will for morality.[3]

Dialectical theology definitively rejected the soothing preaching of liberal Christianity in favour of the uncompromising message of the Gospel; since only the total unexpectedness of the Bible had anything to offer man, caught in the clutches of the unexpected contradictions of life. This message is the message of the inbreaking of the kingdom; of the sovereign act of God, which

[2] A. VON HARNACK, Das Wesen des Christentums (Leipzig 1900) réed. (Siebenstern, n. 27), Munich-Hamburg 1964; in particular pp. 43–8, 70–82.

[3] J. WEISS, Die Predigt Jesu vom Reiche Gottes (Göttingen 1892); A. SCHWEITZER, Von Reimarus zu Wrede. Eine Geschichte der Leben Jesu-Forschung (Tugingue 1906) réed. (Siebenstern, n. 77–80), Munich-Hamburg 1966. Cfr. W. G. KUMMEL, Das Neue Testament, Geschichte der Erforschung seiner Probleme (Orbis Academicus) (Fribourg-BR-Munich 1958), pp. 286–309.

snatches me today from the eon of sin; my existence is at the same time 'already more' and 'not yet'; it is stretched between the past of sin and the future of God.

For Karl Barth this action of God consists above all in his word: God who reveals himself through himself. The Church is the community of those whom he has gathered by his Spirit and in which the word becomes event through preaching. The Spirit ceaselessly creates and renews the Church, and thus embodies Christ, that is to say, gives him an earthly, historical form. This community of saints is ordered and governed by God, by the divine action, or by the Spirit, and not by means of any function exercised exclusively by a number of ministers. Church order is wholly subject to the lordship of Jesus Christ and should therefore be an order of service, as Christ himself was servant. Every activity of the Church – preaching, diakonia, theology – is regulated by this order, which is one of service, and which is entrusted to every member of the community. The heart of the community's life – and so, since the Church is the community of saints, the heart of the Church's being – is to be found in worship, where the community becomes event; the sovereign call of God touches man, and man replies by his confession and praise. But this community does not contain its own end; it is 'between the times'. The kingdom did indeed draw near in the Epiphany of Jesus Christ, but the Church still awaits the Parousia; the Church is in sight of her goal, but has to realise that she is only the Church; that she is pressing forward to the sanctification of the whole human world. The kingdom is thus her foundation and her limit: in the Church the definitive act of God, or his lordship, is already at work; she remains nevertheless provisional.[4]

For Rudolf Bultmann God's act reveals us to ourselves: we must come to a decision in the here and now of our existence. The Church is a community of the Beyond. We live well and truly in the concrete circumstances of existence, but we have received the Spirit; we are already living in the conditions of the future: in freedom with regard to this world and in hope of the life that is

[4] K. BARTH, *Die Kirchliche Dogmatik*, IV. *Die Lehre von der Versöhnung*, I–II (Zürich 1953–1954), in particular Section 62 (I, pp. 718–826); Section 67 (II, pp. 695–824); *Credo* (Zürich 1936), French trans. *Credo* (Genève 1969), pp. 176–90.

still hidden. But the Church, from being an eschatological community turned herself into a sacramental and institutional one. In this way the Church makes herself worldly; she sets herself up as a new religion and thinks she possesses salvation; she becomes an organisation which functions empirically; the community, like Israel, has once again a history, whose origin is Jesus. In short, Bultmann considers that the authentic Church is of a transcendent, but provisional, importance, in the sense that the Church can remain faithful to her essential nature only if the dialectical concept of future and present is maintained – a concept which is overturned by institutions and sacraments.[5]

Recent attempts to describe New Testament eschatology, whether among Reformed (Edward Schweizer, Oscar Cullmann) or Catholic (Rudolf Schnackenburg) theologians also base the Church on the eschatological message of Jesus, but they maintain an historical dimension in their interpretation of the tension; they do not reduce eschatology to nothing more than a dialectical moment of existence. In the Church the way of God is already realised, but she is still travelling towards the kingdom. In the Church Israel is already fulfilled, but the new factor of the eschatological event makes its appearance. The Church presents a tension between salvation and history. It is in this double dimension that the missionary task of the Church and present realities find their meaning. There remain nevertheless considerable differences between Reformed and Catholic in the appreciation of what constitute the original 'data' of the Church, and above all in the evaluation of the constitutive value and the definitive character of the ministries which exist in her.

In his desire to preserve the historical dimension of the eschatological event, Jurgen Moltmann too objects to the subjectivism of the dialectical interpretation, which would reduce the kingdom to a kingdom of intentions. On the contrary, the gospel message reveals the future of the world itself, together with the objective structures which make it up. This message is a promise which goes beyond realities already perceived and gives man hope in a future for the world where death will have been

[5] R. BULTMANN, *Jesus* (Tübingen 1926); *Jesus Christ and Mythology* (New York 1958); *Glaube und Verstehen* (Tübingen 1960 and 1965).

conquered; this hope should infect the world with a spirit of uneasiness and give life to our resistance and opposition to the forces of death which still exist in its structures. It is thus in the world and not simply, nor even chiefly, in the Church that the act of God is realised. This victory over death is given reality not only in souls but also in an efficacious love which creates new institutions in the history of the present world. The Church's mission consists not only in being, by its community life, a circle of interpersonal relationships, but in opening up for the world today the prospect for the future shown forth in Christ crucified. In short we are dealing here with a social Christianity founded on eschatology. The *eschaton* is realised in human history by the new structures which men create.[6]

Harvey Cox's Secular City is incontestably a transposition of the kingdom of the Gospel. This is shown by the theme of the City of the Future, 'this passing age', newness, the eschatological functions of the Church: *kerygma*, *diakonia*, *koinônia*. But eschatology is realised simply in the history of human experience; it is the revolution which God brings about through responsible men who do not 'leave it to the snake'. The Church is the avant-garde of this inbreaking of God; she follows the Lord who always goes before her into the world; she broadcasts the seizure of power over the forces of alienation, she binds up the wounds of technopolis, she makes the future City of Man visible by destroying all separation. If she were not at the head of the revolution of our age she would be nothing but a bastion of the past; that is to say of 'this passing age'. Revolutionary events are thus seen as signs of the world to come. The Christian *par excellence* is the rebel; the guerrilla priest becomes the symbol of the new Christian.[7]

If then one wants to consider the Church – and the priest – from the point of view of eschatology, one must situate her vis-à-vis the decisive event of the reign of God as it is to be found in the New Testament. This will, moreover, enable one to avoid getting

[6] J. MOLTMANN, *Theologie der Hoffnung* (Munich 1964).

[7] H. COX, *The Secular City. Secularisation and Urbanisation in Theological Perspective* (New York 1965); *God's Revolution and Human Responsibility* (London 1969); *On Not Leaving it to the Snake* (London 1964).

bogged down in an abstract meditation on present and future, extension and spirit, body and spirit, religious and social.

The question then is; what is the reign which Jesus proclaimed and how does the Church understand herself in relation to it? The pages which follow make no claim to present a biblical theology, they simply comment on certain data of contemporary exegesis which are stimulating and perhaps enlightening for contemporary ecclesiology.[8]

The kingdom, or rather the reign of God announced by Jesus is not a domain, an establishment which comes down ready-made from heaven; it is an action – the work of God which saves the world. Jesus' thought continues in the same tradition as that of the psalms: 'God reigns' (Pss. 47, 93, 96–9).

This act of God is sovereign: the reign is the work of God himself and of him alone. There is no equation possible between our efforts and his. It is not up to us to construct the kingdom: it is God who gives it. We receive it, we pray that it may come, we have to seek it, we hold ourselves in readiness for the hour of its coming – but it is not up to us to make it: it is a seed which grows by itself. Moreover this kingdom is given us out of mercy: not in virtue of our righteousness; but in virtue of our humility, of our poverty. It is not given to him who wants it, or who chases after it, but to those to whom God shows mercy.

For the Jew, nourished on the prayer of the psalms, God reigns over the waters and over the earth, in nature and in the history of his people. But the preaching of Jesus, like that of the apocalyptic writers and John the Baptist, is concerned above all with the final act of God, through which all human history is fulfilled and brought to its conclusion.

Jesus proclaims a reign which is coming; this reign already sheds its rays among men, but has still to show itself in its completed form. Christ preaches both that the kindgom is here, among

[8] E. SCHWEIZER, Gemeinde und Gemeindeordnung im Neuen Testament (Zürich 1959); R. SCHNACKENBURG, Gottes Herrschaft und Reich. Eine biblisch-theologische Studie (Fribourg, Br. 1967); Règne et Royaume de Dieu, Essai de théologie biblique (Etudes théologiques 2) (Paris 1965); Die Kirche im Neuen Testament, Ihr Wirklichkeit und theologische Deutung, ihr Wesen und Geheimnis (Fribourg, Br. 1961); L. CERFAUX, La théologie de l'Eglise suivant saint Paul (Unam Sanctam 54) (Paris 1965); Le chrétien dans la théologie paulinienne (Lectio divina 33) (Paris 1962).

us, and also that we must still search for it, wait for it, ask for it. He rejoices at its realisation and keeps alive his burning desire for its fulfilment. Present and future, the reign includes two times, or two aspects, which Jesus evoked in the parables: the reign remains hidden, remains the object of opposition, worked secretly; but it will show itself in power. There are two phases: the seed or the leaven, and the final harvest, the great tree, the risen dough.

God already reigns in the preaching and in the miracles of Jesus: these constitute the signs of the reign. The healings are truly the work of him who is to come, they demonstrate, moreover, the merciful or saving nature of the reign; Christ is the servant who bears the sufferings of many. As for the preaching: it is the sign *par excellence*: to those who busy themselves with reading the signs in order to determine chronologically the precise moment of the coming, no sign is given but the sign of Jonah: this sign is at one and the same time the preaching of conversion and the person who dies and whom God raises to life. Not that weakness as such would be a sign of the reign; the sign is rather the power of God which bursts forth beyond death.

The lordship of Christ is thus qualified as salvation and service. Jesus indeed specifically maintains his distance vis-à-vis John the Baptist and even more vis-à-vis Jewish apocalyptic. The final work announced by Jesus and inaugurated in his life is salvation and not judgement. The message about the coming of the reign is Good News, or Gospel, rather than the announcement of the final catastrophe. Christ came to save sinners. The coming of the kingdom is an invitation to enter the kingdom, for God does not come for those who have already provided themselves with some form of righteousness but for the lost sheep of Israel and for all the nations whom he brings into his eschatological banquet.

This reign is exclusively religious; it does not answer worldly, natural or political hopes. It is therefore by a religious attitude – faith, humility, mercy – that a man can enter it. And as soon as he enters it, the elect is called upon to live the perfection of God himself.

The Church exists in the time of the reign of God, but at the time of sowing. She is not one work among others which attempt to make the world more human, nor even a religion which aims at reconciliation with God; she is God's final action; in her, salvation is already shown forth and lived. But she is not yet the harvest. There is of course a continuity between the Church and the final reign, but, as the parables suggest, it is not our labours and our efforts which produce the seed's steady growth, but the power of God himself. The growth of the kingdom, then, operates differently from the growth of the world, for God has entrusted the earth to man in order that he may make the grass of the field grow upon it . . .

Has this Church, whose inmost reality lies beyond our time and in which the definitive work of God is already fulfilled, a history? The New Testament, as Edward Schweizer has well shown, contains evidence of two tendencies, which underline respectively two dimensions of the Church: on the one hand the Church's situation is related to two moments in time, since she is founded on the events of the Cross and Resurrection and she is looking towards the Parousia; on the other hand she looks upwards to the Lord already in glory, who is present when she gathers herself together. From the former point of view she is involved in a history which she brings to completion and which she continues: the history of Israel; from the latter point of view she shares the absolute novelty of the *eschaton*. The stability of the Church lies in the existence side by side of these two dimensions; otherwise she would fall either into a sort of functional or organisational Ebionism, or into an enthusiastic Docetism.

We find the historical dimension of the Church most clearly expressed in St Luke's writings. He recounts a history in which events and institutions have their rightful place. The growth of the community, its decisions and institutional changes form a real history, under the guidance of the Spirit and conditioned by its external situation (persecution, rejection by the Jews, difficulties in the hellenistic community . . .). The Church 'between the times', then, is aware of an historical dimension; she develops during a period of time: the sowing goes on right up to the present day and will continue in the future. The result is a continuity across the centuries from the apostles to ourselves. This continuity is not founded, in the manner of the Roman empire, on an unalterable law or the formal structure of the state: nor, on the other hand, is it a timeless eternity, whose institutions would thereby be preserved from all the vicissitudes of history. Luke, moreover, lets us see the flexibility of the forms created by the guidance of the Spirit when the Church is confronted by new situations. Like the kingdom, the Church is definitive, and she is so definitive that she can and must allow herself to be provisional. The definitive must be lived in continuity and be maintained in fidelity. To protect the identity of the community and the message which enlightens it, the Church does not base herself on a printed document, on a book, but on the word which is always actual.

In the Christian community, such as Paul reveals it to us, the perspective is almost exclusively synchronistic: the community is contemporary with the apostle; and if it includes within itself different rôles, if it assigns internal services to its members, services which are co-ordinated by the Spirit, the apostle exercises authority over it as far as the Gospel and community discipline are concerned. Apostolate and services are finally co-ordinated and given their hierarchic organisation by the Spirit. Nevertheless even here there is clear reference to traditions handed down along the path of history.

In the Pastoral Epistles and the Acts, however, a diachronistic perspective is already evident. There is concern not only for cohesion but also for the continuity of the Church in time: the 'depositum' must be preserved. Functions in the community must guarantee the continuity of the work of the apostles. But in order to realise the definitive in the process of temporal continuity, the Church does not rely upon a divine constitution operating like the formal structure of the state; neither does she rely on the cohesion of the interpersonal relationships which should exist at the heart of the group. In order to ensure continuity she has constituted persons in institutions: she has entrusted functions in a permanent manner to individuals and the latter can rely on the charism which is promised them in consequence. The Spirit and Christ protect the Church in the persons of bishops and elders.

It is undoubtedly true that as a result the eschatological community places itself on the level of history and people have not been lacking to point out the similarities between Christian organisation and those of Judaism and hellenistic associations. It is with the community of the new covenant that one can discover the closest parallels. But for this community too the ministry has an eschatological significance: to preserve the community in its faithfulness to the covenant until the time of the visitation. In fact functions in the Church are exercised in this same perspective of waiting and not from the point of view of an organisation permanently settled in history.

But beyond this, the permanent functions in the Church are always endowed with a gift of the Spirit. The Christian communi- ty has already received the Spirit promised for the last times and it is this Spirit which is shared out to bishops and elders so that they may carry out their service.

The actual style of the ministry in the eschatological community must also differ from that of the kingdoms of this world: 'The kings of the pagans lord it over them, and those who exercise power are called benefactors. But you are not like this. The great- est among you – let him be as the youngest, and the leader as he who serves. . . . I myself am among you as he who serves' (Luke 22:25–7). Functions in the Church are exercised in the way in which the reign of God is realised in the life of Christ: as service. Superficially it would be possible to assume that the ministries should be services which function well, that is to say which answer adequately to the needs of the community. In fact there is no question in the gospel of functionalism, which anyway would be simply worldly, but of a wholly original way of guiding the com- munity: that is to say, in accordance with the model of the servant who bears the sufferings of many. As a result the hierarchic principle, which bases authority on power or personal qualities, becomes equally questionable; church order is, in fact, not essen- tially based on an aristocracy of intellect, on a moral aristocracy, not even on a charismatic aristocracy; the qualities required of a bishop are, moreover, extremely modest. The Church does not choose as her pastors those who possess an overriding charism in comparison with the rest of the faithful, but confident in the promise of the Lord who is with her always, she prays that God will grant his spirit of government and counsel to those whom she has chosen to guide her.

In the 'times between' the Church lives and acts in tension between a history which is in the process of being created from the time of the preaching and work of Christ to the full and final manifestation, and the ever actual presence of the risen Lord: The Church is thus both mission and community, sent forth into the world and the first fruits of the world to come. Her being and her life are defined eschatologically by the fact that she belongs to the definitive reign of God, but at the same time she cares profoundly for the world; she thus possesses different functions, some more instrumental: evangelisation or *kerygma* and the service of the world or *diakonia*; others more expressive and by which the community lives: liturgy, edification, mutual help; in a word *koinonia*.

The Church's mission in the world consists principally in evangelisation. This mission is the direct result of her eschatological nature. Christ refuses to answer the question put to him about the moment of the coming of the kingdom and sends the apostles out to preach the Gospel. Moreover the theophany of the risen Christ, which anticipates his coming in glory and which already manifests his reign, is itself a sending out on mission. [9]

The coming is not the only object of the *kerygma*; for through the *kerygma* God already reigns; the preaching is part of the time of sowing and inaugurates in a humble or hidden way the reign of God over the world. The word which re-echoes today in the preaching of the Gospel is the definitive call which God makes to us; the preaching of the Church is marked by the urgency of the eschatological *hodie*.

God reigns through the preaching in the Church: the word is no longer a human word: 'The reign of God is not in word but in power' (1 Cor. 4:20); he does not reign by means of the persuasive rhetoric of human wisdom but by the manifestation of the Spirit and in power (1 Cor. 2:4). One cannot therefore make an equation between the skill of the preacher and the word to be spoken. Admittedly Paul is no ignoramus, but he lays aside his competence, and anyway he is often better when he avoids overmuch theology! If the priest thinks of himself as ploughing in the same furrow as

[9] O. CULLMANN, *Das Eschatologische Charakter des Missionsauftrags und des apostolischen Selbsthewustseins bei Paulus*, and *Eschatologie und Mission im Neuen Testament* in *Vorträge und Aufsätze*, 1925-1962 (Tübingen 1966), pp. 305-36; 348-60.

the apostle, his profession is a highly unusual one: his competence comes from his fidelity and not from his skill. It is not the priest's business to make his mark as a professional psychologist or even as a wise counsellor; consequently he will avoid being dragged into learned debate and will confine himself principally to recalling clearly the word of God, which is holy and full of mercy, to repeating the call to holiness and to announcing the assurance of salvation which recreates the human heart. Between the human sciences and the Gospel there stretches the distance between the human order and the sovereignty of the *eschaton*.

The word of God then is not of this world. But do not let us therefore understand this abrupt or heterogenous character of the Gospel in an oversimplified way. It is true that God does not simply answer our questions and fulfil our needs, but he does speak and every word is a listening. It is the same for us, we only speak well if we listen to the other person and not to ourselves. We have a duty, then, in speaking to the world on God's behalf to appreciate the cares and efforts of the world, to recognise the Spirit who breathes and works there. The judgement which the spiritual should pass on the world is this: are its aspirations and movements signs of the reign inaugurated by Christ, the servant. That is to say, it is not up to us to give unambiguous answers to the world's questions: we have first of all to pass judgement on the questions themselves.

At the present time there are those who would like the prophetic function of the Church to identify the signs of the reign with some particular manifestation of history, some particular revolutionary movement. Does not such a desire spring from a certain oversimplification? Even at the level of events which concern the Church herself, there is no way, I believe, of writing a theological history of the Church. It is true that the historian could, to some extent, evaluate the fidelity of the preaching and the continuity of the life of the faithful and of the institutions, for signs can be compared with one another and one can judge to what extent they are convergent: but the historian will never say: On such and such a day the holy Spirit inspired this bishop to say just this. . . . Beyond some form of general appreciation history is concerned with the human factor, the rôle of people, the interplay of situations, the perceptible results of recognisable action; it is impossible for us to identify, without ambiguity or qualification, the definitive action of God with the events of the Reformation or Counter-Reformation. *A fortiori*, it is impossible to recognise without ambiguity the signs of the times in any particular human experience, or to identify any particular evening in May with Pentecost.

Does this mean we must make no attempt to pass a spiritual judgement on the movements of our time? The Church, through her ministers, has the duty to form Christians ready to take risks, to engage in works which offer the sufficient spiritual indications that they are an action of God in the world; she will therefore have to admit a certain pluralism in the earthly engagement of Christians.

The eschatological message proclaims both the end of the historical regime of the law and the setting up of the radical regime of the *eschaton*; the Church preaches a new justice: an easy yoke which liberates from the casuistry of the law in favour of a demand without limits; Christian liberty consists in living here and now under the definitive reign of God: the perfection of mercy and service. It is true that, since the Church has its place in history, the temptation to install a rabbinate, to lay down once again the detailed list of what is commanded and what is forbidden, remains tenacious; but in an eschatological perspective the preacher will always try to move beyond the contingent world of precepts by concentrating on conversion to the values of the Gospel.

The message, then, is not a *confirmatur* of the old order of the world since it wrenches us free from the whole idea of a settled, circumscribed world. Is it for all that a revolutionary manifesto? Certainly one cannot confine God's reign to the private domain of our hearts and intentions, but should one for all that make of it a revolution which overthrows established institutions in order to set up new ones in the world? Does the reign of God consist in replacing paternalism by participation? On this question there is a preliminary observation to be made: the eschatological conviction of the New Testament goes hand in hand with the rule of stability; the new condition is of so different an order from the history of the world that the Christian remains free to live for God in most earthly situations; he may even be able to recognise elements of God's reign in the powers of the world, which in other respects persecute it.

However the gospel message which the Church has to proclaim unceasingly in this world contains a force which, in the long run, changes and overthrows both institutions and mental and social structures. Christianity revolutionises the world from within and ends by humanising it. If it were not so, Christ would not truly have thrown down the wall between slave and master, Jew and Gentile, Greek and Barbarian. From the moment one lives fully the reality of Christ's death for all men, of the triumph of his resurrection over the powers which alienate man, the pre-Christian structures – such as temple, sacrifices, slavery – lose their meaning and cease to be tenable options in view of the reign of God towards which the Christian is truly journeying and in which he lives already. The reign of God does not guarantee the Christian that his choices in this world will be effective, but it animates them with the Spirit, which discerns the needs and the longings of the world and evaluates their spiritual authenticity. It is evident that one must give up exploiting Jesus' words about the violent who sieze the kingdom by force, for in the context it is a question of the enthusiasm aroused by the preaching of Jesus or of John the Baptist, perhaps even of the violent opposition which it arouses.

The time of waiting is strongly marked by the love which does not pass away. What service should the Church bring to the present world? To begin with she could, through the inter-personal relationships she creates as a community (*Gemeinschaft*), remedy the shortcomings of a society (*Gesellschaft*) which has become technical to the point of becoming depersonalised. In fact the parochial organisation has for a long time played this social role, and often plays it still; moreover priests fulfill in the animation of the community an extremely valuable social function for the *technopolis*. But one has to admit that such is not the real mission of the Church; the community act *par excellence*, the liturgy, is far from being organised to this end, and the mobility of tourists will render this service increasingly problematical.

If the diakonia of the Church were reduced to this aspect, Christianity would run the risk of being deprived of all impact on the social structures themselves, even if one were to strike a proper balance between the interpersonal (cultural, moral and religious) and the structural (social and economic); even if one did take sufficient account, in the organisation of charity, of the needs manifested by statistics, of laws and of economic and social structures, and of the demands of technical science, to aid the world of today effectively. One has of course to reject all confusion between the coming of the reign of God and the coming of any particular historical reality; since this would have as its result the reduction of eschatology to history and its definitive newness to the novelty of the present age. But on the other hand one cannot prevent the regime of love, instituted through the reign of God, from having a concrete impact on society. These conditions for its efficacity must on no account, it is true, make us lose sight of the fact that the Church in her diakonia – and in particular in the chief of the priests who preside this service – is not formally competent, nor is she responsible for the exact observation of needs and the discovery of appropriate techniques, but she should arouse the love which will animate this scientific and technical research, and stimulate the enthusiasm and disinterest which will elaborate and apply the solutions. More than ever the Hymn of Love puts us on our guard: without love our efforts would be nothing; they would not be the love of God which transfigures the world. It is moreover precisely in the freedom of the children of God that the world will attain its destiny. The urgency of action must not make us forget the extreme discretion of love; more Christians have to accept the form and the characteristics of the ways of God.

Finally the community. It is the very being of the Church; the Church is more than mission and service to the world: she lives salvation. When she withdraws within herself, like a family which is reunited at the end of a day's work, she allows herself the liberty of living in common her communion with Jesus Christ, of enjoying here and now, quite simply the presence he has promised: it is a merciful anticipation of the kingdom (Bonhöffer). It is only at the heart of the community that the deepest level of being of the Church can be discovered: the life which remains hidden in Jesus Christ. The Spirit of the promise has already been given us as a pledge: the Spirit which has established Jesus Christ in his condition of lord has already been given us; the Spirit already produces in us the fruits of the harvest, love, joy, peace, patience, gentleness; he is poured out in us in love. The signs of the kingdom, then, do not consist solely of the word, but also in the transformation of the lives of the faithful. Against the temptation to covet above all the spectacular manifestations of the Spirit, Paul opposes the better charisms: faith, hope, and love. Moreover all the charisms are given in community; for the Spirit is given in different ways, but the charisms work together for the good of the community.

The community is established by means of definitive realities: the spirit of promise and the presence of Jesus Christ. Communion, then, is not the result of sociological homogeneity, nor of human skill. It is the body of Christ and the Spirit which throw down every obstacle to *koinônia*. These eschatological realities make the Church. Consequently it is not surprising that the functions which assure the cohesion of the body are based not on a technique or a talent for leadership, but on the Spirit which guides and builds up the Church; these functions cannot be assumed except by reason of a gift of the Spirit. Moreover if the eucharist makes the Church, one can understand more easily why the presidents of the community were very soon entrusted, exclusively, with the presidency of the eucharist.

As long as the Lord of the harvest has not sent out his emissaries to sort and store, the community of saints remains in the midst of a mixed world: such is the lesson of the parables; unless perhaps they suggest also that in the Church sinners and saints march side by side until the end. In any case, the vivid consciousness that the spirit of promise, and eternal life, have already been given us, always goes hand in hand with a large degree of realism. If conversion constitutes the unique act of entry, the Christian has nonetheless to continue the struggle and to pass continually through the death of Christ. It is from this standpoint, which is both ideal and realistic, that the internal discipline of the community must be understood: to bind and to loose. The presidency of the community does not only consist in keeping alive both love and the awareness of present realities, nor simply in announcing the final salvation, but it must intervene by corrective measures and by gestures of mercy, thus anticipating the day of judgement and grace. The eschatological dimension explains the meaning of the discipline of the Church; it is not simply a matter of making learned decisions about what is allowed and what is forbidden, nor of behaving as a spiritual police force whose object is to maintain good order, both moral and religious, in the community; rather the Church anticipates in the community here on earth the final word of grace.[10]

However it is above all in the liturgical celebration where she commemorates the eschatological event of the death and resurrection of Jesus Christ that the Church already shares the banquet which God has prepared for all nations, and that she is already in communion with the risen Lord under the signs of bread and wine.

But the steadfastness of her faith in this presence, which is so real, and the liveliness of her joy only go to strengthen the fervour of her waiting, which breaks out in the cry *Maran Atha*, 'Our Lord, Come!' Thus her concern for the reign which is still coming takes its place in the thanksgiving or recognition of the salvation which is there present, and this concern gathers up in itself the longing of creation.

[10] J. JEREMIAS, κλεις, in KITTEL, *Theologisches Wörterbuch zum N.T.*, III, pp. 743–753; F. BUCHSEL, δεω (λυω), ibid., II, pp. 59–60.

PART FIVE

INTRODUCTION

In this paper, Adrian Cunningham is not directly or exclusively concerned with the issue of priesthood, for he was asked to discuss some of the ways in which cultural and revolutionary change may demand new theological categories. But the aspects and implications of cultural change suggested here have obvious bearings on the nature and role of the Church, and, within the Church, on the function of priesthood. The Church and its priesthood are permanently confronted with the dilemma which results from its acceptance of the double role of reconciling all men in the peace of Christ, and of dividing them by the sword of the Spirit.

BIOGRAPHICAL NOTE

ADRIAN CUNNINGHAM *is a lecturer in the Department of Religious Studies in the University of Lancaster, where he specialises in modern religious and atheist thought and in the cultural analysis of religion. He is an editor of* Slant *and is preparing a book on the cultural analysis of religion which Penguin are publishing.*

14 Cultural Change and the Nature of the Church

ADRIAN CUNNINGHAM

THE QUESTION OF CULTURAL CHANGE AND REVOLUTION bringing new theological categories into play is inseparable from the continuing problem of the relation between faith and history, for cultural change and revolution are supremely historical phenomena. The question is then, in principle, not a new one. Many of the most difficult and contentious areas of present crisis derive from just this: the problems are of long standing and we have not progressed much towards their solution. If they could be seen as fundamentally new or temporary and transitional then *ad hoc* solutions, sudden transformatory interventions would be possible. If on the other hand the problems are old ones then whilst the present may be seen as an exciting challenge it should be clear that it may be almost too late for theological solutions to be operative in creating a new kind of Christian community. For this reason a glance at longer term matters is not of ancillary interest but central to a correct understanding of the nature, extent and weight of contemporary issues. Questions of faith and history go to the root not merely of the adaptations of faith in different circumstances but to the constitutive nature of faith itself, and thus of the Church in which that faith is articulated and historically available.

To put a major point briefly, Christians have often acted as if the main problem of the last century had been and still is the issue of science and religion or modern technical society and religion. In a long view, both in theory and in practice, the issue is in fact that of social science and religion, modern political society and religion; the rise of historical and social sciences and the social changes they reflect which are most clearly articulated in socialism. In so far as the issue is seen as one of religion embattled with science then the battle has been a phoney one; the real action has, insistently, been elsewhere. If in this phoney battle inappropriate strategies are adopted – primarily individualist existential reactions to both science and social science, the recourse to individual existential certainties in the face of the relativising and historicising surge of historicism – then we get the measure of the problem. The issue is not only misdescribed but the response to it is misdirected. The problems for religious belief and action have been historical; the suggested answers existential. With this degree of polarisation polemics can fly to and fro and the central issues never become clear. It is of great significance that one of the few men to be both a reputable theologian and a competent sociologist, Ernst Troeltsch, ended in an impasse and that for forty years his work has been taken largely as a folly. After Hegel, Feuerbach and Marx we have Kierkegaard; after Troeltsch, Karl Barth; after Blondel and Loisy, Jacques Maritain. In each period or tradition the question has not been faced at its own level of seriousness, rather it has been evaded by polarising recourse to the ahistorical. In this major respect the immense differences of Barth, and Maritain, say, are less important than their similarity. (Of course to get an argument going *between* Barthians and neo-Thomists or any of their variants and analogues is to confuse the long term issues almost beyond hope of disentanglement.) It is one of the ironies of the last few years that many Catholics extricating themselves from ahistorical neo-Thomism are drawn to ahistorical existential categories of individual authenticity, angst, certainty and relationship. The pattern is deeply embedded in modern religious thought and there is no reason why it should be any more successful in its contemporary Catholic guise than at any previous point. The nature of the problems and the inadequacy of the response to them has not substantially changed from the 1840s to the 1960s. This is a deliberately emphatic reading of the question for it is the character of social, historical and cultural analysis that it cannot be divorced from practice, thus theological and 'social teaching' responses cannot be divorced from the question of their practical implementation.

Of course historical analysis has been present in the study of scripture but there are two things to note here: how delayed this was in Catholicism so that it came as a trauma in Loisy and is only really current in the last decade or so, and that no amount of historical techniques in a field will reveal relevant theological categories if the whole field is characterised by a passive ahistoricism. So one is not concerned with the history of history in scripture studies but with the history of history in the tradition of Marx and critical sociology. In this tradition, to put it in an intense and paradoxical form, the very crux of history is that *it* does not exist, of studying the operations of history that *it* does not operate:

> History does nothing; it 'does *not* possess immense riches', it 'does *not* fight battles'. It is men, real, living men, who do all this, who possess things and fight battles. It is not 'history' which uses men as a means of achieving – as if it were an individual person – its own ends. History is nothing but the activity of men in pursuit of their ends (Marx, *The Holy Family*).

In two ways such an understanding of history contrasts with much religious thought. First, it traces back actions existing at the 'providence' 'history' scale to human actors; the forces of history lose their inevitability and become in principle 'evitable', open to conscious creation. But, secondly, in its tracing back of history to human interaction, it does not reduce the large scale events to individuals or individual motivations *tout court*; the historical point of the action may not in any particular case be accessible to the actors. That is, between the polarities of an over subjectivised concern with motives, intentions, will and so on, and over objectivised notions of providence, history, the sin of the world etc. characteristic of religious thinking, historical imagination and analysis is concerned with the praxis – and the various *mediations* of this praxis – in which intentionality and historical agency mesh, attempting to render both of these intelligible and finally comprehensible.

In one sense it is hardly surprising that the religious response has not been to engage in this area but rather to redefine the old polarities in terms of, say, existential authenticity and salvation history. The limit of theoretical integration here is found in the development of modern Protestant thought where integration is achieved at the price of reducing historical questions to existential or ontological ones – in the latter case, especially, making history once more inevitable. Typically, eschatological and other future orientated beliefs are re-interpreted in terms of the present alone (salvation as rebirth here and now, resurrection as the experience of conversion etc.). Such a methodological procedure not only empties history of any meaning, it necessarily produces a static and quietist concept of society – especially when it knits with the constantly reduplicated present of modern consensus politics, in which what we urgently need to do is what we are already doing.[1]

The implications of a substantial historical position emphasise at least the following. (a) A sense of human beings as essentially and constitutively situated beings, not in time but temporal, belonging to – even being – a certain language, culture, time and place. In this view the historical and the social are linked concepts, linked aspects of human praxis, and social science is in the last resort an historical discipline. (b) Historical relations are necessarily interconnected and constantly dialectical, there is thus no external or neutral point from which total evaluations can be drawn; criteria are criteria but immanent rather than transcendent. (c) There is a considerable relativity in such a scheme, its final extent depending upon the degree to which immanent criteria can be deployed; short of complete relativism quite new conceptions of what constitutes objectivity are brought into play. Certainly there is no place for static or immutable absolutes, and this is not only a problem for religious thought though obviously most

[1] The move from statements about 'our own life' (i.e. an historical, social and existential reality) to statements of a wholly here and now existential nature pervades BULTMANN's famous *History and Eschatology* (1957); for a typical and subtle non-theological version see the book by Bultmann's colleague KARL LOWITH, *Meaning in History* (Chicago 1949).

worrying there; the inability to think through this problem coupled with a fascination with the natural sciences led to the pervasive degeneration of Marxist theory.[2]

(d) Such a sense of history by centering upon human action and constant change is essentially critical and future directed, history is seen as a demand rather than a process. (e) It demands new conceptions of action, inter-action, subjectivity and consciousness; rather than see consciousness as a primary agency putting things into action at one remove, it stresses action as an on-going process within which consciousness occurs as withdrawal and re-direction of action (Blondel's *L'Action* is of obvious significance here and especially for theology). It is in this way that Marx describes men typically as producers rather than as conscious beings; for consciousness can be the passive reception of or reaction to stimulus, or essentially an individual phenomenon, whereas production whether of ideas, beliefs, cultures or objects is an essentially creative, active, and inter-subjective reality. So (f) it is the conditions of production, and especially of the material reproduction of social life, which will determine (in the sense of shaping or defining, not of linear causality) social existence in other areas. And, in Marx's case, all developments will remain unintelligible unless finally related to the social conflict engendered by scarcity: the conflict both of social classes and of the potentialities of the conditions of production and the forms of their organisation – private competitive ownership, the confined

[2] It may be worth noting that the hiatus in Marxist theory covers a comparable period to that already noted in religious thought, roughly from the early 1920s to late 1950s. It would be interesting to investigate the possible common roots of these developments in the light of ALASDAIR MACINTYRE's remark that 'the conditions which are inimical to religion seem to be inimical to marxism too', *Marxism and Christianity* (1969), p. 111. What constitutes objectivity is a tricky and neglected question in Marxist theory much of which still labours under the incubus of positivism. For useful approaches see LESZEK KOLAKOWSKI, 'Karl Marx and the Classical Definition of Truth' in *Towards a Socialist Humanism* (New York 1968), and *The Alienation of Reason* (New York 1968); GEORGE LICHTHEIM, *The Concept of Ideology and Other Essays* (New York 1967), ch. 1; GEORGE LUKACS, 'Bukharin's Sociology' in *New Left Review*, and 'What is Orthodox Marxism?' in *International Socialism*, pp. 24 and 25; HERBERT MARCUSE, *Reason and Revolution* (New York 1966) and *Negations* (1968). In general the critical approach to objectivity is indicated in GRAMSCI's remark: ' "What should be" is therefore concrete, and it is moreover the only realistic and historicist interpretation of reality; it is the only active history and philosophy, the only politics.' *The Modern Prince* (1957), p. 163.

bourgeois family etc. In such a conception, revolution is the point where the scale of needs and of demands upon social life can be attained only by a transformation of existing social forms. Questions of the length of time involved or of the peaceful or violent nature of the revolution are subsidiary to this main point. (g) With its stress on social reality as a social product and its openness to creative conscious change such a view tends wholly towards humanism rather than any traditionally conceived theism. Integrating and sociologically founding Feuerbach's theory of religious projection, such a view sees the religious world as a systematic reflection/construction where the legitimation of this world – in *both* its negative and positive aspects – is located. Thus religion is not only to be related in its various institutional and dogmatic forms to the historical and social situations which determine it (and are in turn affected by it) but religion as such, as a totality, is to be seen as a human projection or system of projections.

Even this brief summary will, I hope indicate the nature of the problems associated with cultural change, its analysis and understanding. In what follows I want to introduce discussion under three heads: the possibility of new theological categories which might meet the difficulties; ideological elements in Catholic thought and especially social teaching; specific problems in the nature of the Church which might suggest that even if new categories could be found it may not be possible to make them effective. This last point will be discussed mainly in theoretical terms; obviously what is said here must be related to concrete developments and possibilities – this would require an extended study in itself – the main aim is conceptual clarification without which concrete analysis will remain encapsulated within already degenerate categories.

New Theological Categories

Stated baldly the *desiderata* for adequate theological categories are: (1) specific and delicate attention to the intra-mundane, the socio-historical world which (2) is capable of integrating and going beyond the insights of existentialism by (3) grounding them in a substantial understanding of historicity and historicism which affirms (4) history as possibility and demand centered upon human freedom and aspiration i.e. (5) an ability specifically, to engage creatively with the more developed and critical forms of Marxist theory.

On this reading, and as has been argued for some time, there is little to be drawn from traditional Catholic thought on the relation of religion and society or social teaching: in so far as this tradition is historically concrete it derives from ultramontane and corporatist interests; in so far as it is critical that criticism is couched either in terms of an earlier agricultural and hierarchical society or of a bare recourse to the unspecific primacy of the supernatural: that is, it is not only falsely polarised but wholly encapsulated. In different, but sometimes analogous terms there are severe and even at times stronger limitations in the main forms of Protestant thought. An emphasis of the transcendence of God and the sinful facticity of any human society can provide a ground for polemical rejection of dictatorial regimes (Nazism, Stalinism) but in tending to relativise each and every human order vis-à-vis God it is of little constructive use (Barth). Even where such a critique is associated with heroic opposition to the status quo this is addressed to an emergency and the social norms in terms of which it takes place and which it seeks to re-establish may be thoroughly conservative (Bonhoeffer) – here, even here, theological radicalism and political conservatism may go hand in hand which from the cultural analysts' point of view raises doubts about the reality of the theological radicalism. It may be that Marxism is engaged with but this may be the temporary and purely instrumental adoption of a method *pour épater* the idolatrous bourgeoisie in the name of what is finally a conservative and even establishment Christian political position (Niebuhr). These features of modern Protestant thought and their abiding tug upon adventurous innovators should make for caution in the ecumenical translation of Protestant insights into Catholic terms. There are though features of this earlier period which both in justice and for the investigation of new categories have to be mentioned. Though it seems discredited on all sides the Christian socialism of Rauschenbusch needs re-examination as does the religious socialism of the early Tillich (cf. *The Religious Situation and The Protestant Era* – the most accessible in English) though against the focus on human self-transcendence his stress on *kairos*, theonomy and process – and consequently the weakness of his eschatology – one sees the germ of his later ahistorical absorption in an ahistorical ontology.[3] Although, at this distance of time, many of his arguments would seem to lack sophistication – and he has no interest in what is normally described as theology – I think there are important elements for new categories in the work of John Macmurray thirty years ago.[4] Take the following: his contrast between the organic, factually given and *en-soi* kinship nature of community in the Old Testament, and the freely intentional, non-kinship *pour-soi* community desiderated in the New Testament. Or again his understanding of Christianity as the project of a universal community, of transcendence as the immanent sublation of the given towards the future. And lastly, his understanding of Christian history as the continuity of an historical intention whose integrity in development is not only compatible with but demands radical alterations of practice. Later, in his very sophisticated development of the concept of action and of inter-personal reality,[5] this earlier eschatological interest is less represented but with all its need for correction it does provide indispensable tools for theological investigation.

The limits of eschatological categories in recent thinking have been indicated but since they are again fortunately enjoying a major place in theological preoccupations and are central to our topic, I want to add some comments on its current forms. Moltmann's *Theology of Hope* is undoubtedly one of the great books of our period and if I am critical here the personal indebtedness which makes criticism possible is a very real one. Moltmann certainly re-establishes eschatology as the lynch pin of theological work, but, although his criticisms of Barth are acute and substantial, it is a fair question how far in the end he has really gone beyond Barth's limits. That is the categories opened up by him

---

[3] In Tillich's influence on Altizer this leads to a radical social criticism but of an amorphous and Nietzschean kind; an almost hysterical stress upon the reality of the present means that political problems are reduced to existential ones, locatable and resolvable at that level.

[4] Cf., for example, *Creative Society* (1935) and *The Clue to History* (1938).

[5] *The Form of the Personal, Persons in Relation,* Gifford Lectures, 1958.

are unilaterally concentrated upon revelation and would be modified by a modern natural theology; for example, his emphasis on 'promise' in the Old Testament as the condition of historical experience for Israel tends to miss the point that on the historical view (as Feuerbach glimpsed) man as man is constituted by his future. Israel's consciousness may be crucial, but what it is conscious of is a general human fact of an historical-social kind, thus talk of God's future and man's present must be integrally related to man's historical-social future. On the one hand the future is in process of fulfilment by the eschaton, on the other the Christian role is one of hoping, waiting, witnessing, openness; the question of active human demand as historical agency predominant in the historical view is not finally faced. There is consequently in Moltmann a certain fudging of the terms 'fulfilment' and 'participation' (a pervasive feature of the 1960s . . .) human participation tending to be seen as acquiescence in the right sort of future rather than active achievement of it. I am not suggesting that Moltmann falls into the theological-radicalism: political-conservatism syndrome, this is evidently not so; but if his work is not taken further I think it could be encapsulated in a purely instrumental use of historical categories tending back to a Christian and existential transcendence out of history in a divine future, rather than a transcendence on the basis of history in a divine-human future.[6]

The main issue here is that of the relation between the idea of God's kingdom and its active preparation, between the coming of the kingdom and its being built. It seems to me that Moltmann's schooling in Barth leads him to an over-emphasis on the coming of the kingdom, and hence a weakening of human agency, and

---

[6] The latent ambiguity here can be seen in the different emphases Rahner and Metz, deriving from Moltmann, give to the concepts hope and future (in GARAUDY, *Anathema to Dialogue* (1967), pp. 11–24 and 109–25). Metz's stress upon 'hope as awaiting *and* as struggle' . . . 'we are builders – not merely interpreters – of a future, of which God himself is the dynamism' is not present in Rahner's contribution. Dewart's formulation is also to be noted: 'The fundamental relation of God and man is found in the reality of history. It consists in the mutual presence of God and man in the conscious creation of the world' (*The Future of Belief*), p. 195. Though it is obviously a difficult and delicate matter formulations of this kind still need to be made more historically specific, if we are not to find ourselves with a slightly more up to date version of existential 'salvation history'.

hence again a rather vague notion of its achievement – certain writers in the Moltmann vein seem to envision an indefinitely receding undifferentiated future. Christian tradition demands, I think, something more than this. Although if humanity is constituted by having a future there is a sense of unending human adventure, Christian belief demands a qualitative change in the terms of this adventure. The problem is that if the coming of the kingdom is a unilateral act of God then human agency – beyond witnessing and waiting, no matter how existentially fraught it may be – is of little account. Whereas the whole burden of the historical view is that agency is *the* question. One solution, often concretely found in South America, where the notion of specific links between Christianity and politics is inherently reactionary, is to split the eschatological reality away from human agency so that political activities are what we do simply as human beings. Even outside the desperate situation of South America where such a position may have strategic attractions, and taking account of the truth that men who need the special promptings of Christianity to common human justice are not plausibly the salt of the earth, it remains the case that to radically sever politics and eschatology, is to fall back into precisely that (Catholic) supernaturalist or (Protestant) existential-ontological categorisation which has led to the present impasse. Though it is unfashionable in a time of euphoric secularisation to seek a specific salvific agency for the Church, I do not myself see that it can be evaded. It will certainly not be salvific in terms of universal conversion, but perhaps it may be in terms of a continuing remnant, so that, while the notion is a mysterious one, the coming of the kingdom in its fullness is not only conditional upon (what Christians believe will happen) the building of a secular kingdom but also upon the continued active existence of the Christian community. What I am suggesting is that the required theological synthesis will stress both the purely human construction of universal community, with the Christian community as an area of radical eschatological dissatisfaction and demand, of permanent criticism of every existing and possible society, at the same time investigating the role of the Church as the guarantor of the necessary condition of its own abolition, i.e. a community of God and man which renders eschatological criticism unnecessary. With the cautions here indicated I feel that such a theological integration, a perspective of revolutionary change towards the eschaton which runs actively through and beyond existing politics, is possible, and that the forty years hiatus of Christian thought may be ending. Whether such historically grounded theological views can be operative is another question; if they cannot then in the light of what has been said so far, they are useless.

The Problem of Ideology

The question of the viability of theological categories centered upon eschatology and creatively engaged with cultural change as demand and revolution involves an examination of the ideological elements with which existing categories are enmeshed as well as concrete questions of organisational viability. This ideological analysis needs to be done over a wide field, but for the present purpose I should like to look at one model of the Church, especially prevalent amongst Catholics, in some detail – argue that even when not explicit this has an implicit regulating function and that the measure of progress will be the degree to which we can get beyond it. The analogy or model in mind here is that of the family. The 'Christian family' is not only a basic element in Catholic social teaching it is a basic mode of Catholic thinking about what any grouping is, whole societies, the Church itself, liturgical groups etc. As Macmurray pointed out an essential element of Christianity is or should be its release from familial models (leaving father and mother): for the family is necessarily and basically a conserving unit, it is natural and naturally hierarchical; the division of age and care is simply given and inevitable, the structural relations likewise – X simply is my uncle. The point is that other groups, all other groups, are not so inevitably structured: political relations are in principle free, voluntary and open to structural change, their hierarchy is not biologically given but has to be consciously struggled for and maintained. The reading of societal or political questions in terms of the family is wholly confusing and cannot but reinforce the existing social structure, freezing it artificially and preserving it from human control, demand and change. The family can be plausibly described in terms of personal attitudes, intentions or feelings, and change within it can be achieved by personal adjustment. Again, this is not so with other groups, real change here demanding more than attitudinal change. Even the conceptual tools for analysis and change – class, for example – cannot be engendered from individual or psychological roots, they are only accessible at the level of the whole group or society. (Obviously the family in any given instance cannot be clearly understood unless account is taken of its location within and penetration by categories like class.) It is not surprising that orthodox Catholic social teaching has either denied the term class or else emptied it of its essential conflict and rendered it functionally in familial terms, so that different classes can collaborate as if in a family – justice existing to regulate a given structure of relations and not, teleologically or eschatologically, to create a new structuration. Or, more generally, and I shall take this up later with regard to the unity of the Church, unity is seen as a given fact to be restored or maintained, by coercion if necessary, and not as an eschatological demand whose achievement may involve and necessitate conflict.

A further important aspect of this sort of model links it to a more long term phenomenon. Any human group has both productive and consuming functions (products here being understood in the extensive sense already given) and for the maintenance of the group the productive functions are clearly prior. In terms of models, it then makes an enormous difference if the model predominantly follows either a productive or consumer line. Production is essentially creative and, in fact or in principle, socially interactive; consumption may not be either of these, it can be passive and solitary, of its own bent it tends towards isolation and egotism. If for historical reasons – the absence of collective production – the earliest Christian concepts of community are based on consumption, a pooling of the results, fruits or wages of work, there is no reason why this should any longer be appropriate. In modern societies collective productive relations have increased (they form the historical precondition for the emergence of socialism) and consumptive relations have tended increasingly towards the private. At some times – e.g. when agriculture is pervasive – it may be that the family unit is both a producing and consuming group; but outside that area and in the field of typical collective production which now forms the basic social link (it is where we spend the greatest part of our socially significant time) the family has become almost solely a consuming unit. Along with the privatisation of the family has gone a decline in those social areas most connected with it – in Christian terms for example the geographical parish is increasingly where people are in their families, at leisure in their spare time; it is socially marginal. If one links the features of familial social models noted with the marginal nature of consumer units then the practical irrelevance of the model is confirmed. Except for purposes of social control it is wholly uncreative. The Christian family and the familial analogy of liturgical community, bishops and laity, bishops and pope, etc., may offer itself as a critique of the inhumanity of capitalist society – the warm family appeal is obvious . . . – but it exists in fact as a *mediation* of that society.[7] It is not a matter of adjustment; the time in which that analogy and the whole organisational system which goes with it could operate as an effective sign and efficacious reality has already passed. Until this sort of ideological historical root of existing theological categories is faced and understood a clear formulation of new categories will be of no great significance.

Church: Sect, and Hegemony

The question of new categories is involved on the one hand with the most general questions of the link between faith and history and the critique of religion in terms of projection, and on the other for the appropriate terms and forms for those categories, with a study of Christian ideology. Again let us assume that not only will new theological formulations be available, but that models of society and community can be found in which they will be most meaningful and effective. There still remains a

[7] CARL AMERY's study of the failure of German Catholicism to react to Nazism centres upon the role of the familial milieu in German Catholic ideology, *Capitulation* (1967). Germany was *the* centre of theological research and innovation, even a renaissance of Catholic theology launched from Germany was confidently expected by leading European intellectuals in the 1930s; this is worth noting because the obviousness of the connection of theological radicalism and political conservatism in that horrific instance has still to be properly investigated.

connected set of questions thrown up by cultural change and the critical theory of cultural change. This involves the more precise point at which eschatological categories and actual realisation of the kingdom are imbricated in the understanding of the Church. This is best seen by going back to a problem which greatly exercised Troeltsch fifty years ago and the importance of which has only increased with time. His analysis of Christian history had revealed two major forms of organisation: the Church and the sect. Much modification is needed to Troeltsch's original scheme and there is a wide literature on the subject, for the present I want only to expose the basic problem as graphically as possible. The Church is typically a group in which membership is upon the basis of birth; its social composition is inclusive, often coinciding with ethnic or national boundaries; it is directed towards the conversion of all and tends to adjust to and compromise with the values and institutions of existing society. The sect, on the other hand, is characterised by voluntary joining, an emphasis upon conversion experience, and an attitude of ethical austerity; its social composition is exclusive and it tends towards a separatism from the larger society, a withdrawal from or defiance of existing values and institutions. It seemed to Troeltsch that both types were doomed and he asked rhetorically if the mystics and radically subjective believers who had been carried by these forms could themselves form the continuing basis for the future of Christianity. Sociologically the move is implausible, apart from objections to its stress on mysticism. But the terms of the question are still very real, though in a different form. It might be better put (as Gordon Zahn once suggested) can a Church act like a sect? For if new theological categories are to be centred on eschatology and on historical realities and the religious community is not to be an end in itself or even primarily missionary, but functional in the salvation of the world, then priority would seem to go to the sect; its cohesion and limited basis give it a mobility and possibility of opposition to established values and regimes (e.g. refusal to bear arms) that Churches have not had. Churches typically have been unable to take a decision where two of its constituent elements are engaged (e.g. all Christian Churches or hierarchies claiming their own side is right in all known wars). In a period of increasing realisation of political conflict, both in practice and in conceptual understanding, is not the church type too unwieldy a corporate body to be of any use? Precisely by being all things to all men can it say anything specific to any of them? Precisely by crossing social classes can it really be of any serious use to the oppressed? Can its image of itself as a community be other than at best merely symbolic and at the ordinary level a generalised false consciousness? A lot has been said lately of the Church as a symbol, witnessing etc. but the nub of the debate is the Church as sacrament, a sign which effects its meaning. That is why I said 'merely symbolic', for the church community in a world divided not by attitudes but by historical, economic, social and political conflicts in which every day thousands suffer and die and have died for too long, *cannot* effect what it signifies unless it can in some sense act like a sect, that is be socially divisive, committed. (The title of an earlier symposium *The Committed Church* significantly concentrates on what I have described as consumer topics.)

It is the irony of the post-conciliar Church that the very point of the Church as witness of a universal community has become a prime obstacle to the creation of that community. In sociological terms it is quite possible that a Church may become a sect through a period of decline but it is less likely that it could consciously act like or become one, for it is social position that determines religious views not vice versa. At most religious beliefs connect and articulate in a specific configuration particular independently pre-existing possibilities. Have we then reached an impasse? Not yet I think an impasse although the way forward is an extremely difficult one and of problematic success. There are at least two lines of approach to this to be examined: the question of the unity of the Church and the notion of hegemony.

The Church as community, and unity in that community, is part of the Church's self-definition – although analysis of the familial model of that unity has suggested its concrete speciousness on any large scale. But the category of eschatology suggests that the situation may be misconceived. Unity surely belongs to the witness of the Church and, just because it is witness, the reality of that unity is eschatological – it does not and cannot now exist and its awaited real existence will render the Church and its witness redundant. The unity of the Church is not a given but an aspiration, a shape to be struggled for. The Church should always be attentive to any possibility of integration but at the same time it will itself be necessarily and creatively in practice a battleground as much as any other area of life. It will itself contain differences, enmities, struggles and takeovers (as it always has done if one reads it historically, what one is proposing is not start a struggle but a bringing of it into the open). The mistake – an ultramontane and Vaticanist one in particular – is to confuse eschatological unity with present reality, to think a concrete unity exists when it does not and cannot: the result is a generalised unity of spiritual goodwill, dearly beloveds and the banal universals of encyclicals co-existing with a very direct coercion to enforce what practical unity can be enforced; again a polarisation of the most opposed terms which renders the important middle area unintelligible. The pattern is so familiar as to suggest deliberate cynicism or hypocrisy; such a description in moralistic and psychological terms misses however the essence of the phenomena of ideology and false consciousness, that collective states are not simply reducible to statements about individuals. Yet this should not lead to a false benevolence; it is true that men may know not what they do but that is no reason why they should not be stopped from doing it. Thus it is in the light of eschatological unity as hope and demand that the present sham coercive unity is to be exposed and an intensification of conflict rather than its specious accommodation expected.

Does this mean that Catholicism breaks down into a number of warring sects? Put this way the question is inappropriate as that which asks why bring politics into religion because the Church has always contained barely smoothed over socio-political conflicts. Rather it should be asked what sort of identity across classes and other divisions is possible which is not eschatologically pre-emptive and thus false in itself and falsifying eschatology. It is here that Gramsci's idea of the hegemonic party may prove illuminating. He argued that if Marxism is concerned with the whole man and the whole society then both in terms of values and as a definite political strategy the communist party must seek to provide a universal over-arching scheme of values and political direction which will articulate aspirations and creativities at varying levels of the society so that the party aspiring to victory is as culturally extensive as the system it opposes. In this extensiveness the edge of opposition and combativity is not to be lost, very hard organisation and direction is necessary – he is discussing a party and not a moralo-political campaign. The analogy is not hard to see, the Church is already in many respects hegemonic although in an archaic mode and with no real combativity. Gramsci himself suggests an original index of this situation and a clue to the present crisis when he notes how the Church institutionalised dissent in forming religious elites:

> The fact that the Church has to face the problem of the 'simple people' means precisely that a breach has occurred within the community of the 'faithful', a breach which cannot be healed by bringing the 'simple people' up to the level of the intellectuals . . . but by an iron discipline over the intellectuals so that they do not pass beyond certain limits of differentiation and do not render it catastrophic and irreparable. In the past these breaches in the community of the 'faithful' were healed by strong mass movements which brought about, or were absorbed by, the formation of new religious orders around forceful personalities. But the Counter-Reformation sterilised this germination of popular forces. The Society of Jesus is the great religious order, of reactionary and authoritarian origin, with a repressive and 'diplomatic' character, whose origin signalised a stiffening of the Catholic organism. The new orders which arose afterwards had a very small 'religious' significance but great 'disciplinary' significance over the masses of the faithful. They are ramifications and tentacles of the Society of Jesus or they have become such – weapons of 'resistance' for preserving the already acquired political position, not forces of renewed development. Catholicism has become 'Jesuitism'. The modern age has not seen the creation of 'religious orders' but of a political party, the Christian Democrats.[8]

And we might now add that the Christian democratic containment

1 Prison notebooks, 1926–37, in ANTONIO GRAMSCI, *The Modern Prince* (1957), pp. 65–6.

of the laity has also broken down; there are no institutional or quasi-institutional forms for the new dissenting elites. This is at once their problem and their hope. The absence of institutional forms makes containment difficult but it also makes access to effective power equally difficult; if the new elites were not partly composed of clerics within the present power structure, their frustration would be even greater than it already is.

Seen in this light it is not surprising that the debate about the nature of priesthood – whether a life-long role deriving from episcopal consecration, or possibly a temporary function of the community etc. – is so important politically. Raising such questions threatens the very existence of the insulated co-optive power structure of the old orthodox elites.

There can be no question of the Church trying to substitute itself for a hegemonic political party, but aspects of the analogy hold. The radical elites in the Church try at every level to articulate specific grievances and aspirations, to move simultaneously on matters of theology, church government, culture and education. But the final object of their hegemony lies primarily within the Church; it is to form a hegemonic conception, a set of perspectives and orientations which makes sense of Christian experience and helps link it to the struggle for political hegemony in the world at large, and at the same time furnish a meaningful witness to a reality outstripping even the most perfect society. Such a conception is eschatological by the extremity of its demands upon life, the depth of its dissatisfaction and hope, it is thus an inherently critical hegemony. It would be quite false to suggest that this can be all things to all men, being a critical hegemony it will be quite different from the complacent formal hegemony of the existing Church. Having eschatological unity as its hope it will strive towards integration in the present, but at some points (e.g. being clear that the Church in pre-Castro Cuba was rotten beyond hope of internal reform and had to be suppressed) it will be definitely exclusive and divisive. To the extent that it can in this sense be sectarian, it could be viable. [9]

[9] For a sketch of what priesthood might be in such a church see HERBERT MCCABE, 'Priesthood and Revolution' and TERRY EAGLETON, 'The Priest and the Leninist' in *Slant*, 27.

The major questions posed in my outline have theoretically possible resolutions, combative and not acquiescent resolutions, whether they can in fact be effective is another question and one that cannot be put off much longer. At the same time, as Moltmann reminds us, we can have no certainty, only hope.

INTRODUCTION

Fr Laurence Bright contends that the Church has until recently been a re-actionary force in society, its members formed to accept passively the accepted forms set out authoritatively, and to express themselves in ways remote from the needs of the communities in which they live. Universities are in a similar state, and it is not surprising that both the Church and the universities are being subjected to the same kind of radical criticism. This paper uses the model of the modern, secular university as a means of talking about the Church.

When Laurence Bright read his paper to the symposium it was followed by considerable discussion. Some of the objections which were raised are set out in the note by Dr Coulson at the end of this paper.

BIOGRAPHICAL NOTE

FR LAURENCE BRIGHT O.P., *is an advisory editor for Sheed & Ward, a member of the editorial board of* Slant, *associate study secretary and secretary of the Political Commission of the Student Christian Movement, theological adviser to the Newman Association and editor of its periodical,* Newman.

15 A Pattern for the Future Church

LAURENCE BRIGHT O.P.

Presuppositions

The preceding papers have examined the character of the Church's
ministry in history and at the present day. A wide diversity of
understanding and practice has emerged, and it is hardly surprising that there is also diversity of view about the future of both
Church and ministry. Together with others over the past few
years I have argued that the only way to see where the Church
should be going, and to work towards it, is to accept a specifically
Marxist account of society as a whole and the Church's position
within it. There is no point in going through these arguments in
detail once again, but in order to build on them I shall first summarise them briefly under three heads, and add the necessary
documentation for those who wish to examine them more fully.
I shall then go on to show that on these presuppositions there is
a close relationship between the position of the Church in society
and that of the university, so that the movements for change in a
particular direction now actively developing in the one provide a
model for what we must now begin to do in the other, the Church.
Before closing these preliminary remarks, let me say that for
obvious reasons I am confining my attention to the west, and for
the most part to Britain; that by 'university' I mean any institute

of tertiary education (it is unfortunate that no single word exists to cover the very different areas of university, college of education, college of technology, art and so on); and that by 'church' I mean primarily the Roman Catholic Church but expect my remarks to be generally applicable to other Churches too – indeed, within the perspective of the present paper, denominational differences are not particularly relevant. I must add that for the most part I shall be concerned only indirectly with the ministry and its future, but on any account it is closely bound up with the future of the whole people of God.

The first presupposition, then, is that the purpose of the Church is to be an instrument for the renewal of the world, of which it is a part. Since it is true that the relationships between classes and individuals are exploitative, the Christian community has to help to change those relationships into non-exploitative ones. Theologically this is to say that the Church is Christ acting in the world. But Christ is himself a human person, risen and living with the Father. He transcends human community, and draws it towards himself throughout history. So this is not the presupposition of reductive humanism. Certainly it denies that the Church, or individuals within it, are *directly* concerned with their right relationship to God. But it affirms that this right relationship is given by God through right human relationship (the real meaning of 'justification by faith'). The practical consequence is that Christian life and work is fully describable in human (political) rather than mystical terms, but must transcend contemporary society as a whole. The Church has to drive men forward in hope to fulfil the promise of God, knowing that it cannot be fully realised until men are brought 'to the measure of the fullness of Christ'. The Church is not alone in this, because the Spirit of God is not confined to the Church. But it has been 'officially' given this role by God.[1]

[1] The most important influences have been the writings of EDWARD SCHILLE-BEECKX (see especially *Christ the Sacrament* (London 1963) and JÜRGEN MOLTMANN, *Theology of Hope* (London 1967). Some consequences are worked out in my articles 'The Structure of the Church', *Catholics and the Left* (London 1966) and 'Christian and Marxist', *What Kind of Revolution?*, Klugmann and Oestreicher (eds.) (London 1968). See also H. MCCABE, *Law, Love and Language* (London 1968); S. MOORE, *God is a New Language* (London 1967) and the article by G. HIBBERT, 'Christian Materialism', *New Blackfriars*, May 1969.

The second point, on which there need be little controversy, is that as a whole the Church has failed to fulfil its role. The world doesn't think of Christians as revolutionaries, but as sober, decent, law-abiding folk who maintain the standards of the society in which they live. The Church today is largely identified with middle-class suburbia, and there is nothing of importance to differentiate Christians from their non-believing neighbours. Marks of difference are now private rather than public. Christians are still exhorted to practice forms of piety, but these are given minimal public form in terms of Sunday observance or (until the other day) Friday abstinence, and in the training of ministers in separated institutions by outdated methods. None of this really masks the massive conformity of the Church to the mores of bourgeois society. The weekly sermon, the average Christian's main contact with his leaders, turning as it so often does on obedience to authority, especially in matters of private property or sexual morality, continues to inculcate these attitudes. The Church remains, on the whole, wealthy and privileged, because society recognises, consciously or not, that dividends will be paid in terms of support against any attempt at radical change.

Yet the contradiction between what is and what should be remains too great ever to be wholly ignored. The 'ought' isn't simply a remote ideal in the minds of a few way-out theologians; it is sufficiently present to the Christian consciousness to make people uneasy when it is pointed out. The Church has never fully succeeded in getting rid of the gospel through reinterpretations of it; it remains an irritant, a reminder that we are a people of un-fulfilled promise. Minority groups throughout history have tried to put theory into practice, from the first community in Jerusalem through the early Franciscans and allied movements, to the Christians of the civil rights movement in Ulster or the States. This consciousness is even embodied, however implicitly, in the visible form of liturgical meetings. There is already a certain basis on which to build.[2]

[2] There is now a considerable amount of writing from the Christian left. In addition to the books mentioned above, see B. WICKER, *Culture and Liturgy* (London 1963); B. WICKER, *Culture and Theology* (London 1966); T. EAGLETON, *The New Left Church* (London 1966); BRIGHT and CLEMENTS (eds.), *The Committed Church* (London 1966); B. WICKER, *First the Political Kingdom* (London 1967); N. MIDDLETON, *The*

My third presupposition is that a Marxist approach alone
enables us to understand these contradictions in theory and resolve
them in practice, as part of the understanding and resolution of
contradictions within society as a whole. In briefest terms, since
a huge literature is readily available, the root cause of economic
exploitation and cultural fragmentation the world over is the
private ownership of capital in the west. If there is a root cause in
this sense, then it follows that one can never treat a particular
part of society in isolation from the rest, and that important
analogies between one part and another exist. But rather than
argue this in general, I shall do so by looking at Church and
university from this perspective.

One final word of clarification. I don't take a 'conspiracy' view
of society. The west isn't full of wicked capitalists who are
trying to bend all its institutions to their own needs. The con-
trolling bourgeoisie's main worries concern increase in tax on
private wealth and fall in value of shares. Its main demand is an
efficient, stable, law-abiding society without too much altruistic
concern. The effect of capitalism is to produce a class-divided
society which holds itself uneasily together with the help of consensus politics, in which every institution is there to serve élite
rather than merely human needs. One cannot, however, expect
the bourgeoisie to recognise this. In the classical concept of
alienation, exploiter and exploited alike are equally in the grip of
something they are unable to change. The situation has got out of
human control; instead men themselves are controlled by the
abstractions of the market society and the profit motive.[3]

Since capitalism affects every sector of society in the west,

---

Language of Christian Revolution (London 1968). See also the articles 'Politics and
theology: retrospect and agenda', by F. KERR in *New Blackfriars*, August 1968, and
'Locating Theology', by B. SHARRATT in *Slant* 22, which refer to earlier work
especially in these journals. There is also a considerable non-Catholic literature (cf.
in particular H. COX, *The Secular City* (London 1965)), though this is reformist rather
than radical.

---

[3] For analysis of neo-capitalist society see especially P. BARON and P. SWEEZY,
Monopoly Capitalism (London 1968), and R. WILLIAMS (ed.), *May Day Manifesto*
(London 1968). The series *Perspectives on Work, Welfare and Society*, Clegg (ed.)
(London 1969), is also useful. But there is of course a very large output of books and
articles in journals, some of which are cited below.

partial reforms in any of them are necessarily ineffectual. In the end no solution short of revolution is possible. But as yet we are not, in Britain or indeed western Europe generally, in anything approaching a revolutionary situation. The conditions for it are not yet there. Nor is there any agreement about what to do in these circumstances. Hence the fragmentation of the left, sects and non-sects each choosing a different 'British road' forward. Fortunately I do not need to discuss these in detail. It is enough to argue that as a matter of fact for the university, and of hope for the Church, one way forward consists in setting up radical alternatives to the present institutions with their present roles in society, modelled on the roles they may be expected to play in the society we hope to build. If movements to change the university occupy a large part of the paper this is not, therefore, irrelevant to its main purpose. The reader should already be considering the possible parallels within the Church, something I have often found myself usefully doing in the many consultations on student unrest through which I have had to sit.

The University as an Instrument of Capitalist Society

Until recently few members of the left seriously thought of the university as itself an agent of change in society. It was too firmly part of the establishment. It could not possibly take over the role of the working class. Of course this is perfectly correct, but over the last few years the university movement has shown by its achievements that it is a factor to be reckoned with, and there are theoretical reasons why this should be so. I can put this most concisely by using some words of Marcuse and then developing them. He says:

> The intellectuals usually went out to organise the others, to organise in the communities. They certainly did not use the potentiality they had to organise among themselves not only on a regional, not only on a national, but on an international level. That is, on my view, today one of the most urgent tasks. Can we say that the intelligentsia is the agent of historical change? Can we say that the intelligentsia today is a revolutionary class? The answer I would give is: No, we cannot say that. But

we can say, and I think we must say, that the intelligentsia has a decisive preparatory function, not more; and I suggest that this is plenty. By itself it is not and cannot be a revolutionary class, but it can become the catalyst, and it has a preparatory function – certainly not for the first time, that is in fact the way all revolution starts – but more, perhaps, today than ever before. Because – and for this too we have a very material and very concrete basis – it is from this group that the holders of decisive positions in the productive process will be recruited; scientists, researchers, engineers, even psychologists – because psychology will continue to be a socially necessary instrument, either of servitude or liberation.

He goes on to say:

The educational system is political already. I need only remind you of the incredible degree to which (I am speaking of the U.S.) universities are involved in huge research grants (the nature of which you know in many cases) by the government and the various quasi-governmental agencies.

The educational system *is* political, so it is not we who want to politicise the educational system. What we want is a counter-policy against the established policy. And in this sense we must meet this society on its own ground of total mobilisation. We must confront indoctrination in servitude with indoctrination in freedom. We must each of us generate in ourselves, and try to generate in others, the instinctual need for a life without fear, without brutality, and without stupidity.[4]

The university, that is to say, cannot be treated in isolation from the educational system as a whole, which in turn only makes sense within the economic and cultural system of society as a whole, whose needs determine to a large extent things that superficially seem purely academic; methods of teaching, content of syllabus, recruitment and so on. These are now geared to continuing the capitalist system, whereas they could be geared to satisfying human need. The recognition of this by a minority of students and teaching staff is the real cause of the deep unrest in universities

[4] H. MARCUSE, 'Liberation from the affluent society', *The Dialectics of Liberation*, Cooper (ed.) (London 1968), pp. 188–9.

and secondary schools the world over, not matters of internal reform, important as these are both in themselves and as a means to catch the attention of the majority.[5]

There are two important ways in which the university has got itself more and more geared into servicing the needs of the system, to an extent that is alarming even to the liberal academic who still thinks of it as building the 'whole man'. The first, as Marcuse points out, is to provide the sheer manpower needed for modern technological society. Manpower needs have long determined the structure of secondary education in Britain. At the age of eleven a sharp division is made by which some thirty per cent receive a different kind of education from the rest. The majority are destined to become manual workers or lower-grade clerical workers of one sort or another; these on the whole have a working-class background. The rest are destined for more responsible positions, often after passing through university; these on the whole have a bourgeois background. It is part of the strength of the system that there are plenty of exceptions, but statistical examination leaves little room for doubt.[6] Attempts to combine the two types of education produce comprehensive schools in which they continue in parallel streams, but it is very rare for the barriers to be broken down by an education that treats all alike. While it was admitted that syllabus and examinations in the grammar schools were largely controlled by university entry, this was at least felt to be giving the minority a humane and balanced outlook, producing the leaders of society as it had done in the 19th century. But today it is increasingly obvious that the university too is an instrument of mass manpower training. The Robbins report, one of the few educational reports of recent years to be taken notice of, argued (among other things, of course), that the production of graduates was a good investment for

[5] See COCKBURN and BLACKBURN (eds.), *Student Power* (London 1969); T. FAWTHROP, *Education or Examination* (London 1968). Of the many case-histories, two contrasting extremes are shown in *Ten Days that Shook the University* (London n.d.) (Strasbourg University), and Pettit (ed.), *The Gentle Revolution* (Dublin 1969) (University College, Dublin).

[6] Summaries and bibliography in D. MARQUAND and I. CLEGG, *Class and Power* (London 1969). See also B. JACKSON and D. MARSDEN, *Education and the Working Class* (London 1966).

industry and commerce.[7] The result has been the explosive expansion of higher education in the last few years. The result has also been that students themselves have come to see that their education, far from fitting them to be leaders of the society, is fitting them to be an underpaid teacher, a hack industrial chemist, a personnel manager, an engineer. Hence in part the 'flight from science' and the popularity of the social services, where something humanly useful is being done, and of sociology, which is mistakenly thought to have some connection with this. The influence of technological society on the universities is far greater than the occasional attempts, often successfully resisted by liberal opinion, to engage them directly, through tied grants from a large corporation, in industrial or governmental research, even in connection with chemical or biological warfare. If society too crudely demands results for the money it puts in, university liberal opinion can still fight successfully for autonomy: it is only the end-product, the graduate looking for a job, who feels more continually the contradiction between appearance and reality, and yet more subtle analysis is required to recognise the extent to which the university increasingly serves to absorb surplus manpower as it becomes more difficult to find productive employment for all.

The second way in which the university serves the needs of the society is by ideological training. Here again theory and practice are in contradiction. The theory is still the liberal one that university education involves a sharpening of the critical faculties, makes it possible to see more fully and more clearly the assumptions of those who are upholding the current orthodoxies in politics no less than in academic disciplines. And such a critical sense is crucially important in the very matter of technological development, especially say in the moves to full automation. Who is it for, who is to benefit? As Marcuse says elsewhere, we have reached for the first time in history a point at which no one need be in want the whole world over.[8] Yet the fact is that more than half the world's population is in desperate want. Technology is

---

[7] See the article 'Education as investment?', by T. BEAUMONT, *The Newman*, Jan. 1969.

[8] H. MARCUSE, *One Dimensional Man* (London 1964), especially ch. 2.

being used for capitalist profit rather than human need. And the accompaniment of this in the west itself is increasingly a 'one-dimensional' culture. No one of any sense would wish to return to a pre-technological culture: yet technology itself is rapidly becoming an alien force beyond the control even of those who try to manipulate it for their own purposes. The volume of criticism from the universities and those outside whom they have educated has not been very noticeable. For in fact they are much more skilled in continuing that process of damping criticism which begins in secondary school.

As universities expand, and higher education becomes more general, its quality increasingly suffers. I am not suggesting the connection is a necessary one – indeed I am utterly opposed to the older conception of educating only an elite – but it has in fact occurred, and this is because it is advantageous to the capitalist system generally that it should be so. Society wants consensus, not awkward questioners of established values. Through the educational system the norm is becoming one in which authority hands over information as if it were a commodity to be returned intact at some later date, the yearly (or more frequent) examination. As more and more people are crammed into the courses the pretence of training critical judgement becomes less plausible: the values and attitudes of bourgeois society are to be accepted, at any rate criticism must not exceed certain set bounds, and devoted teachers are there to carry these values to the next generation at school or university. The examination is becoming a kind of sophisticated quiz, marks being scored by approximation to the 'correct' answer, known to authority in advance. The penalty for stepping outside the system, for moving outside the acceptable limits at any point in the process, before the top, is to be refused access to the next step on the ladder: and by the top it is nearly always too late. The system of education itself continues to absorb an increasing number into research and teaching, but the research is all too often fragmented and remote from the real concerns of life, the teaching half-hearted because it is often carried on together with a lucrative consultative post in industry or government. Where learning is not being used uncritically to continue the present system, it has become of little use to anybody. The intellectual who has not sold out to the establishment has all too often become separated from it, an object of mild ridicule and mild respect.

The Critical University as a Means Towards Socialism

Change has to take place in two ways, closely connected. The methods of teaching, the contents too, have to be directed to the real needs of society in its progress to socialism, and the exclusive character of the present institutions have to be broken down. Now while a revolutionary change in society as a whole is unlikely to take place in the immediate future, it is possible to work towards it by building alternative structures within the present society. Of itself this cannot bring about revolution. But where these alternative structures are growing in a direction that, so far as can be seen, corresponds to the way in which they will function in the changed society, they can contribute towards the revolutionary movement. They directly change the consciousness of those who are engaged in creating them, and they may by their example help to persuade others of the need for change.[9] This, I think, is the aim of the more clear-sighted students and teachers now engaged in the university movements.

First, then, a word about future methods and content of teaching. It is significant that the languages of western Europe did not develop a native expression for that combination of theory and practice for which Marx uses the term 'praxis', and that the word has never been naturalised in any of them. It is something that can only be realised by consciously moving away from the present over-intellectualised bias in our schools and universities. The alternative is to base teaching and research much more on involvement in real situations. We learn by what we do, and what we do has to be politically oriented. It will be objected that this is to lose the much-prized 'objectivity' dear to the liberal educator. I believe that this objectivity is always a myth, concealing the presuppositions of the society in which educational institutions are set, and that it is better to be open about it. Economics and sociology, for example, are often thought of as neutral and

[9] For one of the most important examples, see A. R. NIELSEN, *Lust for Learning* (Thy, Denmark 1968) (New Experimental College).

academic. But as we practise them they have the presuppositions of bourgeois society, which they help to keep in being. As Lenin put it: 'where the bourgeois economists saw a relation between things (the exchange of one commodity for another) Marx revealed a relationship between people.'[10] Because we have hardly begun to build institutions in which people are democratically related together – industrial concerns controlled by the workers, for example – we have done little to develop an economics and sociology that relate to people's real needs. It is the same with cultural studies. The critical study of literature is for the most part divorced from the actual creation of literature because that remains an elite concern; we have destroyed popular culture without putting anything in its place. History is still to a large extent the history of government rather than of the people because, for one thing, this is so much easier to examine in. Right through the educational system people are turned away from the study of their own situation to be bored with abstractions. The very divisions of subject from subject are arbitrary. But any experienced teacher knows that this is unnecessary. Get away from imposed syllabuses and far more meaningful, indeed enjoyable forms of study, based on involvement in the actual life we share together become possible. And with this education begins to take on a quite new political dimension, as Marcuse pointed out. All education is political, into one pattern of shared life or another; slowly, here and there, men are beginning to create forms of education into democratic ways of life still unknown to our capitalist society as a whole.

The relationship between pupil and teacher is of course closely connected with the nature of what is being learnt. Where knowledge is still remote from life, compartmentalised, it has to be taught by 'authority'; one person knows the right answer, the rest must be cowed into submitting to it. Where people learn through involvement in the realities of their own lives together, pupil and teacher alike have something to learn and to offer one another. If enough people were allowed to live as responsible human beings throughout the years of their formal education, socialism in the west would be a good deal less remote.

[10] V. I. LENIN, *Collected Works*, p. 26; quoted in *Student Power*, p. 206.

Secondly the educational system that has to be built must be completely open, free from the present divisions of class. A common culture is one to which all contribute, not merely an elite. While this can only come into being on a large scale in a society which has achieved socialism, it is already possible to create situations in which workers and bourgeoisie, despite their divisions, bring their different experience to the common task of understanding and renewal. Moreover this can continue in one way or another throughout life; education isn't something that stops at sixteen or twenty-two.

The problem, of course, is to get these ideas off paper and give them institutional form. But my whole point in writing this paper is that in the case of educational institutions the work has now begun, however inchoately as yet. The ideas, in fact, are not abstract; they have grown from the actual experience of men working together in this way. It is true that the main aim of the 'student protest' movement, whether in school or university, has been to transform existing institutions, and that this can have only limited success. Indeed one of the problems in Britain is the degree to which liberal reform has already gone; though the whole structure is wrong, it is less easy than elsewhere to find particular abuses round which to mobilise mass protest and so achieve the wider aim. But here and there in the west something more radical is being attempted. There have been schools in which for a time at least a common education has taken place. And there have been, mainly in Europe, universities that are 'free' or 'critical' in the sense of being open to all, non-authoritarian, and exploratory rather than tied to syllabus and examination. It is unfortunate that no readily available documentation of these attempts exists. A sociological study of them would be of immense value.

An important point is that such institutions should remain in close contact with existing ones.[11] There can be no revolution where the majority of people are left completely outside. Most students are still unwilling to jeopardise their chances of a career in the present society, and it would be difficult to condemn them for this. But since the present institutions are self-contradictory – people in them are divided by the economic and cultural bases of

[11] This seems to be the case in Amsterdam and Turin, for instance.

class but attempt to work on common tasks – there is at least the possibility of conversion if they are offered a model of something better. As things are the differences of interest can be overcome for certain obvious reforms, such as autonomy from administrative or state pressures; beyond this end the real divisions rapidly reappear. It is then that the majority, the 'moderates', come up against the choice at the heart of all authentic existence. No student revolution has yet managed to get very far. In these circumstances the radical alternative institution offers a firmer basis. The march has begun, even though there are still many *li* to go.

The Critical Church

I would have been happy to end there, and allow anyone who found it useful to work out the implications of my analogy for themselves. But then this would have been less plausibly a paper on the future Church and its ministry. At least I hope certain parallels are now obvious. The Church, like the university, has until the other day been a reactionary force in society, its members formed to accept passively the accepted norms set out authoritatively, and to express themselves in remote and academic ways. As in the university, the last few years have thrown up a ferment of new ideas. But here the parallel ends. Where have these been given institutional form?

Obviously enough not in small elite groups, such as the Downside Symposium, the Teilhard de Chardin society, or *Slant*, who are scarcely candidates for inclusion in something claiming to be a mass movement. Within Roman Catholicism the most likely possibility might seem to be the Renewal Movement in this country. But it is essentially still composed of the bourgeoisie, and as yet its aims have not extended much beyond the issue that called it into existence. Similar groups in other Churches suffer from the same limitations. Though the Student Christian Movement has become much more radical in recent years, it is limited in the way its name implies. Going further afield, the 'underground Church' in the States offers certain possibilities, but represents less a single entity than a set of diverse experiences of varying importance. In the English-speaking world, at least, there is nothing corresponding to the new institutions we have seen beginning to grow in the educational field.

The difference lies, I believe, in the *defacto* different class-structure of university and Church. The university is predominately bourgeois, and is likely to remain so for some time to come; the Church, at least in Britain, retains a large body of the working-class within it. Within the university, therefore, there is no basic contradiction involved in the fact that the critical movement consists largely of bourgeois students, who only in relation to staff and administration form a quasi-proletariat. At the same time this means that the university movement, as events have shown, is unable of itself to achieve its aims in a wider context: links have patiently to be built between it and the workers' movement. The Church, by contrast, is potentially in a much stronger position. But its actual state is worse because it has failed to realise this potentiality; *corruptio optimi pessima*. There is massive contradiction between the principle that within the Church 'there is neither Jew nor Greek, slave or free, male or female' and the actual heavily divided class-structure which so closely reflects that of the society in which it is set. All the renewal-groups that I know of consist largely of middle-class intellectuals, having little or no contact with working-class people and their needs. They have not arisen out of parish life, except in a few surburban parishes, nor have they found any means of reaching people as a whole through popular writing. Theologians, whatever their class origins, if they are priests will usually have been thoroughly trained to speak only to their fellow-theologians, in the accents of the ruling class; if they are lay people (and increasingly this is the case) they are mainly from a university background, and though they have often broken through the barrier of technical non-language appealing only to fellow-technicians, they are still remote from the majority of their fellow-Christians.

The way forward, then, is for small groups of Christians, mainly but not exclusively working-class (since this is the actual structure of the Church in Britain) to come into being in response to the need to transform society and thus, in the process, the Church also. In other words a critical Church has to be created, analogous to the critical university, engaged like it in building socialism, and like it aiming to move the vast bulk of the parent-body to come into line with its truth. The difference is one of size, for the Church claims a greater universality in space, time and above all, class – claims, but signally fails to achieve. In its opportunity lies the magnitude of its failure; yet opportunity remains. The situation in Church and university is basically a learning one, learning from involvement, from praxis. With the Church what has to be learnt afresh in every age, lost and learnt again, is the word of the Gospel, a word which is itself an action and which, seen in action, always has the power to move men. Nevertheless it would be naive not to recognise that Christianity, especially Catholic Christianity, has certain problems proper to itself, and with two of these I shall end, since I think that discussion of them also helps us to glimpse, however dimly, the shape of the church we hope to build.

There is a problem of continuity whenever new ideas arise in old institutions, and this takes particularly acute form in Christianity, with its sense of tradition. But those who are rightly worried about the possibility of a total break with the past, and loss of what was valuable in it, forget that revolutions are not just a matter of ideas; they are made by people. Revolution breaks through the determining factors of past history, but it takes place within them; people carry their past with them so that normally it is a matter of generations before revolution is complete (and due to begin again). Marxists recognise this well enough, but Christians, with their tendency to idealism, often overlook it. In theoretical terms it has been seen as the problem of doctrinal development: crudely, how can new ideas be introduced disguised as old ones? But subterfuges of this kind are unnecessary when it is realised that continuity lies not in statements but in people. There may well be sharp contradiction between old and new at the level of statements, but they have to be lived by the Church, people in space and time, modified through interaction with other ideas as well as by experience, before they are a part of Christian belief.[12] 'If they are of God they will prosper' was the classical way of putting it. For better or

[12] Cf. J. H. NEWMAN, *Development of Christian Doctrine*, 1878 edn., ch. 1, sect. 1, 4-7.

worse complete breaks with the past are humanly impossible, as all revolutions have had to discover. We can trust the body of people, where we may distrust individuals, to carry what is needed from the past into the future. If we are Christians this is all we have to trust, for the body of people is Christ in the world.

But in any case the break involved in my proposals is not perhaps as drastic as it might appear at first sight. The proclamation of the Gospel in word and action has always in principle been the centre of the Church's life. Each age has had to find living expression for the word in terms of its own experience. In this it has had varying success, but the word has never been utterly lost, however obscure it has become. Nevertheless it has often seemed as though it stood over-against the Church, to be imposed on it from an earlier period of life. The task of a critical Church is rather to reach towards it again from its contemporary communal experience, for this is the normal pattern of human learning.[13] Only in this way can anything be made one's own. If the Church really enters the struggle to break free from the dead hand of the capitalist world that has for so long made use of it to control men's lives, then the Gospel will emerge once more in all its revelatory power.

The second problem that will be raised for the critical Church in more acute form than for the university concerns the status of those who teach. The danger of paternalism is in any case greater where there is a larger class-spectrum to cover; it is always a temptation for the intellectual to want to teach the worker his new language. The British worker commands a terse monosyllabic language in which to reply. Increasingly in fact he has tended to vote with his feet and opt out of the situation as early on in life as possible, for he sees the evident contradiction between what is said and what is done as clearly as anyone. But if the danger is recognised it should surely be possible, in the Church as in the university, for men to learn from one another on equal terms, although the greater experience of some will put them for the time being in the position of teachers.

The added difficulty in the Church is that those who minister in

[13] Cf. J. A. T. ROBINSON, *The New-Reformation* (London 1965), ch. 2.

this way have traditionally received an ordination which seems to give them a permanent status independent of immediate need.

I do not see that any answer can usefully be given to this question before the critical Church comes into being and poses it in its own terms. We have no right to force the future to speak our language rather than its own. But it is important to remember that, as earlier papers in this symposium have shown, there is no single pattern of Christian ministry running through the Church's history: we do not have to think of the pattern established in recent centuries as for all time.[14] We have to trust to the inspired common sense of the whole Christian people to find a solution. Those who live in faith do not expect answers to all their difficulties; like the people of old they go forward not fully knowing just where it is that God is calling them to go.

[14] See J. LERCLERCQ, *supra* pp. 53–75 (particularly his conclusions, pp. 73–5), and for the theological justification in the symbolic character of priesthood language, R. MURRAY, *supra* pp. 17–39.

BIOGRAPHICAL NOTE

JOHN COULSON *is Research Fellow in Theology at Bristol University. After teaching at Downside for fourteen years, he spent two years at Oriel College, Oxford, writing a D.Phil. thesis on Newman's ideas of the Church and its common ground with the Anglican tradition. This is to be published by the Oxford University Press as 'Newman and the Common Tradition' in the Spring of 1970. He edited* Theology and the University, *the Oxford Newman symposium* The Rediscovery of Newman *(with A. M. Allchin),* Newman's On Consulting the Faithful in Matters of Doctrine *and* The Saints, *and wrote* Newman, A Portrait Restored *(with A. M. Allchin).*

16 Disputed Questions on the Form of the Local Church

JOHN COULSON

THE PAPERS BY THE SOCIOLOGISTS ESTABLISHED THE extent to which most of the clerical functions traditionally associated with the priesthood – medicine, law, education and now social service – are performed by members of separate professions. All that remains for the priest appears to be his liturgical function – he presides over the eucharistic assembly. The difficulty is to discover how this assembly reflects or is related to the local community. Does the celebration of the eucharist become an end in itself? And, if so, what does a priest symbolise; and what does a symbol do in his spare time? We seem driven back to an older and perhaps more fundamental conception of the priest as he around whom the Christian community is constituted, his vocation being essentially that of the bishop or episcopal assistant. But until we can discover what the form of the local church ought to be, we cannot have a sufficiently definite conception of what a vocation to the priesthood ought to signify.

What we have to begin by accepting is that the idea of simple parochial location has gone with the society that made it possible. This trend cannot be reversed, and to resist it is merely to convert the local church into a club, and Christian membership into one club membership among many others. This tendency is reinforced when, as now, Christianity has ceased to be the religion of the majority and to have the characteristic of a national religion. Its tendency is to be inward looking and defensive and, therefore, in form and spirit, sectarian.

If the local church is to be neither sect not club what ought to be the characteristics of membership? We ought perhaps to be thinking of a community that is territorially larger than the parish and yet composed of much smaller cells or units in which a real face to face relationship is possible for those members of the same neighbourhood. But something more than a federation of house-churches is required. The very notion of membership has to be re-thought. We may have to accept not only a wider but more informal, even socially discontinuous, membership. This is what characterises many societies of Christians who gather together from time to time for common study and reflection. People come and go, yet they remain more closely related than mere acquaintances. Of such a kind was St Philip's first Oratory, or our own Symposium group. We may need to see that these too are valid local forms of Christian community, and for many young people their validity is greater than the existing territorial group or parish. In a society in which people belong to many and varied social groups, and perform differing roles within such groups, Church membership may have to be similarly dynamic rather than territorially static.

But we ought also to realise that our membership of the Church is primarily that of a society of those who speak and practise a common language. Our membership is linguistic and thus, to the extent that a language implies a society of which it is the language, social. In a society in which they form the minority Christians are more and more recognisable as those who talk and act in peculiar ways. They are recognised by a certain kind of moral style for which they have a vocabulary of their own – 'that new language which Christ has brought us' – they wait patiently in hope, act charitably as members one of another, and treat their bodies as the temples of an indwelling spirit. Even when paraphrased or modified a characteristic oddness remains, which will become increasingly remarkable as Christian discourse and secular vocabulary move apart. It will, however, enable us to understand that membership of the Christian body is as evident in remaining within the Christian universe of discourse as in attending Church. We shall have to ask ourselves about those young people who are 'lapsed' but still verbally and morally talking our language. Furthermore we shall have to ask whether our membership one of another ought not to be extended to all who are prepared to speak with us – not only fellow Christians, but fellow travellers who may call themselves agnostic. What this may lead to is whether we must accept the notion of degrees of membership – that some, by virtue of office or conviction or dedication are more fully in membership than others who are on the periphery. Would this be a way of re-discovering the significance of those distinctions of degree upon which the Church has always insisted and the hierarchical model of its membership has been based? We might be led to re-examine what ought to be our criteria for admitting a member to baptismal fellowship. But, perhaps, this is merely to encourage a new form of clericalism; and our understanding of what is implied when we are called to be members one of another must reach out to a wider sense still of social responsibility, such as is expressed in those papers in the symposium which deal with the duty of the Church to bring about the kingdom and to realise itself eschatologically. They also raise the question of the extent to which our theological thinking may be determined by concealed or suppressed social and political preferences. These block our response to the scriptures, which are there to call us out of a world grown too familiar. The essential error of sectarianism is to conceive the form of the local church without having first recognised the shape of our society; and, since our political position will determine how our theological understanding develops, to what extent are Christians obliged to stand for a definable political analysis and commitment?

In its present form this is not a new question. F. D. Maurice and company thought that Christianity in an industrial society required a commitment of a broadly 'socialist' kind; but 'socialism' has now a history of its own, and a simple revolutionary optimism now seems naive. Laurence Bright's paper does not provide me with a convincing answer to these difficulties. The categories of

Marxist analysis, with their undertones of sin, guilt, conspiracy and redemption, are – however much they may be modified – as absolute and politically inflexible as were the Ultramontane categories which prevented an accommodation between the papacy and the open society in the last century. The clear-cut conflict which such categories demand obliges Fr Bright to assume *both* the abolition of private capital *and* the rejection of all existing western forms of its public control. I can only see this as placing a fatal restriction upon the argument, since it appears to confine the alternatives either to an unqualified rejection of what Leavis calls the technologico-Benthamite society, or to pronouncements so utopian as to be acceptable only to a Dr Azziz – that character in Forster's *Passage to India* whose face 'grew very tender' with the tenderness of one 'incapable of administration, and unable to grasp that if the poor criminal is let off he will again rob the poor widow'. Revolutionary zeal is one thing; law-abidingness is another and equally essential characteristic of a just society; and the unasked question remains – what are the duties by which the new revolutionaries are prepared to bind themselves? A political prescription which fails to provide an account of its regulating or stabilising principles is, for me, too incomplete to be convincing.

Having said this, what I would not want to under-estimate is the case for the rejection of industrial society. It has a lengthy Christian pedigree. It has informed the criticism of Ruskin, William Morris and their followers such as Eric Gill and the Dominican Fr Vincent McNabb. It is present in our nostalgia for the organic society. And, in the end, the anarchists or Luddites may be right – our persistent failure to create humane environments out of industrial society may be endemic to the nature of that society itself.

How else are we to explain our continuing inability to think *institutionally*? It was the achievement of the Benedictine centuries, as Whitehead remarked, to embody great ideas in great institutions. Vatican II has had great ideas, but where are the institutions to match them? This failure of what the Marxists call praxis – the ability to conceive institutions as themselves the realisation of principles – is a deficiency not only of our Church but of our society; and the rate of acceleration of social change produces a widening, not a narrowing, gap between cultures and generations.

Is our inability to think institutionally, therefore, merely because the rate of social change is greater than our ability to cope with its problems? In considering the local church we ought to remember the extent to which there exists for Catholics especially a growing and unresolved conflict between what amounts to two cultures. On the one hand there are the existing attitudes which are expressed in inherited structures. These have been entirely managed by a permanent professional body – the clergy – and imposed upon a passive and obedient laity. On the other hand there are the teachings of Vatican II that the Church is the whole people of God, and that the clerical and priestly offices are to *serve* this people. Here the pre-supposition is of a Church growing upwards from a foundation in local diversity, for which the appropriate metaphors of growth are the 'cell', 'co-responsibility' and the over-grazed 'grass-roots'. This takes us back behind the Counter-Reformation to that essentially Renaissance and humanist conception of the local church – St Philip Neri's original Oratory. This was predominantly a lay community, in which after long and effective service to the congregation certain men, including St Philip himself, were called out and presented to the bishop for ordination. They had read their theology already – in the university – and were not youthful unknown quantities, whose celibacy and devotion had yet to be tried in the fire of pastoral responsibility, but men of mature years whose ordination to the priesthood was the Church's *recognition* of distinguished active service. Perhaps this is still too high a notion of priesthood for our transitional condition; perhaps even the transition itself will continue to be frustrated. One thing is certain – our continuing inadequacy goes deeper than merely failing to adapt to change: what we are confronted by seems nothing short of an inherited failure of the imagination. At its most local level and in its most day to day forms the institutional and liturgical life of the Church requires a degree of cultural and imaginative empathy which is less and less to be assumed among ordinary people, and which only certain kinds of educated people are willing to provide. As Catholics we too readily assume that we have successfully *realised* our relationship to our past and its traditions by a mere attendance at or acceptance of liturgical forms. It is precisely this relationship with our past that is, of all relationships, the hardest to establish; and we cheat ourselves if we fail to recognise this problem of continuity for what it is. To achieve a meaningful relationship to the present which is also an openness to the future and a reverence for the past is not a privilege which a Catholic simply inherits by attending Mass. It is to wear the shirt of Nessus, and to fear, with Matthew Arnold, that one may be wandering between two worlds – 'one dead, the other powerless to be born'.

It is for this reason that we cannot speak of the form of the local church in the accents of the simple-minded church reformer. If the Catholic is committed to eschewing both trendy Christianity and a severe secularism (where the Christian and the secular presence are so indistinguishable that there is no longer a space for the Church in the world), then what we have to do is to educate a new generation into an understanding of our religious language of liturgy and sacrament. Yet it is a language whose grammar can be deeply eroded by a hostile and inhumane environment. Even when a child receives an excellent education in literature, film, and painting which is both prescribed and expressed in such text-books as *Reflections*, directly he leaves school and falls back into an over-crowded concrete jungle and earns his living in unskilled and unfulfilling work, the power of the adolescent sensibility to grasp sacrament and symbol is at risk. And the local church will have to be large enough and varied enough in its membership to undertake this essential work of reinforcing the foundations. This is in the broadest sense a theological task: it is also a responsibility for *adult* (as distinct from primary and secondary) education. Until the level of imaginative and aesthetic awareness is raised, we must expect a continuing apathy, even hostility, on the part of those who, nominally Christian, fail to understand the newness and peculiarity of Christian language. The question is not one of whether as Christians we know enough, but of what that knowing involves. It involves the study of our tradition but alongside the problems of the day and, in some instances, by means of those problems. A theology that has nothing to say to politics, medicine, or industry, has written a death certificate for the traditions it claims to perpetuate.

It is here that Newman's use of the university as the model for the Church is of great importance. It shows how the Church can be wider than the society in which it exists when it is no longer the religion of the majority. It must foster the attitudes appropriate to a wider community still; and the local Church must be large enough to be the centre of a highly-informed minority. It must have the resources to be able to undertake a proper adult education of the emotions, the imagination and the intellect; yet be so composed as to provide hearths and homes for lonely people who are haunted by no intellectual perplexities. To rise above the dangers of sectarianism, it must be both. On the one hand there may be house-churches, on the other the characteristically episcopal unity which associates these house-churches but is greater than the sum of its parts. This, the extra dimension, is theological; and its fostering needs to be seen for what it is – not the peripheral luxury of a self-righteous minority, but the source of that dynamic which enables the local church to develop, preserves it from the tendencies to sectarianism consequent upon our minority status, and enables it to work and manifest itself *convincingly* in the social and political life of a pluralist society.

17 Concluding Editorial Comment

NICHOLAS LASH

THE 'PRÊTRES SOLIDAIRES' WHO GATHERED AT THE European Bishops' Conference at Chur last summer, and at the Synod in Rome last autumn, may or may not have been representative of a significant number of priests. They were certainly an eloquent symbol of the extent to which the meaning and function of Christian ministry has become increasingly, and urgently problematic. No collection of papers, however wise or learned, could hope to make more than a very modest contribution to the solution of complex practical problems, but it is worth asking what *sort* of contribution it would be reasonable to expect from a book such as this.

The symposium, at which these papers were originally given, was not convened for the personal benefit of the participants (though we enjoyed it!), but as a form of service to the readers of this book. In the course of three days of intense discussion, connections were made and insights generated which had a considerable influence on the form which the individual papers eventually took. While we cannot share with our readers the experience of the symposium itself, it is the purpose of this book, and of this concluding comment in particular, not primarily to convey information (let alone to provide answers), but to help other people to see the problem in the way in which we came to see it. (It need hardly be added that the perspective adopted in this comment is a purely personal one; the extent to which it is shared by the contributors to the symposium may be estimated from their individual papers.)

Much recent discussion concerning ecclesiastical structures and forms of ministry has been sterile because latent presuppositions have often been insufficiently exposed to critical analysis. Those people who are convinced that, fundamentally, received patterns of ministry and their theoretical interpretation and justification are unchangeable (although they may be modified to meet changing situations) need not be presumed either to have an inordinate affection for medieval Christendom or sinfully to be clinging to the vestiges of power. It may be that they do not appreciate the extent to which the model of priesthood and ministry with which they operate is socially, politically and histori-cally conditioned. At some point in the discussion, the claim is almost certain to be made that Jesus Christ 'instituted' the eucharist and the Christian order of ministry. But, as Dom Sebas-tian Moore put it in an intensely paradoxical phrase which is one of the clues to his paper, the question we have to face is 'whether he did *institute* the eucharist' (Moore, p. 215, my stress). To under-stand that question, rather than to answer it, is, I believe, to grasp the perspective within which Dom Sebastian is querying some widely shared presuppositions.

Those people, on the other hand, who are convinced that everything can suddenly go into the melting-pot, and that re-ceived structures and interpretations can simply be dismissed, in the name of the Gospel, as irrelevant, may be in danger of imagining that it is possible 'to realise the evangelical ideal of priestly service and mediation without any other determining factor than the Gospel itself' (Dom Jean Leclercq, p. 74). It would then be very easy to lose sight of the fact that, whatever our opinion of existing models of ministry, that ministry must employ *some* 'model' if it is to be a public, intelligible and Christian fact in the world at all, and that the models which it does employ must inevitably be conditioned by the period and the culture in which we live.

I have already used the term 'model' rather frequently, because it is impossible to read the scriptural and historical papers in this collection without becoming sharply aware of the variety of models of ministry that have been employed, more or less self-consciously and deliberately at different periods, in the Church's history. It is still possible, however, to acknowledge the relativism of Christian history, and yet to view the variety of forms which the theory and practice of Christian ministry have taken as just so many more or less regrettable deviations from the 'pure' form of New Testament ministry. But, as Canon Houssiau reminded us, even Luke, who places greater emphasis than many of the New Testament writers on the dimension of historical continuity, 'lets us see the flexibility of the forms created by the guidance of the Spirit when the Church is confronted by new situations' (Houssiau, p. 239). Or, as Fr Murray put it in a paper published two years ago: 'the institutional element in Christianity, by which I mean especially social structure and law, *is not part of the Gospel*'.[1]

If, in the New Testament, 'priesthood language is used to express a truth of the Church, but this truth is not a matter of the Church's social and ministerial structure; it concerns the Church's role and status in relation to God and the world' (Murray, p. 25); if, furthermore, 'Christianity stands not for the abolition of priesthood, but for its secularisation' (Robinson, p. 14), then one's first impression of the model of ministry which was dominant throughout the middle ages must be that it represents a very considerable departure from New Testament conceptions of priesthood and ministry in the Church. This impression, although from many points of view clearly correct, is yet dangerously misleading. Far from the medieval 'clericalisation' of the Church being exclusively, or immediately, a process of sacralisation it was, as Don Jean Leclercq's paper shows, more fundamentally an expression of that *secularisation* of the Church which began with the collapse of the western Empire. 'The gradual evolution that took place was nothing less than the secularisation of the clergy' (Leclercq, p. 61), and the extensive use, in the middle ages, of Old Testament terminology and imagery to describe the priestly

---

[1] R. MURRAY, 'Authority and the Spirit in the New Testament', in *Authority in a Changing Church* (London 1968), p. 19; his stress.

status and function was polemically motivated and had 'nothing to do with theology' (Leclercq, p. 71). Doubtless the time would come when the attribution of this language to Christian ministry would be reflexively appropriated and would be presumed to be primarily of theological significance. Then the language of the Old Testament would be employed, although analogically, as a direct description of Christian priesthood. When this point has been reached, the complex logic of the New Testament language of priesthood, as described by Fr Murray, has been seriously obscured, and it is now possible to speak, pejoratively, of the 'sacralisation' of Christian ministry.

One illustration, small enough in itself, of the outcome of this complex dialectical process, is the frequency with which, on cards printed to commemorate the ordination of a priest, the words *Tu es sacerdos in aeternum* are to be found. That these words are applied, not in a 'transferred or figurative sense' (Murray, p. 21), but in a manner which implies more immediately descriptive or ontological claims, is indicated by the fact that, for several centuries, ordination to the ministry has, within the Catholic tradition, been assumed (on an analogy drawn from the medieval theology of baptism) to confer an 'indelible character'. Here the wider issues concerning the propriety of a shift from a functional conception of ministry to a view that would see that ministry as conferring a particular social and religious status, come sharply into focus. It would seem that there is need for a fresh examination, by historians and theologians, of the doctrine of priestly character. To what extent does the Catholic community regard itself as permanently committed to the view that sacramental ordination to ministerial function in the Church is necessarily ordination for life? The practical implications of this question, which the members of the symposium felt should be posed with some urgency, are considerable.

The question which has just been raised would seem, at first sight, to be reasonably clear and precise. Any attempt to answer it, however, would today be forced to take into account a whole range of exceedingly complex, and apparently quite intractable problems of theological method. The symposium found it impossible to explore the problem of priesthood without touching on a whole range of questions concerning the meaning of revelation, the historicity of Christian truth, and the nature of theological discourse. Some people may react to this situation with irritation: why did they have to make it all so complicated? Others, however, may be grateful; to set any particular problem in the context of those wider issues with which it is inexorably, even if subterraneanly linked, may at least be taken as evidence of a desire to get to the heart of the matter.

It is not possible to make even a provisional synthesis of the fundamental questions raised in these papers. I shall restrict myself to brief comments on two of them: the normative status of particular aspects of the Church's history, and the role of theological inquiry in the immediate future.

So far as the first point is concerned, almost every Christian body has ascribed, to some aspect of its history, regulative or normative authority (whether that aspect is 'the Church of the New Testament', the text of the New Testament, a medieval model of ministry, or the statements of popes and councils). Dr Kent says that 'if one appeals to history one must appeal to the whole of history, and accept the consequences' (Kent, p. 87). To ask *how* such an appeal could be made, and to answer that, from many points of view, it is doomed to failure from the start, need not necessarily engender despair. To quote Dr Kent again: the fact that 'Discontinuity has ceased to be a choice ... does not mean that Christianity is impossible but that bibliolatry is improvident' (Kent, p. 86; and, a Catholic might add, so is 'conciliolatry' or 'papolatry').

It may well be that an 'appeal to the New Testament' and, indeed, to subsequent moments in Christian history (leaving aside the problem of the criteria according to which particular significance might legitimately be ascribed to this or that moment in that history) is not only possible, but is a permanent charge laid upon the Church. It may also be the case, however, that such an appeal need not, indeed may not, take the form of regarding any particular model of ministry (even the forms which appear within the New Testament) as mythically 'pure' or ahistorically absolute. It may well be that the appeal might take the form of demanding that we, who live in the 20th century, should come alive to the demand of that challenge put to man by God, of which particular forms of ministry might be seen as the honest, inadequate, socially conditioned responses of the Church. It may well be, in other words, that the element of continuity in Christian history (across the manifest discontinuity which a study of history discloses, and which the nature of history renders inevitable) consists in the questions with which the Church is confronted rather than in those structures (and their interpretation) which have, in different situations, been the form of its response. It is only through examining the response that we can come to hear the question, but it is surely the question and demand of God, rather than the answer of man, which is normative for the future of the Church.

Finally, what is the role of theological inquiry in the immediate future? The question arises from the realisation of the extent to which, in the past, the theology of the ministry has been a rationalisation of structures and forms of ministry whose emergence was largely due to socio-political factors. It would seem that theological statement is doomed to be a commentary on situations in the genesis of which Christian faith was not the only, or even the dominant factor: 'At most, religious beliefs connect and articulate in a specific configuration particular independently pre-existing possibilities' (Cunningham, p. 265).

Such considerations should induce in the theologian a certain sober realism, or humility. And yet, I think that a distinction is to be made between the prescriptive function of prophetic declaration, and the secondary, or descriptive function of most other forms of theological discourse. Were the Church *simply* to follow (in structure and interpretation) the shifting patterns of secular society, it would be merely parasitic upon human history. The Church has *also*, and primarily, to proclaim the kingdom of God. The history of the Church provides ample evidence that this prophetic task has often been misconceived as implying an ability to prescribe detailed solutions to human problems. Prophecy does not say how you must feed people: it says that they must be fed. Prophecy cannot construct, in any particular situation, appropriate structures of reconciliation: it can proclaim the necessity and the possibility of that reconciliation. Prophecy does not liberate man from the darkness and ambiguity of his immediate historical situation: it says that, through meeting the continual challenge of that situation, man has a future in God. And the Church performs its prophetic role, not primarily by talking, but by embodying the hopes of man, the future of man, in a style of life and celebration which, as symbolic of that future, both proclaims the hope of man and criticises the inhumanity of the present moment (including, especially, the inhumanity of its own present moment).

The Church may not evade the internal tensions which result from accepting its prophetic role, because they lie at the heart of man's historicity, and a Church which could not contain them would be unfaithful both to man and to the Gospel. The immediate need is not so much for more and more elaborate theoretical analysis (which could be an expression of that inadequate expression of consciousness which is described by Adrian Cunningham: cf. p. 255), but rather for action. The problem of priesthood will not be solved, or clarified, primarily by more sophisticated exegesis or a renewed theology, but by taking the risk of exercising that priesthood in care and proclamation, in reconciliation and the celebration of the victory of Christ. Action and reflection, the exercise of priesthood and the contemplation of God's saving work in Christ, are dialectically related. But, paradoxically, a more generous concrete obedience to the Gospel must precede the emergence of a clearer understanding of the demands of that Gospel. The light of Easter does not precede the darkness of Gethsemane. And the Church is only likely to have the courage to take risks, to explore new forms of life, of ministry, and of communion, in the measure that it trusts, not so much the insights it has inherited from a world which, from many points of view, no longer exists, but rather the Spirit of God whose creative and salvific activity it celebrates, and on whose covenant-fidelity its life depends.

Index